TABLE OF CONTENTS

Top 20 Test Taking Tips

1. Carefully follow all the test registration procedures
2. Know the test directions, duration, topics, question types, how many questions
3. Setup a flexible study schedule at least 3-4 weeks before test day
4. Study during the time of day you are most alert, relaxed, and stress free
5. Maximize your learning style; visual learner use visual study aids, auditory learner use auditory study aids
6. Focus on your weakest knowledge base
7. Find a study partner to review with and help clarify questions
8. Practice, practice, practice
9. Get a good night's sleep; don't try to cram the night before the test
10. Eat a well balanced meal
11. Know the exact physical location of the testing site; drive the route to the site prior to test day
12. Bring a set of ear plugs; the testing center could be noisy
13. Wear comfortable, loose fitting, layered clothing to the testing center; prepare for it to be either cold or hot during the test
14. Bring at least 2 current forms of ID to the testing center
15. Arrive to the test early; be prepared to wait and be patient
16. Eliminate the obviously wrong answer choices, then guess the first remaining choice
17. Pace yourself; don't rush, but keep working and move on if you get stuck
18. Maintain a positive attitude even if the test is going poorly
19. Keep your first answer unless you are positive it is wrong
20. Check your work, don't make a careless mistake

Introduction to the TExES Series

Why am I required to take this TExES Assessment?

Your state requires you to take this TExES Assessment in order to test the breadth and depth of your knowledge in a specified subject matter. Texas has adopted the TExES series in order to ensure that you have mastered the subject matter you are planning to teach before they issue your teaching license. Because the issuance of your license ensures competence in the subject area it is important that you take studying seriously and make sure you study thoroughly and completely.

Two Kinds of TExES Assessments

The TExES Series consist of two different kinds of assessments multiple choice questions and constructed response test. The multiple choice test consists of questions followed by several answer choices. From these answer choices you select the answer that you think best corresponds with the given question. These questions can survey a wider range because they can ask more questions in a limited time period. Constructed response questions consist of a given question for which you write an original response. These tests have fewer questions, but the questions require you to demonstrate the depth of you own personal knowledge in the subject area.

Communication Processes

Self-concept

Self-concept is simply an individual's sense of himself or herself. Voluntarily or involuntarily, every person brings his or her self-concept to bear during Communication Processes. Some of the aspects that make up a self-concept include personalities, roles, aspirations, and past achievements. To a large degree, our self-concept is defined by our interactions with other people, especially by the responses other people make to what we say and do. Individuals often internalize compliments and criticism they are given, and these qualities may become more present if they are reinforced through the comments of others. Sometimes, individuals dramatize their own self-concept in relation to some admired or despised other person; for instance, an individual might model himself or herself after some famous person, and therefore see his or her own words and deeds in comparison with those of that other person.

Changing through communication
Although it is a nebulous, complicated process, self-concept does change over time. One of the main factors that influences change in self-concept is Communication Processes. Individuals largely base their self-concept in relation to how they see others, and their views of others are primarily developed through communication. Although specific interactions (and especially complements and criticism) can have a major impact on self-concept, it would be wrong to isolate a particular communication event as the sole determining factor in individual self-concept. The development and maintenance of self-concept is too complex and long term to be traced back to one particular communication. Occasionally, communications can cause an individual to question radically his or her self-concept. This event is known as an identity

crisis. Even in its most extreme form, an identity crisis is simply a slight acceleration of the normal changes in self-concept.

<u>Applied to communication processes</u>

During communication processes, all the participating parties filter information through their own self-concept. Every person naturally applies new information to their own self-concept. Oftentimes, these concerns about self-interest can make it difficult for a listener to get a true sense of what the other person is saying. As much as possible, listeners should strive to understand and take account of their own self-image, so that they can be as objective as possible when evaluating an incoming message. A slight degree of egotism or self-centeredness is natural for humans; the goal of speech communication education, however, is to mitigate these distorting factors to allow for accurate and insightful listening.

<u>Images of self and others existing during a two-person conversation</u>

When two individuals have a conversation, their self-images and images of each other exert a great influence on the course of the conversation. For instance, imagine you are talking to your teacher. You have a self-image and an image of the teacher. You also have an image of how you hope your teacher sees you. Finally, you have an image of how you think your teacher really sees you. Your teacher has an identical set of four images in her mind. As you can see, carrying on a conversation is quite a complicated event! Speech communication theorists assert that conversations tend to go better when there is less discrepancy between these various images. For instance, if your self-image is similar to the image you imagine your teacher has of you, you are less likely to have trouble coming up with appropriate things to say. Similarly, if your impression of what the teacher thinks of you is similar to what you hope the teacher would think of you, you are less likely to make outlandish claims or try to justify yourself.

Self-disclosure

According to speech communication theorists, conversations are best when both parties are as honest as possible. In other words, the individual in a conversation should reveal their own self-image accurately as much as possible. This process is known as self-disclosure. To the degree that we hide information about ourselves, we do not give other people what they need to truly understand us. There are a number of reasons why an individual does not engage in total self-disclosure. Propriety, pride, and fear are perhaps the most common reasons for hiding information about oneself. It is also troublesome when one individual in a conversation knows information about the other without the knowledge of the other. This kind of asymmetrical knowledge can create unexpressed tension in a conversation. As much as possible, individuals should strive to constantly increase the level of self-disclosure and encourage their interlocutor to do the same.

If we assume that self-disclosure is a positive value in conversation, we can then consider the ways in which it can be promoted. Obviously, it will not always be appropriate to simply demand of our interlocutor that he or she be entirely open and honest. Instead, the best way to encourage self-disclosure is to establish an environment for conversation that is nonjudgmental and comfortable. If a strong rapport and level of trust are built between the interlocutors, self-disclosure will follow naturally. When trying to cultivate self-disclosure, we should refrain from negative comments and harsh criticism. Conversely, we should remember to smile and be as warm as possible with our interlocutors, so that they will become more comfortable revealing their self-image.

<u>Alienation</u>

If a supportive environment is the ideal state for self-disclosure, a state of alienation is the exact opposite. Alienation is a feeling of estrangement from other people. Alienated individuals view the world around them as cold and frightening, and they are therefore less likely to engage in self-disclosure. Many sociologists feel that the United States has an abnormally large number of alienated individuals. It should be noted that individuals with a long history of alienation will be especially unreceptive to efforts at honest and open communication. The natural response of an alienated individual is to retreat inward and avoid exposure. For this reason, it is especially important to develop a supportive and welcoming environment in order to promote self-disclosure. Over time, formerly alienated individuals can learn to trust other people and experience the value of healthy self-disclosure.

Trust

In order for effective Communication Processes to exist, the parties involved must trust one another. Note that trust does not necessarily connote affection. In fact, most people can think of other individuals whom they do not particularly like but do trust. For the most part, an ability to trust is formed in the early years of childhood, and is based on one's relationship with one's parents. When one's parents honor their commitments and take care of their responsibilities, one tends to develop trust in the correspondence between words and deeds. Although it can be dangerous to be too trusting, for the most part it is better to have a natural trust of others to which healthy skepticism can be applied. Furthermore, we should all strive to cultivate trustworthiness for ourselves, so that others will respond to our communications appropriately.

Perception and meaning

Perception and communication are inextricably linked. Our ability to understand both verbal and nonverbal communication depends on our ability to accurately interpret the information we take in from the world. In large part, our powers of perception are based on our experiences in the world. Over time, we develop patterns of perception and observation that structure and inform our interpretation and evaluation of communication. There is no way to avoid this process of pattern formation, and indeed, we should be thankful that our brains learn how to assimilate the massive amounts of stimuli they are confronted with every day. However, it is necessary to take account of our own perceptual filters so that we can understand where our prejudices lie.

Relationship between perception and meaning

The ability to accurately perceive is closely related to the ability to derive accurate meaning from a communication. The meanings that we ascribe to the communications of others are based on our perceptions. This means in part that our interpretation of meaning is based on our perception of verbal and nonverbal communication elements. We derive our impression of what another person is saying not only from their words but from their tone of voice and body language. Face-to-face conversation is perhaps the most effective form of communication because it provides both parties with the most information about one another. A general rule of thumb regarding communication is that the more information is provided, the more accurate the reception of the message will be.

Encoding meaning

When a person says something to another person, he or she is encoding a verbal message and supplementing that message with nonverbal communication forms. The precise code that is used by the speaker is the set of words, with their agreed-upon meaning, as well as syntax and grammar. To the degree that the speaker has a command of vocabulary and a strong sense of meaning, he or she will be able to construct a subtle and effective code. The process of encoding meaning is also influenced by individual bias, desire, and perception. A person will encode meaning differently based on their agenda. As a conversation progresses, the two individuals should be able to increase the complexity and accuracy of their message encoding because they will have acquired more and better information about one another's intentions, knowledge, and character.

Interpreting meaning

When we are listening to another person speak in conversation, we are attempting to decode their meaning through the filter of our own prejudices and perceptions. Speech communication theorists assert that listeners tend to emphasize the components of a message that are associated with pre-existing knowledge or interests. In particular, we all tend to emphasize the importance of those aspects of a message which directly pertain to us. At first, we are more likely to make mistakes in the interpretation of what a speaker is saying. As we acquire more information and become more familiar with the speaking style of the other person, however, we tend to make beneficial adjustments to our interpretation. The more time we spend with another person, the better able we are to interpret the meanings of their communications.

Impediments to communication

Defensiveness

Defensiveness is a quality that can obstruct effective communication. When one of the parties in a conversation feels threatened, he or she is likely to become defensive and protective of his or her own ego. Such a person is likely to become preoccupied with his or her own interests and fail to seriously consider the content of the other person's message. Depending on past experience and temperament, individuals have varying degrees of natural defensiveness. Unfortunately, this prevents these individuals from obtaining new information and making personal progress which prevents future criticism. In this way, defensiveness can be seen as a self-fulfilling prophecy: stung by criticism, defensive people adopt a behavior style that is likely to lead to more criticism. Defensiveness must be challenged indirectly, as any direct challenges are likely to increase the self protective instinct.

Ulterior motives

When one of the parties in a conversation has ulterior motives, it will be almost impossible for effective communication to take place. When we use the phrase ulterior motives, we are referring to intentions which are known only to one party but kept secret from the other. To a certain degree, we all have ulterior motives in conversation even when we are discussing the most banal and impersonal subjects. In some way, we all have our own personal interests at heart. However, the less forthright we are about our intentions in a conversation, the less likely we are to achieve solid understanding with the other person. When we have a hidden agenda, we are likely to speak in a way that refers to these intentions, rather than to the intentions made public. When this is the case, the gap between stated and real intentions can lead to evasiveness and abstraction.

Holding grudges

At times, Communication Processes will be adversely affected by the unspoken resentments held by one party against the other. Anytime important information is known by one party but not the other, communication is impaired. When this information directly relates to the relationship between the two parties, the impairment is severe. Furthermore, when an individual sits on important information and allows it to fester in his or her psyche, it may eventually emerge in a much more toxic and extreme form. Many times, when an individual seems to overreact to a minor grievance, it is because he or she is consciously or unconsciously reacting to grudges that have been held for a long time. In order for Communication Processes to thrive, conversation must be open and honest, and any important grievances must be made plain.

Effective for communication

Cooperation

One of the most common situations in which two people must communicate is when cooperating on a particular task. Effective communication skills are essential part of performance in the adult professional world. This can be one of the most problematic situations for communication, however, and it takes many people until late childhood to be able to work effectively with another person. Job-related communications combine elements of casual social interaction and pragmatic interaction. For the most part, job-related communications are best when both parties are familiar with the names of all the objects and ideas relevant to the task. In some cases, the two individuals will have unequal power in the situation; for instance, when a boss is collaborating with an employee on a work-related project. Unequal distributions of power also have a strong effect on communication.

Feedback

Basically, feedback is the response that a communication message elicits from the receiver. For instance, if you are talking to your friend and your friend nods her head as you speak, she is giving you feedback that both of you understand to mean, "I agree with what you are saying." Obviously, vigorously shaking her head from side to side would transmit an entirely different message altogether. The amount and quality of the feedback in a conversation has a tremendous effect on the quality of the communication. As a conversation progresses, feedback allows each interlocutor to refine his or her message. This is another reason why face to face conversation is the format most conducive to effective Communication Processes. When we talk on the phone, for instance, we cannot see the other person, and therefore cannot identify nonverbal forms of feedback that

would allow us to refine our message appropriately.

Privacy

In conversation, the general goal of both parties should be to create a positive environment in which self-disclosure is encouraged. Of course, there are limits to the amount of self-disclosure that is appropriate in any social interaction. There are certain thoughts and feelings which good manners and propriety keep us from expressing, even though they may influence our participation in a conversation. This need for privacy is universal. For most people, there is not only a desire to maintain personal privacy but also a desire to respect the privacy of other people. There are certain things about other people that we simply do not want to know. The healthy balance between self-disclosure and privacy will vary in different relationships; for instance, a teenager will usually insist on a greater amount of privacy from his or her parents than from his or her peers. Part of the work of Communication Processes is establishing the boundaries of self-disclosure.

Communication event components

Every communication event has four components: source, message, channel, and receiver. The source is the person who is doing the speaking. The message consists of the words and the nonverbal forms of communication that are used to deliver the desired information. The channel refers to the venues for communication that are used to deliver the message. For instance, if you see your friend and say "hello" while waving, you are using the channels of words and gestures. Finally, the receiver is the individual or group of individuals who are receiving the message. In order for a communication event to be complete, it must have all four of these components. For example, if there is no receiver, we cannot say that a true communication event has taken place, since no information was transferred from one person to another. Similarly, if there is no

- 10 -

message, there is nothing to communicate, and therefore no communication has taken place.

Process model

Most speech communication theorists use what is called the process model of communication to diagram communication events. The four important components of a process model are speaker, message, channel, and receiver. These four elements will exist in any communication event, not just in a 2-person conversation. For instance, consider typing an essay on a computer. During this act, all four components of the process model are represented: the speaker is the person typing, the message is whatever the speaker is typing, the channel is the keystrokes, and the receiver is the computer on which the essay is being typed. In a conversation, the interlocutors will alternate the roles of speaker and receiver. For the most part, though, speech communication theorists find the process model to be an easy way to organize their study of communication events.

Feedback

Communications are constantly being refined and adjusted based on feedback. The process model of communication takes this into account. Indeed, the very name of this organizational scheme indicates that communication is to be thought of as an ongoing process. The process model of communication breaks the feedback process into three components: actor, goal, and observer. The actor is the person who is communicating and the goal is the person or thing to which the actor is trying to communicate. During a conversation, the goal is another person or a group of people, whereas during written composition the goal could be your computer. As the actor is attempting to communicate to the goal, he or she also functions as an observer, taking in whatever feedback is offered and subsequently adjusting the communication. When you receive an error message on your computer, for instance, you are receiving feedback that will influence your choices of communication in the future. This is known as a feedback loop.

Codes

The formulations of words and gestures that we use to communicate with one another are known in speech communication as codes. These are not secret codes; on the contrary, they depend for their effectiveness on our ability to understand them and assume that they will be understood by others. Every spoken language is a code because words are used as representations of things. The names that we use to describe the objects in the world and the abstract ideas in our minds are all part of the code. Furthermore, body language and hand gestures are part of a cultural code in which all of the members agree upon meaning. There is no inherit meaning in the gesture of raising one's hand and waving it, but it has been agreed upon by our culture that this gesture means greeting and welcome. In order to communicate effectively, one must understand both verbal and nonverbal codes, and must know how to make adjustments for the imperfect knowledge of codes found in the receiver.

Evaluation and criticism

Criteria for evaluation

There are three steps in the evaluation of a Communication Processes event: selecting the criteria for evaluation, describing the event, and making the evaluation. The first step, selecting the criteria for evaluation, establishes the qualities of communication which will be subjected to scrutiny. The particular criteria used to judge the quality of a communication event will vary depending on the kind of event. For instance, when evaluating a casual conversation, you might focus on warmth, clarity of expression, and comprehensibility. When evaluating a public speech, on the other hand, you might place more emphasis on audience analysis, appropriate gestures, and argument structure.

- 11 -

In an informal setting, we would not expect a speaker to have his or her message rigidly organized. On the other hand, we would be surprised if a public speaker did not have a firm grasp of his or her subject.

Process of description
After selecting the criteria that will be used in the evaluation of a Communication Processes event, one can turn to the task of describing the event itself. Naturally, the description of the communication event will emphasize those aspects, or channels, of the communication that correspond with the selected criteria. For instance, in the description of a public speech, one will naturally be more concerned with the structure of the speaker's argument and will therefore pay considerable attention to this subject when describing the event. When describing a casual conversation between friends, on the other hand, one might pay more attention to describing tone of voice and body language, as these communicate openness and ease. It is important for a description to make mention of all the communication channels utilized by the speaker.

Process of evaluating
After the criteria have been selected and the communication event has been described, one can set about evaluating the Communication Processes event. This simply means using the information from the description to decide whether the speaker has done an adequate job of meeting the standards set by the selected criteria. For instance, if it has been determined that effective argument structure is an important criterion for a successful public speaker, it will be necessary to evaluate whether a particular speaker has met this criterion. The evaluation is important because it enables progress to be made in communication. In a way, the process of evaluating communication is similar to the response to feedback made by the speaker. Consciously or unconsciously, a speaker is constantly evaluating the effectiveness of his or her communication and making adjustments based on these observations.

Critics as consumers of communication information
In order to be successful in Communication Processes, one needs to become a conscious critic. This does not mean hunting out the flaws in other people, or emphasizing the negative aspects of communication events. On the contrary, being an effective critic means paying attention to both the strengths and weaknesses of a communication event. Whether we realize it or not, we are all, to a greater or lesser degree, critics of communication. For instance, from a young age we are all inundated with advertisements. Over time, we become less and less susceptible to advertising because we begin to identify and discount its communication strategy. We implicitly understand the intentions of the advertiser and are therefore skeptical about the message. Speech communication education seeks to expand this healthy skepticism into everyday interpersonal interactions.

Purposes of rhetorical criticism
When speech communication theorists describe the process of breaking down and considering communication events, they often used the phrase rhetorical criticism. This simply means the critical analysis of rhetoric, or spoken words. Rhetoric often refers specifically to important messages delivered to a large group of people, as for instance in a political speech. The purpose of rhetorical criticism is to improve understanding of the strategies used by speakers. When understanding of rhetorical strategy is increased, speakers can refine and improve their messages, and the audience can develop a healthy degree of skepticism. In other words, rhetorical criticism can help us to become better producers and consumers of communication.

Criticism and advancing a cause

Oftentimes, individuals use rhetorical criticism to promote a particular cause they are interested in. In a democracy, making change depends on rallying the support of the public, and this in turn depends on crafting an effective message. When a group of people wants to promote a particular social or political issue, they need to develop a communication strategy that will positively influence the opinion of the general public. Advocacy groups use mailings, television ads, print ads, and speeches to deliver their message to the general public. Individuals can advocate for a cause through letters to the editor, informal speeches, and just by talking with friends. For all of these channels, a careful study of rhetorical strategy will be advantageous.

Criticism and solving problems in society

Many people also use rhetorical criticism as a means to solving problems. In particular, rhetorical criticism can be applied to the problems of the society. This is especially true in a democracy, where public debate generates most of the changes in laws and social conditions. To the degree that individuals with solutions can effectively communicate their message to the general public, they will be able to persuade citizens to give their votes and support to these solutions. Without effective communication, even the most logical solutions may not achieve the critical mass of public support required to be enacted. In a similar way, politicians are constantly self-critiquing and refining their communication techniques to increase their political capital.

Criticism can lead to greater knowledge

Rhetorical criticism is also able to improve our general understanding of the ways human beings communicate with one another. Most universities have several professors whose job it is to theorize and teach rhetorical criticism. The academic study of rhetoric focuses on the ways that human speech drives social change, unifies groups of people,

explains societal problems, and motivates social change. In particular, the study of rhetorical criticism focuses on the way in which human speech develops and maintains individual and collective identity. Finally, rhetorical criticism takes a close look at persuasion in the way in which language can motivate action in the real world.

Nonverbal communication

Nonverbal communication is any action or gesture which communicates information to another person. Nonverbal communication may be quite intentional, or it may be unconscious and habitual. Vague gestures, like the motions of the hands while explaining a point, are not typically considered as nonverbal communication since there precise meaning could not be understood without the accompanying language. Nevertheless, there are many body gestures which communicate specific meanings. For instance, a shrug of the shoulders indicates indecision or the expression, "I do not know." Although nonverbal communications should be able to stand on their own, their meaning will often depend on situational context. Furthermore, the nonverbal communication observed by one individual may be different from that which is observed by another. To a greater degree than with verbal communication, the interpretation of nonverbal communication is subjective.

Nonverbal effects

Enhancing spoken words: Nonverbal communication is the ability to enhance or elaborate on the words of the speaker. In particular, hand gestures and changes in vocal rhythm and volume have the ability to add expressiveness to what is being said. Many times, the gestures and vocal mechanisms of the speaker simply emphasize his or her message; at other times, however, the speaker may detract from or undermine his or her message with contradictory gestures. Hand gestures and gesticulations have the ability to dramatize a communication event. By giving

- 13 -

the audience other things than words to concentrate on, the speaker engages and entertains them.

Feedback: Although nonverbal communication is typically thought of as supplementary to the words that are being spoken during a communication event, it can also serve a vital purpose as feedback. The gestures, eye movements, facial expressions, and posture of the audience can often indicate their level of engagement more accurately and honestly then verbal criticism. It is very difficult to hide extreme boredom or rapt attention. The nonverbal communication of the audience will indicate their level of interest and acceptance of the message of the speaker. The speaker can then adjust his or her message accordingly.

Can alter the meaning of spoken words: At times, the nonverbal communication produced by a speaker will give a slightly different message than that of the speaker's words. This is often the case when a speaker is attempting to introduce an element of irony into his or her message. For instance, if at the conclusion of a bad movie one friend says to the other, "Well, that was a good use of my time," but smiles while saying the words, the other friend might assume that the message is being delivered with sarcasm. In other words, the speaker does not literally mean that the movie was a good use of time, but rather wishes to indicate that it was a waste of time. A message is being delivered, but the nonverbal communication and accompanying the words creates a complex message different than the mere words being spoken.

Can create contradictory communications: Sometimes, the nonverbal communication given by a speaker is contradictory to the words he or she is speaking. This can often create confusion and conflict. For instance, imagine a person is in distress. In some cultures, it is not considered dignified to ask another person for help, even in emergency situations. So, a person in dire need of

assistance might be saying that he or she does not need help, even though observation of nonverbal signs says otherwise. Obviously, this will create conflict in the mind of the audience, who will want to obey the wishes of the person but will also want to lend assistance to a person in need. When an individual directly contradicts his or her words with his or her nonverbal communication, it becomes much more difficult for the communication message to be interpreted.

Paralinguistics
The study of nonverbal communication is divided into three categories: paralinguistics, kinesics, and proxemics. Paralinguistics emphasizes vocal productions and sounds not strictly considered language. Indeed, the term paralinguistics means "beyond language." So, paralinguistics includes all of those noises a person can make to express meaning, as for instance grunts and snorts. In addition, paralinguistics includes elements of linguistic expression, like tone of voice, cadence, and pitch. A great deal can be communicated through the paralinguistic elements of speech. Indeed, the tone of a speaker's voice can either reinforce or contradict the words he is saying. Paralinguistics takes a look at the ways in which these elements contribute to communication.

The three most important paralinguistic factors are pronunciation, articulation, and voice quality. Pronunciation is the ability to effectively make vocal sounds that achieve communication goals. Proper pronunciation is relative to an individual's culture. Articulation is the ability to make distinct sounds which are intelligible to another person. Voice quality is an individual's ability to pronounce the vowels and consonants that are common in a given language. For the most part, voice quality is directly tied to the pronunciation of vowels, since these sounds last longer and are therefore more responsible for an individual's characteristic sound. The collection of vowels and consonants which make up the tonal repertory of a culture are known as the set of phonemes.

The articulation of consonants: Consonant sounds are created by stopping or redirecting a sound. For instance, an "s" sound is formed by pressing the tongue to the palette to slow down an escaping sound. Because consonants often depend on a percussive motion, it is possible to draw the amount for a long time. Similarly, because of their short duration, consonants do not have as much effect as vowels on the quality of an individual's voice. Because consonants are articulated quickly, they are often more difficult to hear. For this reason, speakers need to be especially sure to clearly articulate them. When a conversation is heard at a great distance, often all that can be discerned is a long string of vowels sounds. Similarly, individuals who mumble are doing a poor job of articulating consonants. Many individuals focus on pronunciation, but clear articulation of consonants is a prerequisite for this skill.

The major errors of articulation: As a child learns a new language, he or she has a tendency to omit sounds from words. Over time, the child will include all of the sounds, but may not be able to effectively articulate some of the more difficult consonants. For instance, the "t" sound is one which is often omitted from words, as for instance in the contraction "don't," which is often pronounced as "don'." As an individual begins to speak more quickly, he or she is even more likely to omit these common consonant sounds. To a certain extent, these errors of articulation are not a problem. When they become chronic and extreme, however, they can make speech extremely difficult to understand.

Vocal pitch: Vocal pitch is the measure of the frequency of a human voice. When the frequency is extremely high, we might say that a person has a whiny or nasal voice. When the frequency is extremely low, we

might say that a person has a rumbling or deep voice. Individuals vary the pitch of their voices in order to emphasize or deemphasize certain words in a sentence. For instance, people often raise the pitch of their voices in the last word of a question. Speech communication instructors consider changes in pitch to be a form of nonverbal communication, since the changes in pitch do not themselves contain a linguistic message. Changes in pitch are often made during the pronunciation of a single vowel sound, or between syllables in a word. In some languages, as for instance Chinese, pitch variations actually communicate meaning and cannot be considered nonverbal communication.

Volume and vocal delivery: The volume of an individual's voice is simply the relative loudness or softness of it. The primary requirement of vocal volume is that it must be loud enough for the intended audience to hear it. As long as this requirement is met, a speaker can utilize varying levels of volume in order to emphasize or deemphasize words and phrases. Obviously, using a higher level of volume draws special attention to what is being said, while speaking softly tends to diminish the perceived importance of the message. However, in the employ of a trained and skilled speaker, changes in volume can be quite artful. For instance, a speaker who has fully engaged the attention of his audience may lower the volume in order to force the audience to listen closely.

Speed and vocal delivery: Speech communication instructors consider vocal speed to be a subdivision of paralinguistics. Vocal speed, or rate of speech, is simply a measure of how fast an individual articulates syllables. In most cultures, a rapid rate of speech indicates excitement or urgency, while a slow rate of speech suggests calm and thoughtfulness. However, some cultures have a naturally fast or slow rate of speech. For instance, Spanish is typically spoken quite rapidly, even when the speaker is communicating information that has a normal level of urgency. English, on the other hand, is a more slowly-spoken language, especially by the citizens of the United Kingdom. In part, these varying rates of speech are determined by the characteristics of the language. The fact that Spanish words tend to end in a vowel makes it easier to string them together rapidly.

Functions of pauses in vocal delivery: Human speech is not just a constant stream of syllables. The placement and use of pauses during speech also plays an important role in forming meaning. The study of pauses in human speech is a subcategory of paralinguistics. A short pause is often used to denote the end of a sentence or clause. In many ways, short pauses are used like commas. Long pauses, on the other hand, are more similar to periods or the ends of paragraphs. When a speaker takes a long pause, he or she may be allowing what has been said to sink into the minds of the audience. Individuals often pause as they search for the right word. Other times, individuals will insert a slight pause into a sentence in order to create a level of suspense before the thought is finished.

Kinesics
Kinesics emphasizes the motions of the body that support and elaborate verbal communication. Gestures, facial expressions, and gesticulations are all considered in the field of kinesics. More generally, posture and overall body language are studied as part of kinesic observation. Note that the body motions of a speaker may either contribute to or detract from his or her message. For instance, an individual's facial expression may contradict what he or she is saying. As an example, consider an individual who is using strong language yet standing with his shoulders slumped and head down. Such an individual will be detracting from the confident message expressed by his language.

Proxemics
The study of nonverbal communication is divided into three categories: paralinguistics, kinesics, and proxemics. Proxemics focuses on the relative positions of the individuals who are taking part in a communication event. The dynamics of a communication event are different depending on the proximity and relative positions of the speaker and his or her audience. For instance, if a speaker is delivering his or her message from a raised platform, the effect is different than if he or she were casually strolling through the audience during the speech. Because of the subtle effects of positioning during a communication message, proxemics is frequently invoked by stage managers. For speech communication teachers, however, proxemic study will focus on unrehearsed and informal arrangements of people during communication.

Four proxemic distances: Speech communication theorists distinguish four essential proxemic distances: intimate distance, personal distance, social distance, and public distance. Intimate distance is the degree of separation common to individuals who know each other very well and are comfortable being physically intimate, for instance parents and children or mates. Intimate distance is at the most 2 feet. Personal distance, meanwhile, is around 2 1/2 feet. It is the distance maintained between two individuals who know each other and are engaged in a friendly, casual conversation. Social distance is usually defined as being from 4 to 7 feet, and is the appropriate distance for impersonal and formal conversations. Finally, public distance is 12 feet or more, and is the amount of distance appropriate for the delivery of speeches to a group of people. Public distance is great enough to focus the attention of the audience on an individual speaker.

Emphasis on geographic relationships in proxemics: In their study of proxemics, speech communication theorists place a great degree of emphasis on geographic location -- that is, the relative positions of the participants in a communication event. To begin with, the distances between the various parties are important; the closer the participants in a communication event, the more intimate with one another they can be assumed to be. If one individual is placed above the other members of the communication event, he or she can be assumed to have some sort of elevated status or authority. When individuals are placed around a round table, on the other hand, we may assume that they are equal in importance, and that a democratic discussion rather than a lecture will take place.

Defining boundaries: The proxemics of a communication event often indicate the boundaries of the parties involved. Individuals have a concept of personal space and territoriality, and tend to be defensive if they believe another person is encroaching on their area. A teacher who lectures from a podium at the front of the class, for instance, would be made uncomfortable if a student got out of his or her chair and stood next to the podium. Similarly, an informal conversation might become uncomfortable for one of the parties if there is too little distance between him and the other participants. For the most part, the appropriate distances between people during a communication event are indicated without explicit mention. In part, the appropriate distance is a cultural designation. However, participants in a communication event can indicate their preferred position through gestures, or simply by moving forward or back.

Defining a communication event: The relative positions and distances between the participants in a communication event can indicate a great deal about the quality of the event, even when none of the content of the message is known. For instance, when two people are standing very close to one another during a conversation, we can assume that they are intimate with one another and are

discussing a subject of personal interest to each. On the other hand, if two individuals are standing at a considerable distance from one another and avoiding eye contact, we can assume that they either do not know each other very well or they are not well disposed to one another. If one party attempts to close the distance with the other party and the other party resists, we can assume that the first party desires a greater degree of intimacy than does the second.

Defining interpersonal relationships: The evolution of interpersonal relationships can be charted by the changes in proxemics. When two people first meet, they are likely to maintain a social distance, between 4 and 7 feet. This distance indicates formality and impersonality. If the two people develop a closer relationship, however, they will likely begin to stand closer to one another during communication. Another scenario in which proxemics denotes interpersonal relationship is when the parties have varying degrees of power. For instance, communication events in which one person is positioned by himself or herself while the others are facing him or her indicate that the isolated individual has a greater degree of power than the others.

How patterns are learned
One of the main issues in nonverbal communication study is the degree to which nonverbal communication patterns are learned or inherited. Researchers are particularly interested in whether certain gestures have the same meaning for individuals from different cultures. In general, they have discovered that the individuals learn basic nonverbal communication patterns from their parents and the other senior members of their community. At the same time, each individual develops his or her own idiosyncratic nonverbal mechanisms, which reinforce that individual's identity. Interestingly, people tend to use more individualized nonverbal communication techniques at moments of high excitement or stress.

Feedback

Nonverbal feedback
In order to be an effective receiver of communication, a person must be able to give clear nonverbal feedback. In particular, facial expressions are a key way of signaling interest and understanding (or the lack thereof). If a person can display subtle gradations in understanding and interest with his or her face, he or she is much more likely to receive a refined and well-adjusted message. Traditionally, smiles and head nods are good indications that the message is being understood, and that the listener agrees. On the other hand, a shake of the head or a frown tends to indicate disagreement with the speaker's message, or sometimes, an inability to comprehend the content. What many people forget is that the receiver in a communication event must be as active and engaged as the speaker in order for the event to be considered a success.

Verbal feedback
In order to be an effective receiver, a person needs to be able to issue timely and thoughtful verbal feedback. For instance, a receiver needs to be able to ask pertinent questions if he or she does not understand a particular aspect of the delivered message. At the same time, the receiver needs to be able to describe his or her reaction to the delivered message, whether it be confusion, agreement, or disagreement. Oftentimes, questioning that encourages the speaker to elaborate and refine his or her message can lead to new insights that were not contained in the original message. In pedagogy, this is known as the Socratic Method. In terms of verbal feedback, however, the most important function of a receiver is to continually indicate his or her level of understanding of the delivered message.

Listening

For most students, the vast majority of information is obtained through listening.

Despite the large amount of reading that most students have to do, they still take in more information through their ears than through their eyes. Good listening is an essential part of the communication process, because it advances the interests of both the speaker and the listener. Obviously, the listener needs to understand and remember what he or she hears so that he or she can consider the information accurately. At the same time, the listener protects his or her own interests by developing an accurate impression of what the other person has to say. Meanwhile, the ability of the speaker to have his or her message be effective is dependent on the listening skills of the audience.

Basic characteristics of the speech listener
The individual or groups of individuals who listen to a speech bring their own characteristics to bear on the quality of the speech. For one thing, listeners will always have their own intentions. That is, they will always be seeking to obtain something from the speech, whether it is information or entertainment. Listeners will also have varying degrees of skill, meaning that some groups will be better at understanding a complex message. Listeners will also bring their pre-existing attitudes towards the speaker and the speaker's subject. In order to deliver an effective message, a speaker needs to perform an audience analysis to determine the characteristics of his or her listeners.

Listening for comprehension
Although listening appears to be a passive process, it must be active in order to be effective. Indeed, the listener should have a purpose for listening. The precise purpose of listening need not be conscious in the mind of the listener. Speech communication teachers generally distinguish four intentions of listening: comprehension, criticism, empathy, and appreciation. These intentions are often intermingled in the same act of listening. When we listen for comprehension, we are trying to understand the message the speaker is communicating. In order to listen for

comprehension, we need to know the standards of grammar and punctuation in English. We also need to know the common forms of argument. We also need to have an understanding of the context in which the words are spoken so that we can understand the relationship between message and context.

Listening for the purposes of criticism

Most speech communication teachers will say that in order to listen for the purposes of criticism, one must also be listening for comprehension. It is true that in order to accurately assess the quality of a verbal communication, you will need to understand the content of the communication first. To a certain degree, however, we all apply critical listening skills to communication we have yet to fully understand. For instance, when we hear an advertisement on the radio, we know immediately that the speaker is trying to sell us something, and so we are naturally receptive or skeptical of the message, depending on our preexisting interest in the product or service. In this case, our critical listening skills are influencing our listening even before we have begun to comprehend the content.

Listening for empathy

Oftentimes, people listen to one another as a demonstration of empathy. Empathy is the ability to understand and appreciate what another person is going through even though you are not going through it. One of the ways a person can express their understanding and compassion for another person is simply by listening to them. By listening to other person, you are indicating that the other person's problems are worth your time. Most people find that not only is listening a good way to demonstrate empathy, but it is a good way to develop empathy. It seems that when we listen to one another, we gradually develop a sense of each other's internal worlds, and we come to treat each other with more compassion.

Listening for appreciation

In many cases, the person is listening not necessarily for information but simply to appreciate the quality of what the other person is saying. Many conversations are designed for the entertainment of the listener so it is not absurd to say that one listens to another person talk with the same appreciation one would have when listening to a piece of music. At the same time, it is important to take the speaker seriously on his or her own terms. If the speaker is trying to be gravely serious, it may not be polite to simply listen for appreciation. In many cases, though, and especially when listening to a speaker who is exceptionally fluent or more interesting, it is appropriate for a listener simply to appreciate the sound and meaning of the speaker.

Physical, mental, and emotional obstacles

There are a number of things that can prevent a person from listening effectively. Perhaps the most common is an external distraction, like background noise or confusing motion. There are also the internal distractions on the part of the listener, however, as for instance, anxiety or other preoccupations. Many people are desperate to express themselves, and fail to listen to other people because they are so focused on what they want to say. Also, many people have personal biases regarding what the other person is saying that prevent them from listening effectively. Any of these problems can prevent effective communication processes.

Listening for content

In almost every listening situation, the audience is required to listen for information. A communication can only be considered effective if the message communicates the information intended by the speaker. The feedback issued by the audience indicates the degree to which the information has been received accurately. When the audience is required to ask for clarification or repetition of the message, it is possible that the speaker has been ineffective in delivering his or her information. Moreover, if the audience provides no verbal feedback about a delivered message, it is possible that they either did not understand any of the message or are simply not interested in the message. Of course, when there is no verbal feedback it is also possible that the audience simply understood the transmitted message perfectly and they require no clarification or elaboration.

Unwillingness to listen
Communication can be significantly obstructed when the intended receiver is unwilling to listen. This is a common situation on television talk shows, when all of the guests and the host try to talk at once. When this occurs, no one is listening and therefore no messages can be considered complete. In order for a communication events take place, all the parties involved must accept that there can only be one speaker at a time. Frequently, the unwillingness to be a receiver is a symptom of a poor interpersonal relationship. Unwillingness to listen is a classic sign of disrespect. Other times, however, a failure to listen is simply product of unfamiliarity between two parties. With a little bit of patience and practice, this obstacle can be overcome, and complete communication events can take place.

Effectively receiving information
In order for a communication event between two people to be effective, both parties need to alternate the roles of speaker and receiver. Moreover, each receiver should ensure that the message of the speaker is fully understood before delivering his or her own message. Through the use of feedback, like clarifying questions and comments, the message of the speaker can be elaborated and made plain. A conversation cannot really move forward until both parties understand what has been said. This is not to say that the two parties are required to agree on what has been said. On the contrary, some of the best conversations are those in which two parties calmly and descriptively elaborate their differences. In order to be effective communicators, people

need to be able to play both the role of speaker and the role of receiver with skill and dexterity.

Creative listening
Speech communication instructors often use the phrase "creative listening" to describe extremely engaged receivers who are constantly encouraging the speaker to develop and specialized his or her message. An extremely good listener can often discern implications and ideas inherent in the message that may not have been known even to the speaker. In this way, a creative listener can actually add value to the content of the message. Some of the best conversations involve interplay between speaker and creative listener, as each plays ideas off the other until new and exciting conclusions are reached. Creative listening also demonstrates the receiver's interest and respect for the speaker. Often, this has the effect of encouraging the speaker to improve and expand his or her message.

Psychological effects of listening
Simply listening to another person can have profound psychological implications. Indeed, the entire field of psychoanalysis is largely based on the idea that having a sympathetic audience for one's problems is profoundly therapeutic. Many people pay a great deal of money simply to have a sympathetic listener who can offer some professional advice. Psychoanalysts are especially skilled at creative listening. That is, they are able to unpack the message of the speaker and discern new, possibly hidden meanings. Numerous studies have indicated that the process of verbally elaborating and describing personal issues eases the burden of stress on the mind, regardless of whether the interpretation of these issues is accurate or constructive.

Defensiveness and good listening
Defensiveness can be extremely limiting to an individual's ability to listen properly. When a person is defensive, he or she is overly

concerned with protecting his or her own interests. Defensiveness is especially prevalent in communication processes where the two parties do not trust one another. However, some paranoid individuals may be naturally more inclined to defensiveness than others. The problem with defensiveness is that it indicates that the attention of the listener is on his or her own concerns, rather than with the content of the message being delivered. To the degree that a listener is not focusing on the message being delivered, his or her ability to understand and respond to the message will be impaired.

Speech communication theorists identify a number of ways in which defensiveness can impair effective and accurate communication. These ways are basically defined by the attitude of the listener. For instance, some defensive listeners adopt an overly evaluative posture in which they indicate that it is up to them to decide whether the speaker is competent or not. Other defensive listeners adopt a self-consciously apathetic attitude, as if to indicate that they are above being interested in the message of the speaker. Another common listening attitude for a defensive individual is certainty, or the assumption that he or she already knows the content of the message. This attitude draws the speaker up short and makes it difficult for him or her to continue communicating.

Active listening
Active listening is a technique of communication reception in which the listener tries to develop an empathic relationship with the speaker. Proponents of this form of listening declare that too much of listening contains an unhelpful evaluative aspect, such that the speaker continually feels in danger of being criticized by the listener. In active listening, on the other hand, the listener makes an effort to fully experience the thought process of the speaker before even beginning to judge. Perhaps most importantly, active listening is a skill that is developed over time. In order to fully engage

with what someone is saying, the listener must practice subverting his or her own ego and focusing instead on the perceived interests of the speaker.

Listening versus hearing
For most people, listening and hearing are synonyms. However, in the world of speech communication, there is a subtle distinction between the two acts. Hearing is simply receiving a sound in the ear. In other words, hearing is the physiological and neurological act of converting heard sounds into meaning. Listening, on the other hand, is the more active process of taking what is heard and interpreting it. All the time we are listening to the words of those around us, using our knowledge of language and cultural values to determine the meaning of what is said. Listening, then, is a more subjective act than hearing.

Listening styles
RRP listeners: Experts in speech communication distinguish between three listening styles: RRP, VAT, and SUR. The first category, RRP, includes reasons-oriented listeners, results-oriented listeners, and process-oriented listeners. Reason-oriented listeners will be interested in hearing the logical support for a given argument. Results-oriented listeners, on the other hand, are interested in the overall intention of the idea or argument. Process-oriented listeners, finally, are interested in the way a particular idea or argument was conceived. All of these types of listeners will be very interested in the specific details of a speech. In order to impress an RRP listener, you will need to have your details in order and possess an extensive knowledge of the subject.

VAT listeners: Experts in speech communication distinguish between three listening styles: RRP, VAT, and SUR. VAT listeners are so called because their listening style emphasizes the visual, auditory, or tactile elements of a speech. A visual listener will focus on the aspects of the presentation that can be seen, whether it is body language and physical presentation of the speaker or any visual aids accompanying the speech. To engage an audience of visual listeners, the speaker should be sure to have sufficient visual aids on hand. An auditory listener, meanwhile, will be most interested in the words spoken by the speaker. Auditory listeners will not need the presence of visual aids to hold their attention during a speech. Tactile listeners, finally, need to have some physical contact in order to truly appreciate what is being described. Physical demonstrations, handouts, and sample materials are all good ways to engage the attention of tactile listeners.

SUR listener: Experts in speech communication distinguish between three listening styles: RRP, VAT, and SUR. The SUR listening style gets its name because those who practice it are self-absorbed, unfocused, and rules-driven. Self-absorbed listeners are preoccupied with their concerns and have a hard time paying attention to the ideas or interests of another person. Unfocused listeners are not skilled or knowledgeable enough to listen well, and have a hard time understanding an argument or complicated idea. Rules-driven listeners, meanwhile, tend to obsess about minor points of reason and logic instead of paying attention to the most important aspects of a speech's message. In other words, rules-driven listeners "cannot see the forest for the trees."

SUR is an acronym for a listening style in which the audience is self-absorbed, unfocused, and rules driven. Unfortunately, there are some other common obstacles to listening besides being self-absorbed, unfocused, or rules driven. Many individuals simply do not pay attention or they allow their minds to wander off in a digression from the major ideas of the message. In scientific studies of listening behavior, researchers have observed that information can be processed by the human mind much more quickly than it is capable of being delivered in a speech, which means that the brain often performs other tasks alongside listening. Obviously, these other tasks run the risk of hindering effective listening and concentration. Some research has suggested, however, that many individuals require a small amount of distraction in order to concentrate effectively. For instance, many people are able to study more intensely when listening to music at the same time.

Intentional listening
The ideal speech listener will not simply sit back and allow the words being spoken to wash over him or her. Rather, an effective listener will engage in what is known as "intentional listening," an active state of processing, interpreting, and thinking critically about a speech. It is always good for the audience members to ask themselves what they hope to gain from a speech before it begins, as this will focus their attention and give purpose to their listening. As a speech is being given, audience members should be attempting to place each successive idea into an overall framework.

Appreciative and therapeutic listening
Speech communication researchers have identified five basic kinds of intentional listening: appreciative, therapeutic, discriminative, comprehensive, and critical. Appreciative listening is perhaps the most passive form of listening. An appreciative listener is simply seeking to obtain as much pleasure as possible from the words being spoken. Although the intention of many speeches is to entertain the audience, an appreciative listener may not pay enough attention to the actual message being delivered by the speaker. Therapeutic listening, on the other hand is listening with the intention of obtaining as much emotional support as possible. Many times, individuals who listen to sermons and motivational speeches are engaged in therapeutic listening. The message of the speech empowers them and makes them feel better.

Critical listening

Speech communication researchers have identified five basic kinds of intentional listening: appreciative, therapeutic, discriminative, comprehensive, and critical. Critical listening is the most active form of audience behavior. It entails organizing and interpreting the information contained in a speech. As a speech is given, the critical listener will be evaluating the arguments or ideas presented by the speaker, weighing the evidence given, and thinking of possible problems with the speech. As consumers, we are engaged in a form of critical listening every time we hear an advertisement. During a speech, however, many people sympathize with the speaker rather than evaluate the message of the speaker critically.

Discriminative listening

Speech communication researchers have identified five basic kinds of intentional listening: appreciative, therapeutic, discriminative, comprehensive, and critical. Discriminative listening focuses on the aspects of a speaker's message that are implied rather than spoken directly. A discriminative listener is paying attention to the sound of voice, body language, and implicit argument of the speaker. To a certain extent, we are all always involved in discriminative listening, though some of us focus on it more than others. A sophisticated listener obtains information not only from the message but from the medium in which it is delivered.

Listening for comprehension

Speech communication researchers have identified five basic kinds of intentional listening: appreciative, therapeutic, discriminative, comprehensive, and critical. Listening for comprehension is probably the most familiar form of listening. Students in a classroom are engaged in listening for comprehension when they take notes during a lecture. Whenever we listen to an informative or persuasive speech in order to obtain information about a subject, we are engaged

in listening for comprehension. The validity and accuracy of other forms of listening, as for instance critical listening and discriminative listening, depend on effective listening for comprehension. If an individual is unable to understand the message that is being presented, he or she will not be able to critique it insightfully.

Detached, intentional listening

When speech communication instructors describe the ideal listener, they often refer to detaching or decentering. They are referring to the process of considering the speaker's message on its own terms rather than in the context of the listener's experience and emotions. Basically, this just means giving a speaker a fair hearing before applying critical thinking to his or her message. Too often, audience members prejudge a message based on their past experience or existing opinions. This not only prevents the audience member from acquiring a better understanding, but it significantly handicaps the audience member's ability to listen for comprehension. Even when a speech is being delivered on a familiar subject, the audience should try to keep an open mind to gain as much as possible from the speech.

When speech communication instructors refer to the five kinds of listening (appreciative, therapeutic, discriminative, and comprehensive, and critical), they do not mean to suggest that these forms of listening exist independent of one another at all times. On the contrary, the members of an audience may be engaged in several different kinds of listening at the same time. Furthermore, it is quite common for the members of an audience to adjust their listening style during the course of a speech. For instance, whereas at the beginning of a speech an audience member may be strictly listening for comprehension, as the speech goes on he or she may begin to listen more critically. Similarly, an audience member may at first pay attention strictly to the explicit message of the speaker, but may later become more interested in the implications of the speech, and may therefore be engaged more in discriminative listening.

RRA technique for active listening

When speech communication instructors describe active listening, they sometimes refer to the RRA (review, relate, anticipate) technique. This technique breaks the process of active listening down into three easy steps. To begin with, an active listener is constantly reviewing what has been said and placing new information into the evolving model of the message. As the listener considers the speaker's argument or idea, he or she relates it to his or her foundational knowledge. In other words, the audience member tries to compare and contrast the speaker's message with his or her own knowledge of the subject. Finally, an active listener tries to anticipate the rest of the speaker's message. Not only is this a good way to stay engaged with a speech, it provides an excellent measure of attention. When a listener is able to confidently predict the direction of a speech, he or she can be certain that his or her understanding of what has been said so far is sound.

Listening and the emotions

In order to be a good listener, a member of the audience needs to keep his emotions in check. Of course, this is not always easy. Sometimes, the fiery rhetoric or sentimentality of a speaker is designed to sweep the audience into a heightened emotional state. However, as much as possible audience members should try to retain control of their critical faculties in order to give an accurate and objective appraisal of the merits of the speech. Indeed, part of an objective and comprehensive analysis of a speech will be the methods by which the speaker attempts to engage the emotions of the audience. If the audience member finds that his or her emotions are roused by the speaker, he or she can say that the emotional appeal of the speaker has been successful. This, however, does not necessarily speak to the merit of the speaker's argument.

Critical listening and public speeches

Critical listening is perhaps most important in the context of public speeches, since there will be less opportunity for each audience member to clarify the remarks of the speaker through questions after the conclusion of the speech. In other words, each audience member will be on his or her own in the task of deciphering and evaluating the speaker's message. For this reason, many audience members try to make brief notes and chart out the structure of a speaker's argument. Speeches delivered to large crowds often involve appeals to the emotion. A speaker can get away with histrionic gestures and exaggerated vocal mannerisms before a large crowd, when these same techniques might seem ridiculous before a small group.

Considering content of a speech

When considering the content of a speech, audience members should pay special attention to three basic areas: main ideas, organization, and supporting evidence. The main ideas of the speech are the fundamental arguments or concepts the speaker is trying to convey. If the speech is effective, the main ideas will be obvious. Audience members should be paying the most attention to the articulation and elaboration of these main ideas. The way in which the main ideas are expressed and supported is referred to as the organization of the speech. In order for a speech to be effective, the speaker needs to organize his or her ideas clearly and avoid long digressions that obscure his or her main points. Finally, the audience member needs to consider what supporting materials the speaker is using to provide evidence for his or her ideas or arguments. The audience member needs to consider whether these supporting materials are appropriate and credible.

Assessing the situation in which a speech is given

In order to get the most out of a speech, a listener needs to consider all of the various factors that contribute to the speaker's

- 24 -

message. One of the factors that does not receive a great deal of attention is the situation in which the speech is delivered. Many times, the physical and interpersonal setting in which a speech is delivered has a great deal of influence on the message. For instance, an audience member might consider whether the speaker has been required to make his or her address more or less formal for the occasion. The audience member also might consider whether the occasion on which the speech is being delivered has influenced the quality of the speaker's message. Finally, the audience member should consider whether the physical environment in which the speech is delivered has been more or less conducive to his or her understanding and appreciation of the speaker's message.

Assessing the characteristics of the speaker
As part of the overall critique of a speech, an audience member should consider the personal characteristics of the speaker. For instance, the audience member might consider what he or she knew about the speaker before the speech, and then decide whether this information had any influence on his or her interpretation of the speaker's message. The audience member might also consider whether the speaker's personal presentation indicated credibility or made his or her message difficult to believe. Many times, a speaker with a good message and solid supporting materials comes across as vague and disorganized because of his or her physical appearance and vocal mannerisms. Audience members should try to distinguish between weaknesses in the speaker's message and weaknesses in the speaker's personal presentation.

Analyzing the message of the speech
When the member of an audience listens to a speech, he or she should be attending to three fundamental factors: ideas, organization, and support. The most important thing to consider is whether the speaker's main ideas are logical and clearly expressed. If the ideas

are comprehensible, an audience member can then consider whether they have been expressed in the logical order, or whether the speaker has presented them in a disorganized fashion. Finally, the audience member needs to consider whether the speaker's main ideas have been adequately supported by argument or factual evidence. Does the speaker provide enough support for his arguments to remain credible? Is the evidence provided relevant to the main ideas of the speech?

Importance of deciding to listen
It sounds strange, but it is actually a good idea to consciously decide to listen when involved in Communication Processes. Most people fail to listen properly because they are not intentional listeners and they allow themselves to become distracted by secondary stimuli. When a person makes a conscious decision to listen, he or she naturally ignores all the other kinds of activity that is going on in the background. Also, once a person gets into the habit of consciously listening to other people, he or she will find that his or her listening skills improve exponentially. Many people do not realize just how satisfying Communication Processes can be until they make a conscious decision to listen.

Maintaining proper attention
It is essential to maintain attention throughout the delivery of a speech. In order to get the full value of a speech, each member of the audience has to understand the entire structure of the speech, and this can only be done by maintaining attention throughout. If, for example, one misses the beginning of the speech, one will not understand what all of the supporting arguments and evidence are supporting. On the other hand, if one listens to the beginning of the speech but allows one's attention to trail off, one will come away from the speech without knowing the precise reasons why the thesis statement of the speaker should be believed.

Concentrating on message structure

An effective member of the audience for a speech will be able to outline the structure of the speech in his mind. The basic outline of a speech will include the main argument, supporting arguments, and supporting evidence and reasoning. Only by making sense of structure can an audience member truly diagnose the strengths and weaknesses of the speech. For instance, an audience member should be able to tell whether the speaker has done a good job of ordering his points. If the speaker makes the mistake of initiating his speech with minor points and only later working in more essential arguments, the audience members should be able to identify this error and determine whether it reflects poorly on the speaker or on the argument as the whole.

Demographics

Cultural demographics

One way of looking at culture is through the lens of category distinctions. The process of dividing people into categories is commonly known as demographics. The most common demographics are age, gender, sexual orientation, religious affiliation, ethnicity, and socioeconomic status. When an individual considers his or her own culture, he or she typically considers it as a set of memberships in these various categories. In speech communication, we are constantly considering the prejudices and values that influence speech and the interpretation of the spoken word. Part of the process of speech communication instruction is to bring the implicit cultural information in speech to light so that it can be analyzed and critiqued.

Identification with demographic categories

In speech communication, one is required to view speech through the lens of received and lived culture. In other words, one is required to consider how elements of culture influence the medium and message of speech, as well as the interpretation of the spoken word. One of the most important aspects of an individual,

then, will be the extent to which he or she identifies with various demographic categories. Some people, for instance, have a strong identification with their ethnic or religious background, while others base their self conception more on their gender or age. Age, of course, is a demographic identification that changes with time. Indeed, all demographic identifications may change with time, as an individual acquires more information and critically evaluates the prejudices and values of his or her culture.

Cultural ideology

Whether consciously or not, every individual has adopted certain ideas, patterns of thought, and prejudices from his or her native culture. This native worldview is known as a cultural ideology. The cultural ideology of a particular group permeates every aspect of the group's existence. It defines what is important in the group, what is right or wrong in the group, and how members of the group should behave. Oftentimes, the aspects of an individual's native ideology are so ingrained that they are considered "common sense" and are never really held up to scrutiny. Ideologies are important because they provide individuals with a moral compass and a sense of pattern in the world; however, it is important to develop an ability to think clearly and objectively about one's own ideology.

Cultural hegemony

Cultural hegemony is any relationship in which one party is dominant and one party is submissive, and in which both roles are agreed upon by the participants. Every culture establishes basic hegemonies, in part as a way of organizing the populace. For instance, in Asian cultures it is typical for the husband to impose his will on the wife, although she may subtly exercise power in her own right. Both partners agree that this is the proper hegemonic relationship between married couples. The hegemonies are not necessarily bad; in fact, they are useful ways of distributing power and responsibility in a society. As students of speech communication, though, we need to be conscious of the ways in which language establishes and reinforces hegemony. Over time, it may be necessary for a culture to modify its hegemonies in response to the repressed needs of certain people.

Cultural enactment

Cultural enactment is the process in which an individual fulfills with his or her words or behavior the expectations of his or her culture. In other words, cultural enactment is the "acting out" of cultural values. All of us are engaged in cultural enactment throughout our lives. When we rise in the morning, go off to work, and fulfill our roles as professionals, we are adhering to the expectations of our society. When we relate in a certain way to our family members, we are fulfilling our roles as mothers, fathers, brothers, sisters, etc. In speech communication, we study cultural enactment as it is performed in language. Whether consciously or not, we are constantly adhering to the expectations of society with our manner of speaking and with the message we present. Speech communication seeks to analyze this process.

Cultural embodiment

Although every person grows up and develops with a particular cultural background, very rarely do we take the time to objectively consider it. In part, this is because it is very difficult to put into words the ideology that supports our worldview. Nevertheless, we are constantly producing and reinforcing the values shared by the members of our community with our speech. This process of expressing cultural assumptions is known as cultural embodiment. Literally, cultural embodiment means giving a body to the unconscious values and beliefs held by a particular culture. In speech communication studies, we are particularly interested in cultural embodiment through language. One of the goals of studying speech communication is to acquire an objective

understanding of one's own culture as it is produced by speech.

Demographic analysis

Before delivering a speech, a speaker should, if possible, engage in some basic demographic analysis. The following are the most important demographic categories: age, education, gender, group membership, and cultural background. In many groups, all of the audience members will be of the same age, and the speech can therefore be tailored to their maturity level. As far as education, it is important to know about the audience's experiences and knowledge regarding the topic before the speech begins. Many times, the members of the audience will all be members of a specific group such as a school class or a civic group. Finally, the cultural background of a group should be considered because the group's values, taboos, predilections, and ethics could be offended by the speech.

Media and Their Influences

Role of media

Informing the public

The mass media plays a central role in informing the general public about local and global events. When most people think about information disseminated through the media, they think about news programming. But there are a number of other venues through which information is transmitted to the public. For instance, nature documentaries and talk shows inform the general public on issues which are perhaps less immediately pertinent to their lives. The federal government uses channels of communication, like the radio and television, to broadcast emergency messages and promote governmental policies. Magazines and newspapers can also disseminate detailed information on behalf of government agencies.

Changing attitudes and behavior

Although the precise power of the media is a matter of controversy, it is beyond question that the major media outlets have an ability to persuade the general public. To take the most obvious example, advertisements on television clearly have a positive effect on sales. Many of the ways in which the media can influence attitudes and behavior are more subtle, however. For instance, simply by providing information about a particular subject, the media can influence popular opinion. As for its influence on behavior, it's easy to think of examples where people choose to spend time with the television or radio rather than doing other things.

Entertaining the public

In public surveys, people cite entertainment that is the number one reason for engaging with mass media. This data is produced by Nielsen ratings, which indicate that sports, comedy, and drama programming is watched much more frequently than news. Moreover, the line between information and entertainment is often blurred. For instance, many documentaries which purport to be informative are also quite entertaining. Indeed, the inherently entertaining nature of mass media communication is an amazing tool for engaging an audience in educational and informative programming. Many people acquire a broad knowledge of the world through television and radio without ever realizing that they are engaged in a process of education.

Spurring public conversation

One of the key roles of the mass media is to inspire and shape public dialogue. For instance, the news media's coverage of a political issue can set up debate. Many people have alleged over the years that the news media in the United States has a particular political bias. Some people claim it has a liberal bias, while others claim it is a

conservative bias. Perhaps the safest criticism one can make of the news media is that it has an inherent interest in conflict, because controversy and disagreement is more interesting to viewers. Most critics of the mass media agree that it is influenced in large part by the desire to sell advertising space.

Framing discussion

One of the media's greatest responsibilities is to frame public discussion in a fair and objective way. In other words, the media is charged with reporting the news in a way that gives ample space to all reasonable points of view and does not ignore pertinent facts on either side. The role of the media in influencing discussion in a society has led some critics to refer to news outlets as "information gatekeepers." It is important that there be vocal critics of the news media, to identify and remedy problems of objectivity. To a certain degree, all citizens are responsible for casting a skeptical eye on the news media, and making sure that they enable free and fair discussion.

Radio

At one point in American history, radio communication was the most important means of mass communication. The first commercial radio station began broadcasting in 1920. At first, radio was not very popular, because most people could not afford home receivers. As these devices began to infiltrate American homes, however, programming expanded, and the radio became a source of information and entertainment. In 1941, the first FM station began broadcasting, allowing signals to be transmitted over long distances with a very small amount of static. Although radio communication has been somewhat superseded by television and the Internet, it is still an invaluable source of information and entertainment for millions of people.

When it was first introduced, radio was the most important form of mass communication.

Unlike telegraphs, radios could deliver complex messages about events as they happened. Also, radio allowed for dramatic use of the human voice and special sound effects. In general, radio is just a more personal medium than telegraph communication. Eventually, however, the ability of television to transmit images and sound would allow it to dominate radio as a form of mass communication. Still, radio is the predominant medium for the transmission of music and is an important player in the transmission of news.

One of the most important periods in the history of radio communication was the development of radio networks. Radio networks first started as a way to offset the costs of maintaining radio towers and transmission equipment. Radio networks began to sell commercials to advertising businesses. The businesses would pay the radio station for the right to air their advertisements. Various radio stations joined together in networks and gave one another permission to air each other's shows. In this way, radio stations around the country standardized programming and made radio a viable business. Each station was able to produce a smaller amount of better programming.

Motion pictures

The first motion pictures were developed by Thomas Edison and his associates in 1893. After a few years of tinkering, motion pictures were introduced to the general public and were immediately popular. Many stores offered nickelodeons, in which patrons could watch a brief presentation for a nickel. Around 1910, a small film industry began to develop in Hollywood, California. In 1912, the first full-size theaters were introduced. In the mid-1920s, sound was added to motion pictures, which had previously been silent or accompanied by live music. By 1929, all new films had sound.

Motion pictures have played an important role in the economic and social life of the United States. Perhaps the first example of the effect of the movies was during the Great Depression, when motion pictures continue to portray images of success and wealth in spite of widespread poverty outside the theater. It is at this point that people first began to remark upon the escapism inherent in the movie watching experience. Subsequently, movies have also proven to be a powerful medium for exploring real and tragic events. A good example of this would be the newsreels of battle footage from World War II, as well as the many powerful movies that have been made on the subject of the Vietnam War.

Television

Television is so entrenched in daily American life that it can be hard to remember that it has only really been on the scene for the past sixty years. The first television broadcasts took place in 1939. It was only after World War II, however, that television truly burst onto the American scene. At first, televisions were extremely expensive and only broadcast in black and white. Also, when televisions were first introduced, radio communication was still the most popular medium. Over time, however, televisions became smaller, less expensive, and began to broadcast quality programming. After approximately a decade, television supplanted radio as the most popular form of mass communication in the United States.

Because of its ability to deliver visual images and sound, television has proven to be an excellent medium for transmitting news. Many people get all of their information from the television. Television transmission has allowed people to learn about life in the far reaches of the world which they would never have a chance to visit on their own. At the same time, many television news programs seek to provide in-depth analysis and evaluation of local, state, federal, and global issues. Television has proven to be an excellent medium for interviews and documentaries, as well.

For most people, television is primarily a source of entertainment. Comedies, sports, dramas, game shows, and reality programs are among the most popular forms of television entertainment. Perhaps the most venerable form of television entertainment is the soap opera, so named because the first programs targeted housewives and were sponsored by soap companies. Some television programs aired at a regular time for years on end, while others (called miniseries) are only on the air for a limited period. Television executives decide which entertainment shows to keep by evaluating Nielsen ratings, which measure the number of viewers for each program.

Over time, television has become big business. Television stations make most of their money by airing commercials. Although television stations must pay for their transmission equipment, they primarily pay for the development of programming. Television networks, similar to radio networks, developed as a way to share the costs of program development. Broadcast television, which is available just with an antenna, is free for the general public. Cable television, on the other hand, must be purchased by subscription. The advent of cable television in the 1950s allowed television stations to fund special-interest programming for a limited audience.

Radio and television programming is primarily a matter of economics. Networks want to place their most expensive and most popular programming at the times when most people are likely to see or hear it. For radio this means during the morning and afternoon, when people are likely to be in their cars, while for television this means the early evening hours. New television dramas and comedies are usually introduced twice a year. Networks usually produce from 10 to 15 new

episodes in each television season. A show may have two seasons in a year and during the remaining weeks, reruns will be broadcast. Traditionally, news programs are broadcast in the early morning, at noon, around dinner time, and in the late evening.

Internet

Although the Internet has been around for approximately 20 years, it did not first burst into the mainstream until the mid-1990s. Now, it has become a ubiquitous part of our culture and an integral part of the way we communicate with one another. E-mail, instant messaging, blogging, and video conferencing have all become available to people who formerly would have been shut out from these instantaneous forms of communication. The result is that it is now possible to communicate with people around the globe at virtually any time. The Internet has brought formerly isolated geographic areas into contact with other parts of the world, and has provided forums for members of every special-interest group in existence. At the same time, many critics charge that the instantaneous communication afforded by the Internet has impoverished communication on the local and community level.

Mass communication

Mass communication is defined as one-way transmission messages to a large, diverse audience. Radio, television, and the Internet are the typical vehicles for mass communication. Some people include print media as a component of mass communication, though others declare that mass media requires almost instantaneous transmission. One of the signature qualities of mass media communication is that it can be reproduced and replayed in exactly the same way more than once. In other words, since it has the capability of being recorded, it can be played more than once and for more than one audience.

Media diary

Many people would be shocked if they realized just how much time they spent engaged with mass media. A half-hour here, forty-five minutes there; it can add up to a huge chunk of time. One way to gain control over the time spent engaged with mass media is to maintain the media diary. A media diary is simply a daily catalog of the amount of time spent engaged with different forms of media. For instance, a student today might want to keep a media diary listing the amount of time spent listening to the radio, watching television, or surfing the Internet. It might also be a good idea to include activities like watching movies and playing video games. Students should mark down how much time they spend in each one of these activities, and then calculate it as a percentage of their total free time.

Media evaluation form

Another way to keep track of individual media intake is through the use of a media evaluation form. Unlike a media diary, which simply indicates how much time was spent with media, a media evaluation form keeps track of the quality and content of the media that is consumed. For instance, a media evaluation form will include a list of the various television programs the individual watched during the week, along with a brief summary and evaluation of the programs. Many people are shocked to discover how much time they spend every week engaged with programming they do not particularly enjoy. The use of the media evaluation form is a great way to streamline media intake, so that the individual only spends time with those programs which he or she most enjoys.

Applying critical analysis

When there is a free and unfettered news media, it is essential for all citizens to maintain a skeptical attitude and apply critical analysis skills to informative programming.

Television viewers should keep in mind that the way a subject is photographed can influence the way it is perceived; for instance, individuals who are shot cast in shadow tend to seem more dangerous or malevolent. Most people are good at critically appraising commercials, but do not necessarily apply the same skills to avowedly informative programming. Viewers should remember that there is a persuasive element in every communication, no matter how impartial, and should remain alert to signs of bias.

Offering feedback

The providers of mass media communication receive general feedback from a number of different sources. Television companies, for instance, are constantly organizing focus groups to view and offer feedback on new television shows and commercials. Sometimes, networks will arrange for a focus group to be composed entirely of members of a particular demographic, as for example women or African-Americans. Perhaps the most famous example of general feedback for the mass media is the Nielsen ratings, which are used to determine how many people watch a particular television program. The providers of mass communication use all of this general feedback to refine and tailor their messages to the audience.

The media receives a great deal of personal feedback from individuals in the general public. Any time a person writes or calls a television or radio station to give a response to a program, they are giving personal feedback. Many television and radio programs explicitly call for audience participation, which is to say they ask for personal feedback to use as content in their programming. In a way, consumers provide personal feedback to the media in their choice of purchases, since these consumer decisions indicate which television and radio advertisements are successful. Individual voices actually do play a great role in affecting the quality of the content of media presentations.

Funding

In large part, television and radio networks are funded by commercials. The Nielsen ratings indicate how many viewers watch a particular television program. The more viewers a program receives, the more expensive is the advertising space during the program. Every year, the Super Bowl marks the most expensive four hours of programming on television, with some 30-second advertising slots going for more than $1 million. There are alternatives to commercial-funded television and radio. Public television and radio stations are funded by viewer donations and contributions from grant organizations. Also, some small public access television stations are funded by a local government.

Commercials in mass communication
All the programming on the radio and broadcast television is funded by commercials. Cable and satellite television receives part of their funding from distributors, but are in large part also funded by commercials. Commercials are generally more expensive when they are placed during programs with a large viewership. Businesses also like to position their advertising during programs which attract viewers who are likely to buy their products. So, for instance, one is likely to see a lot of truck commercials during football games, since presumably a large number of males are watching. Similarly, commercials during the weekdays are often for products preferred by senior citizens and housewives, who are more likely to be watching television at this time.

Mass communication advances

Changed the legislative process
In the past fifty years, the legislative process has been subtly modified by advances in communication technology. To begin with, television made it possible for the president to speak face to face, as it were, with the American public. This meant that he could push his legislative agenda without having to spend as much time currying favor among members of Congress. Perhaps the most important change has been the introduction of C-Span, which televises all the proceedings in the Senate and House of Representatives. This has made members of Congress even more conscious of their appearance, and has led to much more grandstanding and public displays on the floor of the legislature. Also, the acceleration of the news cycle has put perhaps unfair pressure on Congress to move quickly on legislative decisions.

Politics
The Internet has influenced politics in unpredictable ways. For one thing, it has made it possible for citizens to acquire political information from sources other than the traditional mainstream media. Many people have complained in the past about the prejudices of the news media, and now people have an opportunity to get news from sources that share their same personal ideologies. Many people complain, however, that the hyper-partisanship of many Internet news sources has polarized the country. Another area in which the Internet has radically changed politics is in campaign financing. Candidates can now solicit donations over the Internet, which has led to amazing increases in the amount of money available to popular candidates.

Advances in communication technology have drastically altered the political process. Before the advent of television, political candidates could only reach large audiences on the radio or by delivering addresses to enormous crowds. The development of broadcast television made it possible for presidential debates to be transmitted to the entire country. At the same time, candidates began to pay much more attention to the visual elements of presentation. With the advance of the first 24-hour cable news networks, it became more and more important for ambitious politicians to supply ready-made news events. This has spawned the omnipresent, continuous cycle of political news and campaign coverage. Many critics complain that the incessant need for fresh news by the cable networks has devalued political discourse in the United States, even as these networks provide information to many more people than were reached in the past.

Production

Radio drama
Some of the best oral interpretation of famous stories and plays has been done over the radio. In order for oral interpretation to work on the radio though, the performers need to have excellent vocal control. For one thing, they need to be able to indicate excitement or nervousness with their rate of speech. An excited speaker tends to talk more quickly. Radio drama performers will also have to indicate their emotional state by varying the volume of their voice. For instance, in many radio dramas a speaker will almost whisper during the most dramatic parts, because the audience will then be forced to listen more intently to what he or she is saying.

A great deal of effort goes into the preparation of most radio dramas. Not only do the performers need to become familiar with their roles and practice the performance, but the producers need to decide on the appropriate sound effects to accompany the performance. Like television programs and movies, radio dramas have directors, who are responsible for organizing the actors and overseeing the general interpretation of the text. Typically, a director will go through the text before auditions or even held, so that he or she can get a good idea of the particular themes that should be emphasized in the performance.

It is just as important to rehearse a radio drama as it is to rehearse a scene in a movie or a television program or a play. The director of a radio drama usually organizes a rehearsal right after the parts have been cast,

so the group can run through the entire script together and get a general idea of the direction in which they are having. During this rehearsal, members of the cast will make notes on their script. In subsequent rehearsals, the director will probably interrupt the cast in order to offer suggestions and make corrections. It is typical to do a final rehearsal a short time before the premiere presentation.

Radio dramas have famously been enlivened by the use of sound effects. Sound effects serve a number of purposes in the presentation of a radio drama. For one thing, they can be used to differentiate between scenes. Often, a bit of background noise helps to establish a new scene in the minds of an audience. For instance, a scene might begin with the shuffle of feet and low conversation, to indicate that the scene is a hallway or street. Sound effects also add depth to a radio drama. Instead of just listening to the human voice, the audience is given a variety of noises that advance the action, from ringing telephones to slamming doors. Because radio only transmits through the medium of sound, radio producers of drama have become extremely creative with the incorporation of sound effects.

Video and television
Video and film production has a basic terminology, which includes the following:
- *Angle:* The viewpoint from which the camera shoots the action.
- *Establishing shot:* A shot from a long distance, used to establish the setting in the mind of the viewer; often a shot of the building in which the action takes place.
- *Close-up:* A shot in which the camera only focuses on one person; even closer shots are referred to as tight close-ups and extreme close-ups.
- *Dolly:* The platform on which a camera moves while filming in order to maintain stability and follow action or change perspective during a shot.

- 33 -

- *Medium shot:* A camera perspective in which an individual is framed to the waist; a medium shot contains enough width for two people; sometimes used to frame people as they walk or run.
- *Long shot:* A camera perspective in which several people can be included from head to foot; a long shot is often used to establish a conversational group at the beginning of a scene.
- *Wide angle:* Camera perspective that has an extremely broad horizontal distance.
- *Reverse angle:* Camera perspective in which the object being shot is seen from the opposite perspective to the last shot.
- *Pan:* A filming technique in which the camera is turned horizontally on an axis; often used when the subject is in motion, as for instance when a character is walking.
- *Tilt:* A camera technique in which the camera is moved up and down vertically on an axis; sometimes used to shift the frame from an individual's feet to the individual's head.
- *Cut:* Sometimes called a take; a transition from one scene to another
- *Zoom:* To move closer to or farther away from the subject with the camera.
- *Fade:* A gradual dissolution of the scene; most often, movies and television shows use a fade to black.
- *Dissolve:* A gradual transition between scenes, in which the first scene is slowly replaced by the second scene.
- *Wipe:* A transition between scenes in which one moves in as the other moves out, with no overlap
- *Over the shoulder shot:* A classic camera perspective in which one individual is seen from the perspective of a point over the shoulder of another person

The preparation of a camera shot sheet: One of the most important tasks of a television or film director is to prepare a camera shot sheet. A camera shot sheet is a detailed set of instructions to be followed by the various camera operators during filming. For each shot, the director should list what is to be framed, the type of lens to be used, the length of taping to be expected, and the sound requirements. All this information needs to be condensed into a format small enough for all the camera operators to carry around during shooting. It is very important that the sequence of shots be accurate, so the camera operators can spend their time preparing for their next shot.

Producer and director: The producer of a television program has a variety of different roles. Perhaps most generally, the producer can be called the overall boss of the production. He or she arranges the financial backing, hires the crew, and assigns a director to the project. Once the production is underway, the producer acts as a liaison between the financial backers and the director. The producer may also have a role in assisting publicity. As for the director, he is hired by the producer to interpret the script, cast the parts, and to manage the crew that will film the program. The director is responsible for creating an interpretation that is acceptable to the producer.

Associate director, floor manager, and production assistant: An associate director has several tasks on the set of a television production. For one thing, the associate director is usually in charge of directing the background action. That is, he makes sure future shots are being set up while the director concentrates on what is being filmed at present. The associate director also tries to keep the director organized and on schedule. The associate director is often responsible for managing the logistics of production as well. The floor manager, meanwhile, is responsible for organizing the facilities that will be used in the production, and maintaining the operation schedule. A production assistant typically takes care of the finer details of production, from the making of cue cards to set design.

The use of microphones, switchers, and mixers: A variety of specialized equipment is required for television production. For one thing, television requires the use of hidden microphones. The most common microphone used on a television set is one suspended from a long horizontal pole, called a mike boom. The microphone can then be suspended above the performer, but out of sight of the camera. Television production also requires the use of a switcher, which is a mixing panel that allows scenes to be placed end to end on a videotape. Finally, television production requires the use of a mixer, which is an electronic board on which various sources of sound and video can be spliced together.

Basic phases of television production: There are four basic phases in television production: preproduction planning, rehearsal, productions, and postproduction. During preproduction planning, the director familiarizes himself or herself with the script, and a production assistant arranges the facility and the production equipment. Also, during this period the cast and crew are hired. During a rehearsal phase, the actors and director figure out their roles and do the blocking. During the production phase, the program itself is filmed. Finally, during the all-important postproduction period, the program is edited in mixed. Also, it is during this period that corrections are made, art and music are inserted, and any necessary dubbing is performed.

Personal media inventory: Individuals can create a personal media inventory to compile their intake of media communication during a particular time. A comprehensive personal media inventory would include categories for television, radio, movies, Internet, recorded music, and any other form of mass media. Most people are very surprised when they realize how much time they actually spend engaged with media. In particular, many people are shocked to realize just how much television they watch each week. One way to gain control over the amount of time one spends with mass media is to catalog this activity in a personal media inventory.

Communication classroom

Basic audiovisual teaching materials
These days, educators are expected to have a firm grasp on the latest audiovisual teaching technologies. Whereas in the past a teacher might only be expected to operate an overhead projector and photocopy machine, now he or she is required be fluent in the use of computers, DVD players, and stereo equipment. Most public school classrooms are equipped with a computer with Internet access. Also, teachers almost always have access to a video or DVD player. Educators are increasingly asked to provide their students with a multimedia approach to their subject. Some theorists believe that this is the only way to hold the attention of students who have been raised in an era of nonstop information and constant Internet access. Other experts worry that the emphasis on audiovisual teaching materials comes at the expense of critical thinking skills. For most teachers, the challenge is to find a balance between these viewpoints.

Essential audiovisual materials for a communication instructor
An enterprising communication instructor will discover a wealth of instructional resources on the Internet and in recorded audio and video. The Internet provides an excellent arena for students to examine the creation and reception of written messages. There are a wide variety of audio and video recordings which can be used to illustrate concepts in speech communication. Even the most inane soap opera can be mined for examples of paralinguistic and proxemic communication. When teaching a lesson on oral interpretation, it is always appropriate to

show the class examples of classic performances.

<u>Use of the Internet</u>

A speech communication teacher in the modern age is required to be familiar with some of the popular audiovisual teaching materials. Specifically, a communication instructor will need to be familiar with the workings of computers and the Internet. The World Wide Web provides an excellent resource for students to examine the various modes of communication. Many students will already be fluent in the ways of email and instant messaging. It is the job of the instructor to show students how the theories of communication can be applied to these formats. Namely, a teacher can demonstrate how identity construction, meaning formation, and message interpretation take place in electronic communication.

Oral Interpretation

Basics

Although oral interpretation is a kind of public speaking, it is very different than the delivery of a speech. For one thing, oral interpretation does not require the speaker to have written his own words. On the contrary, an oral interpretation presentation is a reformulation and expression of words written by someone else. In a sense, oral interpretation is a public and social form of storytelling. The work being interpreted may be a dramatic text, a work of prose, or a poem. Before the advent of radio and television communication, oral interpretation was the predominant form of information and entertainment. It is still very prevalent, although much more oral interpretation occurs through other media than in person.

Text selection

Perhaps the most important step in oral interpretation is selecting a proper text. Works of prose, poetry, and drama are acceptable texts for oral interpretation. It is important for the chosen text to be appropriate for the audience. For instance, storytellers often take fairy tales as their text. This is appropriate for an audience of children, but may be too simplistic for an adult audience. Also, it is important to make sure that the text is of an appropriate length given the time constraints. An effective oral interpretation may require significant dramatic pauses and periods of nonverbal communication. All of these features should be taken into account when determining whether a text is the right length.

Composite recital

In the form of oral interpretation known as composite recital, two or more people will interpret various texts. All of the texts interpreted by the performers will have some common thread, whether it is author, theme, cultural background, or subject matter. It is typical for there to be an introductory speech before a composite recital. In this speech, the unifying thread will be detailed, and the various pieces to be interpreted will be introduced. In a typical composite recital, all of the performers will be grouped together on a stage, and will take turns interpreting their material. There is usually minimal set dressing for oral interpretation presentation.

Choral speaking

In the form of oral interpretation known as choral speaking, a group of people join their voices together to pronounce a single text. Perhaps the most famous example of choral speaking is the dramatic chorus in Greek drama. Only texts with a regular meter or rhythm can be used in choral speaking; other, more various texts are too difficult to say in unison. Different kinds of poetry have been incorporated into choral speaking with great results. Sometimes, an individual speaker will deliver the verse, and the group as a whole will deliver the chorus. Other times, each individual will read a line, and then the group as a whole will read the refrain.

Use of scripts
Typically, all of the participants in choral speaking will be given a script to use during the performance. Each participant should indicate on his or her script those lines which he or she will be required to speak. If there are any stage directions, these should be indicated on the script. It is a good idea to print the text in double space and to number the lines, so that cast members can easily find their places. The scripts should be distributed in advance of rehearsal, so that cast members can practice finding their place during a performance.

Clarity, motion, and position
In order for a choral speaking performance to be effective, the cast members need to practice speaking in unison. Only by beginning and ending each word at the same time can they achieve the clarity necessary to be comprehensible. Also, if the cast is required to make any synchronized motions, these should be practiced as well. The intended effect will only be successful if the motion is performed precisely in unison. Finally, the director of a choral speaking group needs to organize the group by voice. Typically, any soloists will be positioned towards the front of the group. The deeper and stronger voices are usually placed in the back.

Reader's theatre

Reader's theatre is a form of group oral interpretation in which two or more individuals present a dramatic interpretation of a literary work. The presentation of reader's theatre is similar to that of a play, except the text is a work of prose or poetry rather than of drama. Also, reader's theatre typically has little set direction and scenery. Participants in reader's theatre often use elements of pantomime to suggest props. Because there are so few accessories in reader's theatre, the presenters tend to make exaggerated movements and display broad emotions. Reader's theatre is similar to the run-through performed by actors during the rehearsal of a play.

On occasion, the participants in reader's theatre will use a work of drama rather than one of poetry or prose. Obviously, works of drama lend themselves to oral interpretation, and therefore will require much less in the way of suggestion in the place of costumes and scenery. On the other hand, plays often have elaborate set directions which may be beyond the scope of reader's theatre. When this is the case, the participants should either select another text or should include an introductory in which the potentially confusing aspects of the presentation are explained. In a more formal presentation, the participants may hand out a program that gives this information.

Folklore

Folklore is any story passed on by word of mouth. In other words, folklore is the set of narratives that circulate among the members of a community through oral interpretation rather than through writing. Various categories of folklore include legends, jokes, fairy tales, and fables. Even though we usually associate folklore with a bygone age, there is a great deal of modern folklore as well. Although most scholars declare that folklore must be fictitious, it often is based on real themes and issues. For instance, there is a great deal of folklore surrounding the figure of Davy Crockett. Even though most of this folklore is exaggerated or untrue, it is based on events that actually happened to a real person. There are many scholars who concentrate solely on the characteristics of folklore in various cultures.

Because it is an oral exercise, the creation and dissemination of folklore is by definition an act of performance. Folklore is traditionally allied with storytelling, though there are other ways in which it can be delivered. For instance, one of the most common forms of folklore at present is joke telling. Whenever we tell a joke to a friend, we are engaged in a form of performance. This performance can be subjected to as much scrutiny and evaluation as a formal dramatic presentation. Indeed, all of the elements which define a successful performance (vocal control, nonverbal communication fluency, rapport with the audience) are essential to the delivery of folklore.

Storytelling

Storytelling is the craft of using words, gestures, and sounds to convey a narrative to an audience. At one time in human history, storytelling was the predominant form of information, entertainment, and self-knowledge for communities. Societies defined themselves based on the stories they told about themselves. By studying the stories that have been told in the past, scholars can gain appreciation for which qualities were particularly valued by a culture, and which were the issues that caused the most anxiety for those people. Many people assume that storytelling is a dying art, though in fact it continues to thrive in various media. Television and radio, for instance, both use traditional elements of storytelling to develop powerful narratives.

Storytelling as a form of oral interpretation remains a popular form of entertainment even in this modern age of computers and televisions. Storytelling requires a narrative, which means it must have characters and a plot. Outside of these requirements, there is a great deal of creative freedom for the storyteller. Many storytellers incorporate sound effects and simple props into their performances. In any case, a speech communication instructor can assess a

storytelling performance in the same way as he or she would any other oral interpretation. The success of the performance will depend on the fluency, preparation, and rhetorical skills of the storyteller.

Oral history

Oral history is any account of events in the past which is transmitted through the human voice rather than through writing. In the distant past, many cultures developed their self-identity primarily through oral history because they did not have mechanisms for maintaining a written history. At present, many historians focus on oral histories that are tape-recorded or videotaped. Many historians claim that oral history is a good way to give a voice to members of a society who, because of their marginal status, would otherwise not be able to make their voices heard. Also, oral history lends a human element to large, formerly impersonal historical events.

Because it is a serious source of scholarly information, it sounds strange to speak of oral history as performance. In the broad sense of performance, however, by which we mean any instance presentation involving and other forms of communication to an audience, it is clear that oral history fits the definition. Indeed, oral history is an important supplement to written history because information can be conveyed in the speaker's tone of voice and vocal mannerisms which cannot be expressed through printed language. Oral historians make a point of emphasizing those aspects of vocal performance which differentiate oral history from other forms of record-keeping.

Text principles

Theme and mood
In order to present an effective oral interpretation of a piece of literature, one must be able to discern the predominant theme and mood of the work. In order to

discover the theme, one must read the text in its entirety and consider the general point the author is trying to get across. Even if the selection to be interpreted is only a portion of the entire work, one needs to understand how the selection fits into the work as a whole. This comprehensive reading should also discover the mood of the piece. The mood is essentially the emotional content of the text. Obviously, the predominant mood of the text will have an enormous impact on the interpretation. Note that the mood of a text can change numerous times during the course of a selection.

Characterization

When interpreting a work of literature, one is often required to assume the point of view of a character in the text. In order to do this effectively, or to provide appropriate emotional emphasis to discussion of a given character, one needs to pay special attention to the author's use of characterization. Characterization is simply the way the author describes a character. Characterization may be direct, as in descriptions of the characters appearance and personality, or it may be indirect, as in things that the character does or the ways in which other characters react to a given character. It is important not to take whatever characters say about themselves at face value because often an author wants us to learn to distrust the words of a character.

Structure

With experience, a reader will develop a sense of the structure of a literary work. This sense of structure is invaluable when developing an oral interpretation. First of all, a sophisticated reader will be able to identify the climax of a text. The climax should be at the point of highest emotional content; therefore, the reader will know that his interpretation should also peak in emotional content at the designated climax. Furthermore, a reader should be able to identify when an author is attempting to build tension in the text. The interpreter will want to convey this mounting emotion in his or her delivery.

Dialogue

If a selection for oral interpretation includes dialogue, the interpreter will have to make some important decisions on how this dialogue will be handled. For instance, the interpreter might decide to use different voices for the different characters in a conversation. Also, the interpreter will need to practice adjusting his voice to accurately represent the various moods of the seekers in a dialogue. It is important as well for a speaker to understand the motivation of the participants in a dialogue, as this information will allow him to produce a more sophisticated, nuanced interpretation of the words. Conversations have their own rhythms, with rising and falling amount of tension. A good interpreter will be able to capture these rhythms in his presentation.

Diction

An author's diction is his choice of words. In order to interpret a work of literature effectively, a person needs to understand both the denotative and the connotative meanings of all words used by an author. If necessary, the interpreter should look up all questionable words in the dictionary. Most importantly, the interpreter needs to understand how to pronounce all of the words. A dictionary will provide pronunciation guides as well as definitions. Besides understanding the pronunciation and definition of each word in the text, the interpreter also needs to know which words deserve special emphasis. Identify key words in the text allows the interpreter to convey the appropriate meaning.

Punctuation

It is easy to gloss over the punctuation in a literary text, but in oral interpretation is important pay special attention to the punctuation. For instance, the following punctuation marks require pauses of various durations: periods, colons, semi-colons, dashes, spaces, and spaces between sections of text. When printing a question, on the other hand, it is typical for the voice register to be lifted at the end of the sentence. Obviously, when quotation marks are used it is to indicate that a character is speaking. The interpreter will have to decide whether he wants to use different voices for direct quotations from the various characters in a text.

Prose

In the interpretation of a work of prose literature, it is especially important to have a sense of the point of view. The point of view is simply the perspective from which the story is told. For instance, in first person point of view, the story is told by one of the participants. First person perspective is distinguished by words like "I," "me," and "mine." When installed from the third person point of view, however, this means that it is told by a narrator who stands outside the story. A narrator may be omniscient (meaning that he or she knows everything, including the thoughts of the characters) or may be limited (meaning that he or she only knows certain information).

Poetry

In the oral interpretation of poetry, one needs to be conscious of these rhythms and repetitions of the poet. Poetry is almost always written in a meter, or rhythm. Rhyming poetry will have what is known as a rhyme scheme, which is a pattern of rhyming in the last word on each line. Furthermore, poems often repeat a single word, phrase, line, or set of lines frequently. An interpreter needs to pay attention to these repetitions and vary his reading of the repeated words. The enunciation of the repeated words should evolve throughout the performance, so that the audience gets a sense of progress within the interpretation.

In the oral interpretation of poetry, it is essential to recognize the words in a line that deserve special emphasis. Too often, interpreters simply emphasize the last word in each line. Not only does this give their performance a repetitive and boring quality, it also is incorrect in cases where the line does not end with a comma, semi-colon, or period. When there is no punctuation at the end of a line of poetry, the interpreter should continue reading to the next line with no special emphasis. It is only through close study of the language and punctuation of a poem that an interpreter can learn the proper points of emphasis.

Dramatic works

Occasionally, a single individual will attempt the oral interpretation of a dramatic work. The obvious advantage of this selection is that the text has been designed for public performance, so the language and points of emphasis should be fairly clear. On the other hand, works of drama may call for elaborate staging and costumes which are beyond the scope of an individual oral interpretation. The interpreter will have to study the text to determine whether it can be adapted for oral interpretation. If there is too much action called for in the stage directions, or if understanding of the text depends on the presence of other characters, the interpreter would do well to look for another text.

Condensing selections

In order for a literary selection to be of an appropriate length for oral interpretation, it may be necessary to trim some areas. When editing a selection, it is important to leave all the text that is essential to the meaning. For instance, when condensing a selection from a work of prose, it is a good idea to trim any references to characters or events that do not appear in the selection, unless these references have bearing on the meaning of the selection. The best rule of thumb is to always review the selection after the condensation has been performed. If it still makes sense and conveys the same thematic meaning as before, then the condensation process has been successful.

Introductions

In some cases, an oral interpretation presentation will be preceded by a short introduction. If a selection is being taken from a larger work, or if a selection requires some context in order to be understood, it will be especially important to provide some guidance to the audience. There are a few key components to this kind of introduction. To begin with, the presenter should outline the selection, including the major characters, back story, and any other information that is required to understand the selection. A speaker also will often describe why he has picked the selection and why the selection might be of interest to the audience. If the selection has any relevance to current events or to the lives of the audience members, this information would be meaningful to an introduction.

Practicing

It may seem obvious, but it is absolutely essential to practice before an oral interpretation presentation. Practice begins with learning the text inside and out, but it is not complete until the performance has been fully rehearsed several times. During these rehearsals, the performer should be clocked to make sure time constraints are obeyed. If possible, the performer should rehearse in front of an audience (perhaps of friends or other performers) so that he can practice making good eye contact and directing his voice to the different parts of the room. Multiple rehearsals also give the performer a chance to experiment with different deliveries and gestures.

Analysis and interpretation

During the preparation for a dramatic presentation, the director and his crew will need to analyze and interpret the text. The director will want to identify the central character (known as the protagonist), the supporting characters, and the main conflict in the text. The director should also identify the mood and theme of the play, as these factors will influence all of his other decisions, from casting and staging to vocal emphasis and lighting. The director should outline the general structure of the play, so that he can bring the action to its appropriate climax and resolution.

Rhythm

One of the aspects of drama which receives less attention than it should is rhythm. Every player has a natural rhythm, or periods of intense action, followed by lighter action. In order to avoid overtaxing the audience, a dramatist has to mix moments of high and low intensity. Typically, a play will have several small climaxes before reaching the dramatic point in the major climatic scene towards the end of play. Afterwards, there is often a period of resolution, known technically as the denouement. During the analysis of a play, the director and his staff should pay close attention to the rhythm of the text, so they can honor it.

Character interaction

During the planning phase of a dramatic presentation, the director and his staff should pay close attention to the relationships between the various characters. Each actor should note the attitude of his character towards all the other characters in the play. In some cases, the relationships between even distantly-related characters will change subtly during a performance. The director needs to be able to indicate these slight changes to his actors and actresses so that they can be conveyed in the performance. Also, there are natural relationships between people that must be demonstrated in a dramatic performance; for instance, characters who are father and son or brothers will have a unique relationship.

Group oral interpretation

There are a number of advantages of performing group oral interpretation. For one thing, it encourages more than one person to familiarize themselves with the text. Also, group members can motivate one another to higher achievement. It is also easier to perform works with more than one character in a group. It can be very difficult for one person to make all the different voices required by some texts. Group interpretation is also a good venue for people to gather and share their various ideas of interpretation and of literature. Finally, rehearsals tend to be more productive when there are other people present to critique each other's performance.

Actors

Motivation
When we describe the motivation of an actor, we do not mean the actor's reason for participating in the play. Rather, we mean the actor's identification of the motivations held by the character he or she is playing. In order to effectively interpret a role, an actor needs to understand why the characters behaving as he or she does. Without the right motivation, an actor will not be able to demonstrate effective emotion. Even the nonverbal aspects of a character's interpretation are dependent on the character's mood and motivation. Therefore, in order to transmit the right thematic message to the audience, the director and the actors need to have a good sense of each character's motivation.

Establishing character background
Actors often talk about developing the background of the character. By this, they mean establishing the life and history of the character before the events of the play began. By understanding where a character is coming from, and actor can gain insight into that character's motivation and emotional range. Sometimes, this information can be discerned from the author's description of the character. For instance, if a character is handicapped, it might be assumed that he or she has been in an accident in the past. Information can also be obtained from the character's dialogue and behavior. The director and actors need to collaborate to establish character background in order to accurately diagnose the motivations of the characters.

Vocal control
In order to effectively interpret his role, an actor needs to have excellent vocal control. An actor needs to be able to pronounce words clearly, so that every member of the audience will be able to understand the dialogue. In some cases, an actor may need to incorporate a regional dialect and have it be both credible and comprehensible. Some characters have particular vocal mannerisms, like a stammer or a lisp, which must be interpreted accurately. Finally, an actor needs to be able to convey the appropriate emotion with his voice at different times during a play. An actor needs to have a sense of his own emotional vocal range, so that he saves his most exaggerated vocal techniques for the climactic sections of the play.

Vocal technique of projection
Actors often refer to the vocal quality of projection, by which they mean the level of force in volume with which words are delivered. In order to perform in front of a large audience, an actor needs to have enough projection so that of audience members can hear and understand all the lines. Actors cultivate strong abdominal muscles and lungs so that they can maintain their ability to project. Also, actors constantly work on combining clarity of expression with volume. A specific technique that actors used to increase the quality of projection is called pointing. This is the technique of emphasizing particular words in a sentence, either by pausing before them or extending their enunciation. Pointing helps the words of the actor to be understood.

Nonverbal communication
There are a number of different ways for an actor to handle nonverbal messages during a dramatic presentation. It is important for the gestures to be appropriate, consistent, and

tailored to the audience. Any nonverbal communication used must be appropriate to the character being portrayed; in other words, the gestures and vocal techniques need to be such that they seem right for the character. Also, the mannerisms used at the beginning of the play must be the same as those used at the end of the play. Finally, the nonverbal communication used by the actor must be expressive enough that it can be seen by all members of the audience. When performing for a small audience, an actor can get away with more subtle nonverbal communication than he can when performing for a large audience.

Movement
There should be no random movements during a dramatic presentation. That is, all the positioning of the actors should be choreographed ahead of time. The entrances and exits of the characters are usually indicated in the text, but the proxemics may be at the discretion of the director. A sophisticated director can convey information about the characters and their interrelationships through their positioning on the stage. At all times, however, the director needs to keep in mind the necessity of making the actors visible to the audience. Positioning should be one of the main focuses of rehearsal, and the director should experiment with different arrangements.

Memorization
In order to be truly expressive, an actor needs to memorize his or her lines. This is in large part because the actor's concentration needs to move from the recitation of the mere words to the development of nonverbal communication methods and interpretation of character. If an actor is looking at cue cards or holding a copy of the script in his hands, he will not be able to gesture or move about the stage freely. Furthermore, he will not be able to make eye contact with the other actors or with the audience. It is really important to memorize lines before rehearsals begin in earnest. Even if the lines are memorized

imperfectly and the actor requires a prompt during rehearsal, is still better to start working without a script as soon as possible.

Parts of the stage

In a basic dramatic stage there is a single floor and an arch that extends from one side to the other. The section of the stage closest to the audience is referred to as downstage. The section of stage farthest away from the audience is known as upstage. When the stage directions call for movement to the right or left, this means from the perspective of the actors. Although most of the major set directions are included in the dramatic text, a director will have to come up with supplementary directions. These supplementary directions are known as "blocking."

Choosing a script

When selecting a dramatic script for presentation, a producer needs to keep in mind the makeup of the audience. For instance, when a work is to be presented to a group of children, it should not deal with mature or violent themes. One of the best places to find a dramatic text is the local library. Most libraries have numerous anthologies containing famous plays. Once a player has been chosen, the producer needs to procure playbooks for all the members of the cast and crew. It may be necessary to pay royalties to the author or publisher of the play.

Holding auditions

When holding auditions for a dramatic presentation, the directors should have a basic idea of what type of actor they prefer for each role. At the same time, the directors should keep an open mind. Sometimes, the unique performance of one actor's audition will change their minds about what they need for a given role. If an audition is open, that means that anyone is allowed to show up and

- 43 -

try out. If an audition is closed, it means that only invited actors are allowed to attend. If there are particular qualities that an actor must have to fill a given role (such as the ability to sing or play an instrument), these should be made known before the audition.

Making casting decisions

There is a general policy used by directors in making casting decisions. To begin with, everyone who participates in an audition fills out a form with contact information. This audition form should also include space to indicate any conflicts of interest that might interfere with the dramatic presentation. During the audition itself, actors may read from a script or be asked to improvise. Sometimes, actors will be instructed to prepare a short scene ahead of time. If an actor is going to be required to sing or dance during the presentation, the skill should be tested during the audition. Usually, casting decisions are made by a committee including the director and producers after all of the auditions have been completed.

Giving feedback

During a rehearsal for a dramatic presentation, it is essential that the director and producers provide constant and specific feedback to the cast and crew. Rehearsals are a good time for everyone involved in the performance to experiment with different techniques, so it is important for the director to let the actors and crew know what is working and what is not. In some cases, it may not be appropriate to give feedback immediately. In order to provide a venue for feedback, they get director will set up regular meetings with each member of the cast and crew. By the time of the dress rehearsal and first performance, the performances of the cast and crew should be fully reviewed and approved by the director.

Responsibilities

Student director and stage manager
A student director (also known as assistant director) helps to facilitate the work of the director. He may transcribe notes dictated by the director during rehearsal, may help to implement the director's blocking plan, and may coordinate activities with the costuming, lighting, and sound departments. A stage manager, meanwhile, has a number of practical responsibilities. He or she is responsible for overseeing construction of the set and making sure that any sets changes can be accomplished quickly. He or she is also responsible for organizing and managing the crew. A stage manager needs to be intimately familiar with the light and curtain cues in the play, and must also have contingency plans in case things go wrong.

Business and house managers
In a dramatic presentation, the business manager is responsible for looking over all the financial aspects of the performance. These include ticket sales, the cost of promotions, and the costs of production. In the case of professional presentations, the business manager will need to handle the wages paid to cast and crew. The house manager, on the other hand, is responsible for handling the admittance and seating of the audience members. The house manager runs a crew of ushers, who help audience members find their seats and clean up the auditorium after each performance. The house manager is also responsible for maintaining the heat or air conditioning system in the auditorium.

Makeup, costumes, and props

In order to be performed professionally, a dramatic presentation needs to have a makeup, costume, and props committee. Makeup is necessary to counterbalance the effects of bright stage lighting. The members of the makeup crew will need to practice applying makeup to each cast member before the first performance, so that they can get a good idea of what makeup scheme is appropriate. Costumes, obviously, are required to create an air of verisimilitude in the performance. The costume committee acquires the necessary wardrobe and makes sure it fits the cast. The props committee is in charge of all the movable items used in a performance. These items must be acquired, cared for, and stored.

Speaking and Listening in Different Contexts

Group discussions

Purpose
One special form of Communication Processes is the discussion group in which a small number of people gather together for a particular purpose. The purpose may be to solve a problem, to organize a collective effort, or simply to elaborate and analyze a controversial issue. Sometimes, discussion groups are held in a ritual fashion, as for instance in the case of book clubs or Bible study groups. Speech communication theorists assert that regular and organized discussion groups typically have better communication. Also, discussion groups seem to function better when there is a clear and explicit hierarchy among the members, whether there is one leader of the discussion or none at all.

Characteristics
In order for a discussion group to function effectively, there must be a good sense of rapport and understanding among the members of the group. These positive sentiments are more easily cultivated in groups that meet regularly. For new groups, establishing a positive environment for discussion is the responsibility of the chairperson, leader, or moderator. Unless a comfortable discussion environment is established, it will be difficult for the group to accomplish its goals. Time and again, research studies suggest that relationships between people have far-reaching effects on the progress and ultimate success of organizations both great and small. Discussion groups are no exception to this trend.

Morale and efficiency
In order for a discussion group to be effective, the group needs to have a high sense of morale. Morale is a general expression used to describe the attitude of the members of the group in regards to the activities of the group. If the members of the group enjoy one another's company and feel like the group meetings are worthwhile, morale will be high. Morale is also linked to situations in which the members of the group know their respective roles. When everyone knows his or her job and responsibilities, there is much less resentment and blaming for unaccomplished work. Similarly, the degree to which a discussion group is productive in pursuit of its goals will determine the effectiveness of the group. If, after several meetings, the members of the discussion group observe that progress is being made towards long-term goals, they will be more likely to commit themselves to the group and make any necessary changes to promote its effectiveness.

Togetherness
Research into discussion groups suggests that a sense of togetherness is essential for the promotion of discussion group goals. When the members of the group feel tied to one another, they are more likely to go out of their way to help one another and promote the progress of the group. In other words, the members of a cohesive group subvert their own goals in the interest of promoting the group goals. Also, the members of a cohesive group are more likely to communicate any personal problems which may affect the progress of the group. Communication becomes highly efficient and constructive criticism does not derail group activities. Cohesiveness can be built by creating an atmosphere in which the group members take an interest in one another and are respectful of each other's feelings.

Positive social environment
There are a few different ways that discussion group leaders can actively promote a positive social environment. One easy thing to do is to allow the members of a group to get to know each other during the first group meeting. Many group leaders will do a few

"icebreaking" activities, in which the members of a group share a little bit of information about their personal lives and therefore become more comfortable. It is especially useful to have all the members of a discussion group describe what they are hoping to get out of the group work, as this establishes a climate in which all the members of the group are openly working towards communal goals. It is natural for the members of a new group to feel a bit of apprehension during the first meeting. As much as possible, the group leader should seek to mitigate this apprehension by promoting warmth and positivity.

Disagreement and cohesiveness

It may seem like a paradox, but groups with a high level of cohesiveness tend to have a higher incidence of disagreement. The simple reason for this is that in a cohesive group, the members feel comfortable enough with one another to disagree. In other words, the group members do not worry that this agreement will destroy the group. Also, a cohesive group has likely established positive channels for constructive disagreement, so members are assured that conflicting opinions will not be viewed harshly by the other group members. Furthermore, cohesive groups often discover that frequent disagreement can be a stimulus to effectiveness in group discussion. When all the group members agree with one another, they do not raise pertinent objections and do not subject ideas to enough scrutiny.

Establishing roles

In order for a group discussion to be effective, it is important for the members of the group to have established roles. Speech communication research suggests that even if roles are not made explicit at the beginning of the discussion, after an hour or so individuals will naturally assume specialized roles. For instance, once the discussion gets rolling, it is natural for one or two leaders to emerge. Similarly, a discussion usually has two or three individuals who do not advance the

discussion necessarily, but offer insightful critiques of what has been said by others. The formation of an individual's role within a group is a constantly evolving process in which the individual's personal desires and thoughts are combined with the needs and reactions of the group.

The basic principles of role emergence: The emergence of individual roles in a group discussion is the result of interplay between the individual and the group. In other words, an individual is not solely responsible for his or her role, and neither is the group solely responsible for designating that individual. Once the members of the group have assumed tentative roles, the other members of the group assess the value of each role. That is, a hierarchy begins to develop within the group. Those individuals who have emerged as the leaders of the group are given a higher status. Group members look to them for direction, their opinions carry more weight, and the other group members tend to listen to them more closely. Lower status group members, on the other hand, may feel that their opinions are not valued and that they are not really being given the full attention of the group. Over time, however, group roles can shift, and individuals can gain or lose status.

Characteristics of a leader: Perhaps the most important role within a discussion group is the leader. Research suggests that most people, given the option, would prefer to be the leader. Indeed, most people lead in at least one area of their lives, whether at school, at home, or at work. However, some people have a natural gift for leadership. In a discussion group, these individuals tend to speak more, be more forthright with their opinions, and project more confidence with their nonverbal communication. Of course, individuals can also develop leadership traits over time. Some people do not really blossom as leaders until they reach adulthood. Although our society values democracy, it seems plain that discussion groups function effectively when there is some form of

- 47 -

leadership. Perhaps the essential point is that leadership must be a designation that is agreed upon by all the members of the group in order for it to be effective.

Characteristics of a central person: Speech communication instructors often refer to a "central person" in a discussion group. A central person is one who has such a strong personality that he or she cannot help but influence the group. A central person may have a positive or negative effect on the group. Central people are often funny, charming, and charismatic. However, their charisma may distract the attention of the group from its intended goals. Speech communication instructors are interested in central people because of their random and destabilizing effects on groups. At times, the presence of an influential central person can lead a group to high achievement; at other times, the manipulations and distractions of the central person can negatively affect the group.

Changing membership
For a discussion group that experiences changes in membership, the effect is destabilizing. When new members are added to a group, they must quickly assume roles in order to avoid obstructing the current progression of group work. If a group member is removed, on the other hand, the remaining members must try to fill the void by assuming different responsibilities. In general, it seems that when the members of a group change, the roles of every other group member are affected to a greater or lesser degree. Afterwards, there is a brief period of instability in which the group is less effective than before. It is important for discussion groups to recognize the inevitability of this down period, and to be patient as roles are reestablished.

Principles of formal leadership
Sometimes, the roles in a discussion group are determined ahead of time. The speech communication instructors refer to this kind of group as having a formal organization. A formal organization will almost always have a designated leader. Furthermore, the other members of the group will probably have their relative status designated over time, as well. Unlike in a free-form group, where roles emerge and evolve over time, a formal discussion group features static group roles. At times, this can create inefficiencies in the group, as for instance when the designated leader is ineffective at discharging his or her duties. Similarly, group members with lower status may gradually develop skills that would otherwise lead to an increase in the importance of their role. The rigid nature of a formal hierarchy, then, can inhibit discussion if it is not managed properly.

Group discussion characteristics
When speech communication instructors use the phrase group discussion, they are referring to a single meeting or group of meetings of a small number of people who have a similar, agreed-upon set of goals. The minimum number of people required for a small group discussion is three, and while the maximum number is not set in stone, it is generally agreed that a group of more than fifteen will have a hard time managing a democratic discussion. Ideally, a small group discussion will have about five members. This seems to be the maximum number of people who can participate fully in a discussion. When a group has more than five members, it is common for the extra members to remain silent for the most part.

Discussion group advantages
Provide information: Group discussions are a useful source of information. The various members of a group discussion will naturally have different levels of experience and expertise on the subject at hand, and will hopefully be able to fill in gaps in each other's knowledge base. Indeed, many discussion groups are organized simply for the purpose of assembling a comprehensive body of knowledge on a particular subject. It is always useful to ask participants to prepare

- 48 -

for group discussions which have information-gathering as their explicit purpose. Sometimes, a group discussion will begin by compiling all of the information on the subject, and then will move into analysis and evaluation phases.

Yield solid evaluations: Group discussions are often used to evaluate a given subject. This is especially the case when the members of the group discussion are attempting to solve a particular problem. In this scenario, the group may outline the problem, describe the various proposed solutions, and then evaluate them. A small group discussion is most effective at evaluation when all of the members have equal standing. Also, evaluation is most effective when all of the members have a similar body of knowledge on the subject. If only a few people in the small group truly understand the problem, they may be the only ones who can contribute meaningful evaluations of the proposed solutions.

One-time meetings

In some cases, a small group discussion meeting will be held only one time. The dynamics of this kind of meeting are slightly different than those of a set of meetings which will be held regularly over a period of time. For instance, in a one-time meeting, there will be no time for roles to develop and emerge, so it is beneficial if a group organization is established beforehand. As much as possible, the members of the group should become familiar with one another rapidly so that the business of the discussion can be begun. Effective leadership is especially important when administrating a one-time meeting, as there will be no time to waste on role development and making acquaintances.

Ad hoc meeting
Sometimes, small group discussions are organized to attack a particular problem. Speech communication instructors refer to these meetings as ad hoc groups, from the Latin phrase meaning "for a particular purpose." An ad hoc group may meet only once, or may meet several times until the intentions of the group have been realized. It is likely that the members of an ad hoc group will not have met each other before the first group meeting. However, unlike the members of the one-time meeting, the members of an ad hoc meeting group can assume that they will be in contact with one another until their mission is complete. This tends to encourage a bit more solidarity. Also, there will be more of a chance for role emergence and development in an ad hoc discussion group.

Role of a chairperson
A discussion group that will only meet one time requires effective leadership more than any other kind of group. In order to swiftly and effectively lead a one-time discussion group, a chairperson needs to establish ahead of time the precise purpose of the meeting. This purpose should be known to all group participants. The discussion should be structured to achieve the goal and, as much as possible, environmental distractions should be minimized. Any preparatory materials that will be required for the discussion should be procured ahead of time. It is also important to determine the necessary outcomes of the meeting. A chairperson needs to know what sort of information constitutes a conclusive decision by the discussion group. He or she needs to know what details have to be decided upon before the group can adjourn. Finally, the chairperson needs to know and explain the mechanisms for putting into place the decisions made during the discussion.

Structure for leading
Although every one-time meeting will be slightly different, depending on the structure, membership, and intentions of the meaning, there is a basic structure a chairperson can follow. To begin with, the chairperson should call the meeting to order and announce the intentions of the discussion. The chairperson should then lead the discussion, heading off any digressions, and maintaining the group's focus on its overall goals. After a sufficient

amount of discussion, the chairperson may need to stimulate decision-making by calling for a vote. If there are time constraints on the meeting, the chairperson needs to keep track of these and truncate discussion when necessary. At times, the chairperson should summarize what has been decided so far, and indicate what the group has left to do. When all of the goals of the discussion have been reached, the chairperson needs to be able to summarize them and indicate what will then happen in the future.

Participation

Individuals to participate in a one time meeting need to be conscious of the particular characteristics of this kind of discussion. They should not waste any time worrying about their personal concerns or role within the group, but should focus their efforts on the achievements of group goals. Participants need to maintain an open mind during discussion, and keep their own contributions on topic. In a one-time meeting, it is important that all perspectives receive an airing, so participants should avoid dominating discussion. In general, participants should maintain a civil and respectful tone in their remarks, as a one-time meeting group is typically made up of individuals who do not know each other very well and need to maintain a decent rapport in order to achieve their mission.

Small groups

Attention span

One of the obstacles in any small group discussion will face is the limited attention span of its members. Sometimes, a discussion veers off in a direction that is only interesting to one or two of the group members, causing the other members to lose interest and become disengaged from the discussion. If there is a designated group leader, it is his or her job to make sure digressions are avoided and all members of the group are engaged. After the group has fully discussed a subject and can no longer continue with the topic, a group leader needs to summarize the positions of the group members and introduce a new topic for discussion. This is especially true when a group has a limited amount of time for discussion or a large number of things on the agenda.

Freedom and structure

In their consideration of small group discussion, speech communication instructors often focus on the balance between freedom and structure. In order to be effective, a discussion needs to have a discernible and appropriate structure. On the other hand, in order to be engaging, a discussion needs to allow group members to follow their own ideas and interests. For a group leader, maintaining the balance between freedom and structure is the difference between success and failure. With experience, discussion leaders can learn to moderate in such a way that the goals of the group are accomplished without repressing the interests of the participants. Occasionally, a group leader must refer members of the group back to the original goals, or at least reframe the current discussion in light of the avowed intentions of the group.

Benefits of small group conversation

There are a number of potential benefits of small group conversation. For one thing, information can be exchanged during these discussions. Small group discussions are also a useful forum for individuals to share their ideas and experiences. People are often able to convey emotion much more effectively in a small group discussion setting than through writing or communication with a larger group. A small group discussion is a fantastic way to develop individual speaking and listening skills, since it is likely that each member of the group will be called upon to contribute frequently. Furthermore, a small group discussion is an excellent place to persuade other people of something because the intimacy afforded by the limited membership is conducive to building rapport.

Qualities that improve discussion

Certain individuals seem to thrive in small-group discussions. Although the charismatic qualities that make for effective small group discussion may seem abstract to many people, they are actually quite simple. For one thing, good discussion members are always sincere in what they say. They do not make the other members of the discussion group guess whether they are being serious or not. Good discussion members are also versatile, and can adjust their comments and questions depending on the flow of conversation. Good discussion members exercise tact and courtesy in regard to their peers. Finally, good discussion members are good listeners, capable of demonstrating through their actions and responses that they take all the other members of the group seriously.

Making decisions

Group discussions are often used to make decisions. Oftentimes, a group will gather and compile a body of information, evaluate potential solutions to a problem, and then decide on a course of action. Group discussions that are intended to end with decision-making seem to work best when there is an established and agreed-upon format for this process. For instance, many groups adopt parliamentary procedure as a way of organizing a discussion. For many groups, though, this may be excessively formal. In a small group, any system of decision-making is fine as long as it is agreed upon by the members. In small groups, there is enough time and space for all members to contribute their opinions before holding a vote.

Types of discussions

Panel discussions

Panel discussions are probably the most common form of small group discussion. They typically consist of between four to eight individuals, one of whom is designated by the others as a leader. The members of a panel discussion do not prepare formal speeches in advance of the meeting. In addition, there is no prescribed order to the proceedings, other than the discussion will be led by the designated individual. Panel discussions are typically organized to discuss a specific problem or theme. They are not really the best format for decision-making. Panel discussions often occur at conferences. When this is the case, a small group may discuss an issue before a large attendant audience, and then open the floor to questions.

Lecture format

When a group discussion is held in a lecture format, there is a clearly defined leader. The leader will deliver a long prepared speech on a given topic. Before the meeting, various members of the discussion will have been given assignments. During the course of the leader's presentation, he or she will call on the various group members to elaborate on key points or provide specific information. During the leader's presentation, group members will have the opportunity to interrupt and ask questions. Once a subject has been covered in its entirety and is understood by all of the discussion members, the leader will move on to another topic.

Round table discussion

In a roundtable discussion, there is very little hierarchy among the members. There may be an acknowledged leader, but he or she often is not responsible for providing more information or direction to the group than any other member. All the members of a roundtable discussion are expected to have done some preparation before the beginning of the meeting. This kind of meeting format is especially appropriate for groups in which all the members can be assumed to be reasonably informed and competent in the area to be discussed. Also, roundtable discussions often are held by groups whose members have different areas of expertise. When this is the case, a leader might informally direct the conversation to various members as different points in the overall subject are being discussed.

Progressive group discussion

In a progressive group discussion, a large group is divided into several smaller groups. These smaller groups simultaneously discuss the various components of a larger problem. For example, one group might focus on the consequences of a possible solution, while another group might focus on the roots of a problem. It may be that all of the members of the discussion are asked to prepare to discuss all subjects, or they may be told ahead of time which particular aspect of the subject they will be discussing. Once all the small groups have come to a general consensus, the group as a whole will reconvene and one representative from each small group will present his or her group's findings to the rest of the people.

Symposium format

In a symposium, the participants in the discussion are allotted a certain amount of time and are placed in order ahead of time. It is typical for a symposium to have a designated leader. This leader will introduce each of the participants in the discussion. All of the speakers in a symposium will be discoursing on the same subject or theme. Oftentimes, the leader will take a moment between speakers and attempt to organize what has been said so far. At the end of the symposium, the speaker will offer some concluding remarks. There is no prearranged interaction between the participants in a symposium, although the leader is free to open the panel to discussion at his or her discretion.

Reflective thinking

In order to be productive, a group discussion needs to follow a logical sequence. Speech communication instructors have delineated five basic steps in successful group discussion. To begin with, the group defines the problem or topic to be discussed. Next, the group compiles all the information they have on the subject. After this, the group evaluates the possible solutions to the problem, or possible insights to be gained from evaluation of the topic. The fourth step is selecting the best solution which may require deliberation and even voting. Finally, the group will outline practical ways that the agreed-upon solution can be put into action.

Discussion techniques

Introduction of new material

One sure way to improve the quality of a group discussion is to assemble a greater amount of information. One of the common fallacies of participation in a discussion is that it does not require preparation. On the contrary, discussions are only successful to the degree that the participants can offer reasoned, well-considered examples and evidence. If necessary, group members should bring published material that is relevant to the discussion. Also, group members may want to consider how the subject or problem to be discussed has impacted their personal lives. Although group members do not want to spend a great deal of time discussing their personal lives, in some cases personal experience may have a direct influence on the discussion.

Better listening

By listening more carefully and creatively, the participants can improve group discussion. In a sense, group discussion is a creative, collaborative enterprise. Group members expand upon, elaborate, and modify one another's ideas, until a group consensus is reached. By listening attentively, group members achieve a good understanding of what is being said by their fellow participants, and improve their ability to modify and embellish ideas. At any given time, every group member should be able to summarize what has been said so far in the discussion, as well as the general topic that is being discussed.

Discussion group leadership

<u>Non-directive leadership</u>
Although group discussions are basically a democratic arrangement, it can be useful to designate a leader of the discussion. A leader is someone who has a special responsibility for being prepared and keeping the business of the group on track. There are three basic kinds of leaders: non-directive, directive, and supportive. A non-directive leader participates in the group discussion like any other member. This kind of leader exercises very little control over the actions of the group. Mainly, a non-directive leader is designated just in case the group needs someone to help them get back on track or come to a conclusion. If the discussion flows smoothly, a non-directive leader will not have to assert himself or herself.

<u>Directive leadership</u>
Studies of group discussion leadership identify three kinds of leader: non-directive, directive, and supportive. A directive leader is assertive in controlling the activities of the group. Unlike a non-directive leader, who only leads when the discussion gets off track, a directive leader is constantly arranging the activities of the group. A directive leader initiates discussion, calls upon members of the group to speak, and suspends discussion when he or she believes it is time. Directive leaders are more appropriate in situations where group participants are unfamiliar with one another or unfamiliar with the general dynamics of group discussion.

<u>Supportive leadership</u>
Studies of group discussion leadership identify three kinds of leader: non-directive, directive, and supportive. A supportive leader exhibits elements of both directive and non-directive leadership. The supportive leader is a bit more hands-on than a non-directive leader, but is less assertive than a directive leader. Basically, a supportive leader is responsible for suggesting possible solutions and discussion strategies to the group. A supportive leader does not attempt to influence the course of discussion or the decisions made by the group, but rather seeks to aid the group in whatever direction is chosen. Supportive leaders are appropriate for groups that understand the topic thoroughly, but may need some help with coming to a decision.

<u>Opening and closing a meeting</u>
A discussion leader is responsible for opening and closing a discussion meeting. To begin with, the leader should introduce the topic or problem to be discussed. If the members of the discussion group do not know one another, the leader should take a moment to introduce all the members of the group and allow new members to introduce themselves. The discussion leader should always make sure that every member of the discussion group fully understands the problem or topics to be discussed. Once a resolution to the problem has been found or the topic has been fully discussed, the leader should close discussion. At this time, the leader should offer a brief summary of what has been discussed as well as the agreed-upon solution. The leader should also ask if there are any remaining questions from members of the group.

<u>Preparation</u>
In order to lead a discussion group effectively, a discussion leader needs to be well prepared. Of course, all the members of the discussion group need to be prepared in order to contribute in a positive way to the discussion. This is more true of a leader, however. A leader needs to be able to summarize the topic at the beginning of the meeting, and needs to have a rough idea of the potential solutions or conclusions that will be reached by the group. A leader also needs to be fluent enough in the discussion topic to summarize it to the group at various points during the discussion.

Maintaining group focus

It is imperative for a group leader to maintain the focus of the group on the task at hand. All too often, a group discussion goes off down a blind alley or follows unproductive digressions. Even a non-directive leader needs to be capable of stepping in and refocusing the attention of the group. One easy way to do this is by restating or summarizing what has been discussed so far. This tends to draw the attention of the group members back to the original task at hand. A group leader may also indicate discussion topics that still need to be addressed, or try to refocus the group by asking a general question about the central issue of the discussion.

Performing discussion critique

After a discussion is over, it is advantageous to spend some time considering which aspects of it were successful and which were not. To this end, many people find it is useful to complete a discussion critique. A discussion critique is simply a standardized form on which people can indicate their opinion of the discussion. Sometimes, participants are asked to grade the quality of discussion in a number of different areas on a scale of 1 to 10. On some discussion critique forms, participants are asked to grade the individual performances of their fellow group members. When this is the case, it may be appropriate to make the forms anonymous.

Interaction and participation diagrams

Individuals who are studying group discussion often use participation and interaction diagrams as tools for analysis and evaluation. These diagrams indicate how many times every participant in a discussion has spoken, on what issues they spoke, and to whom they directed their comments. The members of the group are represented in boxes or circles on the form. Lines drawn between the participants indicate interactions during the discussion. These diagrams can be useful because they indicate when certain members of the group are primarily talking

amongst themselves as opposed to involving all the members of the group. Sometimes, a group leader will study an interaction and participation diagrams and realize that conversation has been unfairly dominated by a few members of the group.

Different contexts

Oral communication builds community

Speaking and Listening in Different Contexts is an act that creates and reinforces the bonds of a community. When a person speaks in public, he or she is expressing his or her own opinions and beliefs, which may echo or stand in contrast with those of the community. In either case, public speech requires the listeners to consider their own shared beliefs. Public speech draws attention to the similarities and differences between various communities through a process known as cultural maintenance. Through the creation of a public discourse, the members of a community learn about each other and think critically about their social mores and cultural values.

A transaction

Speech communication instructors often refer to speaking and listening in different contexts as a "transaction" or a way of indicating the important active roles of both the speaker and audience. Too often, people consider speech-giving as a process in which one person actively provides information while another group of people passively receives information. Instead, the ideal speaking and listening in different contexts relationship is one in which the speaker presents a message and the audience presents feedback. Even when the audience is not given an opportunity to speak, they provide feedback in the form of attention or inattention. By referring to speaking and listening in different contexts as a transaction, instructors emphasize the roles and responsibilities of both speaker and audience. In general, speech communication instructors would describe any communication as a transaction, in which information passes from speaker to listener and vice versa.

Purpose of studying

There are a number of reasons for studying Speaking and Listening in Different Contexts, but the most commonly cited are social, intellectual, and consumer motives. People need to learn to speak in public in order to function in society and to manage relationships, administrate social events, and minimize conflict. Intellectually, a study of Speaking and Listening in Different Contexts gives insight into human thought, ethics, and persuasion. The thoughts and emotions of people can be influenced and even produced by public speeches. Finally, it is important to study Speaking and Listening in Different Contexts not only to improve one's own speaking skills, but to improve one's ability to analyze and interpret the speeches of others. Students need to be able to understand the forum of public expression, the rhetorical vocabulary, and the various methods of thinking critically about speech.

Methods for studying

An effective speech communication teacher will incorporate different pedagogical modalities into his or her instruction so that students receive a wide range of exposure to different methods. Students should practice giving different kinds of speeches in both formal and informal settings. Some examples of speech types include technical lectures, extemporaneous speeches, and entertaining monologues. Students should get some practice interpreting and analyzing different kinds of public speech, whether in the form of advertisements, political speeches, public service announcements, or editorials. Students should also get some exposure to acclaimed historical speeches.

Basic goals

For most people, the obvious goals of speaking and listening in different contexts are political victories and support for social movements. These indeed are common

motives of public speech, but they are not the only recognized intention of public communication. Public speech is often used to define an individual or a community. For instance, people use speeches to describe the particular attributes of themselves or of the group to which they belong. People also use speeches simply to disseminate information. Speeches can be used to inspire other people to action. Famous addresses like the "I Have a Dream" speech of Martin Luther King, Jr. exemplify this kind of speech. Finally, speaking and listening in different contexts can be used to introduce arguments and to debate controversial questions in a community. The presidential debates before the general election are a good example of this.

Speeches

Speech types

Informative speeches

When one is delivering an informative speech, one's primary goal is to instruct the audience on a particular subject. If the speech is effective, the audience members will leave with more knowledge and understanding. College lectures are a great example of an informative speech. Although informative speeches may be entertaining, the humor or color of the speech should not distract from the overall intention which is to disseminate information. Informative speeches often contain specific statistical data and an organized set of arguments and supporting evidence. Many informative speeches contain mention of counter-arguments, including rebuttals.

Impromptu speeches

An impromptu speech is one delivered off-the-cuff; that is, one delivered with a minimum amount of preparation and in an informal style. Of course, not everyone is capable of delivering an effective impromptu speech. For most people, an impromptu speech can only be successful when it is delivered on the subject with which he or she is extremely familiar, or a subject on which he or she has spoken before. Of course, we all make impromptu speeches as a matter of course in our daily lives. Every time you are asked to give your opinion on a subject or to explain an idea, you are in effect making an impromptu speech. By studying speech communication, however, one can learn the elements of effective impromptu speeches, and improve one's ability to deliver them.

Any relatively informal speech on a light subject can be referred to as an impromptu speech. An impromptu speech may be given on very short notice, and will therefore give evidence of much less preparation. Even so, impromptu speeches tend to follow a similar pattern. There are four basic steps in a typical impromptu speech: an engaging introduction, a brief overview, elaboration, and summary. Notice that the four components of an impromptu speech directly parallel the components of a proof speech. The only real difference is that the delivery will be looser and the style of delivery will endeavor to be more entertaining. An impromptu speech often begins with a humorous or intriguing anecdote, and often ends with a light touch as well.

Extemporaneous speeches
An extemporaneous speech combines elements of preparation and improvisation. When one is delivering an extemporaneous speech, one is drawing on prepared research but not reading directly from a sheet of paper or reciting the speech from memory. An extemporaneous speech is more conversational and informal than a written speech, and is therefore more appropriate for casual gatherings. The colloquial and informal nature of an extemporaneous speech can be extremely helpful in cultivating a good rapport between speaker and audience. In order to deliver an effective extemporaneous

speech, however, the speaker needs to be extremely familiar with his or her source material.

Proof speeches
Speech communication instructors often refer to what is known as a proof speech. This is a common type of speech, in which the speaker introduces his argument and then attempts to prove it. Proof speeches abide by a consistent pattern. In brief, a proof speech has four components: introduction, argument, development, and conclusion. A speech that follows this pattern allows the audience to become acquainted with the thrust of the speaker's arguments before substantiation is offered. The lengths of the various components of a proof speech will vary, depending on the speaker's interests and the knowledge level of the audience. For instance, an audience that is already familiar with the subject matter may not require as much supporting material to be convinced.

Problem-solving
In a problem-solving speech, the speaker outlines a particular problem, attempts to diagnose the cause, and then suggests a potential solution. Problem solving speeches are at their heart persuasive speeches, since they attempt to convince the audience of the merits of adopting a particular strategy to solve a given problem. In order to be effective, however, a problem-solving speech needs to follow a logical pattern. These speeches typically begin with an introduction and a definition of the problem in question. The speaker will then summarize the possible causes of the problem, and will discuss some of the possible solutions. The speaker will then make a case for one of the solutions and provide supporting evidence and argumentation. Finally, the speaker will attempt to rebut some of the possible counterarguments to the proposed solution.

Call-to-action
When speech communication instructors describe a call-to-action speech, they are

referring to a speech that intends to inspire the audience to follow some recommended course of action. A call-to-action speech has five typical components: engaging the audience, describing why the audience should want to change something, explaining the best way to change, describing the positive consequences of making the change, and directly indicating how change can be made. It is not really possible to rearrange the steps in a call-to-action speech. Unless the argument is delivered in this order, the speech will likely be ineffective. It is important to end by outlining the positive consequences of change and making an emotional plea, as this leaves the audience on a high note that is most likely to translate into direct action.

Memorizing versus reading

When delivering a speech, the speaker may need to decide whether to memorize or read the text. There are advantages to each approach. When a speech is memorized, the speaker can make eye contact with the audience and use his or her hands to make illustrative gestures. However, memorized speeches run the risk of sounding overly rehearsed, and the speaker may falter if he or she loses track of the speech. Some speakers prefer to read their speeches, often because they prefer to have a copy of the speech for reference. If the speaker plans to read his or her speech, he or she should become extremely familiar with the speech so that it is not necessary to read every word from the paper. Regardless of whether a speech is memorized or read, the speaker should practice delivery to increase fluency.

Persuasive speeches
Persuasive speeches are designed to change the minds of the audience or motivate the audience to action. The precise goals of a persuasive speech are dependent on the particular cause promoted by the speaker. Moreover, the methods employed in a persuasive speech will depend on the subject matter and the rhetorical style of the speaker. Some speakers employ a dry, data-driven style when making a persuasive speech. They hope to overwhelm their audience with the strength and breadth of information. Other speakers seek to beguile their audience by amusing and entertaining them. This kind of speech is appropriate for general audiences and non-technical subjects. When a persuasive speech is being delivered to an audience of experts, or is centered on a complex issue, it will need to include cogent reasoning and supportive data.

Entertaining speeches
Some speeches have as their only goal to entertain and amuse the audience. Standup comedy is a sort of entertaining speech. Many speeches which also contain information or persuasive content are primarily entertaining. The keynote speakers at conferences and conventions often cloak their arguments in witty anecdotes and jokes. Obviously, serious subjects will not be appropriate content for entertaining speeches. However, many speakers will introduce some elements of an entertaining speech in order to capture the attention of the audience and persuade them to engage seriously with the more weighty elements of the speech.

The eulogy
A eulogy is a speech which takes as its subject the good qualities of a person. Eulogies are often given at funerals as the speaker remembers the deceased in a positive light. Eulogies are not appropriate times for criticism or objective analysis of a person's life. On the other hand, if they are excessively laudatory, they will not be believable to the audience and will therefore fail. In some cases, a sort of eulogy may be given in praise of a particular event, community, or culture. Typically, a eulogy is delivered to an audience of individuals who are already disposed to think favorably of the subject. The giver of a eulogy is typically someone who has extensive personal experience with the person in question.

The introductory speech

It is common for a speech of introduction to be given before a keynote speaker, a presentation, or a public performance of some kind. For instance, a symphony director will often give a brief speech of introduction before a concert. The best speeches of introduction do not simply list the achievements or characteristics of the person or event that is to follow. Rather, they engage the interest of the audience and whet their appetite for what is to come. A good speech of introduction should not include any criticism of what is to follow. It is always a good rule of thumb for the introductory speaker to confer with those who are to follow so that his or her message can be as appropriate as possible.

The welcoming speech

A welcoming speech is often given at the beginning of a convention, meeting, or special event of some kind. Typically, it is given by some representative of the group or organization that is putting on the event. For instance, the chairman of a professional organization administering a business convention might deliver a speech of welcome to convention attendees. The speeches are typically light on substance, and primarily deal with a rundown of the events that will follow. Also, a welcoming speech typically includes a message of thanks to the organizers and administrators of the event. The speaker will often indicate his or her personal goals for the event, and may tell the audience how to make their questions and comments known to the event administrators.

Purposes for a speech

In order to focus the preparation of a speech, it is a good idea to lay out the specific purpose of the speech ahead of time. This will enable one to procure appropriate research materials and make the right points of emphasis within the speech. The specific purpose of a speech might be informing the audience on a particular point, changing a few minds on a particular subject, raising some money, or simply entertaining the audience. It is a good idea to make the specific purpose of the speech explicit in the speech. Although you do not want to beat your audience over the head with your intentions, there should be no question as to what is meant to be accomplished by the speech. In general, the specific purpose of a speech is defined in terms of the desired reaction from the audience.

In preparation for making a speech, one needs to establish a strict definition of the purpose of the speech. Unless one has a firm idea of the intention of the speech, it will be too easy for the content to miss the mark. To begin with, one should consider one's own intentions and the intentions of the audience. As much as possible, the intentions of the speaker and the audience should be made to overlap. One should define the central argument or idea to be expressed in the speech, and make sure that this argument or idea is consistent with the intention of the speech. One should also develop a title for the speech which indicates the intention as well as the central theme of the speech.

Persuasion

Persuasion is the art of changing the attitudes, beliefs, and actions of other people. It can be used for any number of purposes: to sell a product, to make a friend, to advance a cause, or simply to win an argument. To a certain degree, even primarily informative speeches contain an element of persuasion. The speaker is encouraging his or her audience to understand a given subject in the same way that he or she does. In order to be persuasive, the speaker has to have a clear idea of what he or she is trying to accomplish. Also, he or she needs to understand the best persuasive strategy for accomplishing these goals. Persuasion can be a matter of direct argument or more indirect, even subversive suggestion.

Persuasion and likeability: Students of rhetoric have long noticed the correlation between a charismatic personality and

- 58 -

persuasion. Basically, if a speaker is able to establish strong personal relationships with his or her audience, he or she is much more likely to be an effective persuasive communicator. The most important thing for a persuasive speaker is to establish trust from the outset. If a speaker can convince the audience that he or she has their best interests at heart and is a competent source of information, the work of persuasion is largely done. Establishing trust and respect with the audience is as much a matter of one's credentials as one's appearance and presentation. Speakers who can demonstrate expertise and empathy are likely to find success with the audience.

Persuasion and competence: In order to be persuasive, an individual needs to be seen by the audience as being competent. Competence manifests itself in a number of characteristics: preparedness, poise, thoughtfulness, and clarity. A competent individual should be able to answer questions from the audience on a specific subject, or least should be able to describe where the answers could be found. A competent speaker needs to have supporting evidence for his or her arguments, and needs to make this evidence clear to the audience. A competent speaker will also be able to organize his or her message effectively, such that the audience can best educate themselves. Finally, a competent speaker will appear unhurried and calm.

Personal conviction and persuasion: Audiences seem to have a sixth sense for insincerity. They can tell when a speaker does not really believe his or her message. For this reason, effective persuasion is greatly benefited by the speaker's deep conviction in what he or she is saying. It is often said that before a speaker can persuade anyone else, he or she needs to be persuaded. When the strength of a speaker's convictions is evident in his or her delivery, the natural empathy of the audience will assist in persuasion. Historically, a survey of the great persuasive

orators (Martin Luther King Jr., Abraham Lincoln, Pericles, etc.) confirms that strong belief is a boon to persuasive rhetoric.

Reputation and persuasion: Another factor that can greatly influence a speaker's power of persuasion is reputation. When a speaker has a reputation for upright behavior and responsibility to the truth, an audience is much more likely to believe his or her message. The credibility of the speaker is imperative, regardless of the topic. If the content of the speech is highly specialized, the audience will want to know that the speaker has some advanced training in the subject. When an audience arrives for a speech already knowing the positive reputation of the speaker, the work of persuasion is almost complete. For many politicians and orators, building a reputation that encourages persuasion is the work of a lifetime.

Value of direct familiarity with sources: It can be extremely beneficial to a speaker's power of persuasion to have direct knowledge of sources. For instance, imagine a motivational speaker on the subject of weight loss. If that speaker has had the experience of being overweight and regaining his or her health, the audience will be much more likely to take his or her words to heart. When a speaker can claim direct experience of the topic on which he or she speaks, the audience is unlikely to attribute motives like personal gain or manipulation to the speaker. The most effective speakers are able to present their personal experience as a model for the examination and consideration of the audience.

Mimicry and persuasion: Unconscious mimicry or imitation can be one of the most powerful forces for persuasion. Human beings have a natural tendency to imitate the behavior of someone they perceive as a leader or role model. Oftentimes, people will do and believe things contrary to their normal behavior in order to mirror the behavior of a leader. This phenomenon is in part due to the tendency of human beings to minimize differences between one another and as a means of preventing conflict. Of course, in order to inspire imitation on the part of the audience, a speaker needs to have a good reputation and must appear competent. The members of an audience should be particularly skeptical of speakers who encourage them to adopt a point of view simply because others are doing so.

Being persuaded with following directions: Human beings have a natural tendency to believe things that they are told by any designated authority figure. In part, this is an inherited characteristic. In order to survive in the wild, humans often had to rely on the advice and guidance of their peers. In many cases, people will follow directions from an authority figure without considering the ramifications of their actions. This phenomenon was evidenced during the Nuremberg trials after World War II, as numerous Nazi officials defended their actions as "just following orders." The educational system also encourages people to trust authority figures and follow directions. Audience members should be aware of this tendency, and should guard against blindly accepting the recommendations of a speaker.

Being persuaded with accepting a suggestion: Sometimes a persuasive speaker uses a suggestion rather than a direct command to achieve his goal. A suggestion is simply a less forceful recommendation; it implies that the audience has the ability to decide for themselves whether or not to accept the guidance of the speaker. Suggestion is a good strategy for dealing with naturally skeptical audiences, who will resist any overt attempts to change their minds. Because it is an indirect form of persuasion, however, it requires a bit more subtlety on the part of the speaker. Suggestion can be more effective than direction, since it gives the listener the impression that he or she has arrived at the conclusion independently.

Persuasion and dramatization: Often times, a persuasive speaker will use the language and techniques of drama in order to capture the interest of the audience. In other words, the speaker will frame his or her arguments as part of a larger narrative. The speaker may introduce certain representative characters and may spend a little bit of time describing the human characteristics of these people. The speaker may then introduce some conflict against which these characters must struggle. This kind of generic dramatic scenario gives the audience a sort of hook on which to hang its attention. Instead of being required to pay attention to dry statistics and formal arguments, the audience can become enmeshed in the stories of the characters. Many speakers find that this captivation is a spur to positive persuasion.

Persuasion and the motivation of the speaker: When the audience is considering the elements of a persuasive speech, they will likely give some thought to the motivations of the speaker. For instance, when approached by a salesperson, a customer is likely to assume that the salesperson has a vested personal interest in making a sale, and does not necessarily have the best interests of the consumer at heart. In other contexts, however, the motivation of the speaker may be harder to discern. In an academic speech, for instance, the audience will be aware that the speaker is attempting to promote a certain viewpoint, but they may not be able to determine exactly why the speaker supports that point of view. To the extent that the audience can discern the motivation of the speaker, they will be able to intellectually consider the merits of the speech, and not be swayed by emotion.

Resistance to persuasion: Audiences will naturally be resistant to persuasive arguments that attempt to take them out of their normal routine. Individuals of all ages have a tendency to fall into habitual behaviors which can be difficult and even painful to interrupt. A persuasive speaker, however, is by his very nature one who attempts to

- 60 -

convert the audience to a new way of living or thinking. He will therefore be encountering the resistance of the audience's entrenched habits. There are a few ways of attacking habitual behavior. One is to persuade the audience that these habits are detrimental. Another is to suggest the advantages that can be gained from a new way of living or thinking. In all cases though, the speaker should remember that most behavioral change is incremental, and not the result of sudden conversion.

Unique qualities of persuading the audience to change something: One of the most common kinds of persuasive speech is one in which the speaker attempts to persuade the audience to change something. The speaker may be asking the audience to change their behavior, their opinion on some subject, or the way some issue is handled in their community. These kinds of speeches usually follow a similar arc: first, the speaker describes the disastrous state of affairs at present. Second, the speaker introduces his or her proposal for remedying the situation. Third, the speaker indicates the rewards that the audience will obtain by accepting the proposal of the speaker. If the speech is effective, by its conclusion the audience should be practically intoxicated with the expansive vision of a positive future that has been outlined by the speaker.

Unique qualities of persuading the audience to not change something: Another kind of persuasive speech which is delivered often is one in which the speaker attempts to persuade the audience to not change something. Like the speech in support of change, the speech against change has three classic components. First, the speaker argues that things are fine as they are. Second, the speaker argues against any proposals for change that have been made. Third, the speaker describes the negative consequences for the audience if changes are made. As with the speech in support of change, the speech against change begins by setting the general

scene, and only gradually works its way around to addressing the individual concerns of the audience members. In this way, the lasting impression of the audience is of the effects of change or stasis on their own lives.

Immediate versus ultimate aim: On occasion, a speaker will have a slightly different intention in making a speech than is apparent from the speech itself. In the field of speech communication, this is known as the distinction between immediate aim and ultimate aim. For example, a particular speech may be a small part of achieving a long-term goal. A prominent businessman, say, might make a speech about ethics in public policy. While on its face the speech might seem to be a simple address about local community issues, it might be also part of the businessmen's plan to develop his reputation in advance of a political campaign. The immediate aim of the speech, then, is to inform, while the ultimate aim is to advance the political ambitions of the speaker.

Presentations

Basic elements
Over the last few years, the presentation has emerged as the most common speech form in the United States. Presentations are frequently given in the business community, but are also used in academic lectures, community discussions, and religious gatherings. One of the defining characteristics of a presentation is that it contains other media besides simply a speaker. It is common for a speaker to include PowerPoint slides, photographs, brochures and handouts, short videos, audio samples, and a presentation. Presentations are often designed to be given over and over again to different audiences, and so they may be complex, detailed, and highly coordinated.

Basic presentation aids
One of the defining characteristics of a presentation is the presence of presentation aids. A presenter will often bring audio or

- 61 -

visual supplementary materials in order to elaborate upon or reinforce his or her points. At present, the most popular presentation aid is PowerPoint, a computer program that allows speakers to put together basic collections of slides to accompany their speech. It is also very common for speakers to bring video samples into a presentation. In business, tables and charts are frequently used to illustrate the points of a presentation. In the classroom, a teacher might use handouts or overhead projector transparencies as presentation aids. Basically, any media used by the speaker to supplement his or her spoken message is considered a presentation aid.

Increasing importance of the presentation in the United States

Most speech communication experts believe that presentations will increasingly become the most popular form of public communication. In large part, this is because the citizenry of the United States has been raised on television and radio commercials. That is, they are well used to multimedia presentations. For many people, a simple speech is boring. It requires presentation aids like audio and video to hold the interest of such a modern audience. In the future, then, the most successful persuasive speakers will be those who can apply the traditional elements of direction and suggestion to a presentation containing enough multimedia to engage the interest of the audience.

Audience analysis

Basic premise

In the study of speech communication, audience analysis is simply the practice of examining the characteristics and background of the audience in order to tailor a speech appropriately. For instance, one would want to know the general age, socioeconomic status, culture, and gender of an audience while preparing a speech. The type of speech appropriate to a group of elementary school girls will be quite different from that appropriate to a group of older men, even if both speeches are on the same subject. The prejudices and pre-existing opinions of these two groups will be wildly different, and therefore in order to be effective, a speaker will have to deliver his or her message in a much different way.

Primary factors

When a seasoned public speaker performs an audience analysis, he or she focuses on a few specific characteristics of the audience. For one thing, the speaker wants to know the audience's background as it relates to him or her and his or her subject matter. Although much of audience analysis consists of determining the approximate ages and socioeconomic backgrounds of the audience, this is primarily done because such information enables the speaker to guess the audience's degree of familiarity and opinions about the subject matter and speaker. A speaker who is well-liked by the audience can employ a different rhetorical strategy than one with whom most of the audience disagrees.

The audience's capacity to act

When developing a speech, one should always remember the characteristics and capabilities of the audience. This is especially important when producing a persuasive speech. It does not make sense to encourage the audience to take an action of which they are not capable. For instance, a politician would be foolish to make an impassioned plea for votes to a bunch of elementary school students, all of whom are years away from voter eligibility. When developing a persuasive speech, then, it is essential to remember the capacity of the audience to act.

Audience attitude

It is important for speaker to gauge the attitude of the audience before delivering his or her speech. Attitude is a more subtle quality than age, ethnicity, or belief system; it can only be determined through direct observation. This is one reason why it is helpful for a speaker when he or she has the chance to observe the audience before making the speech. He or she will then be able to tell whether the audience is generally in a good mood or a bad mood. If the audience is in a hostile mood, the speaker may want to avoid trying to joke with them. An audience that seems jovial and engaged, on the other hand, should not be alienated with strident rhetoric or harsh words. The job of the speaker is to establish and maintain a good rapport with the audience.

Beliefs
In order to have an accurate conception of what an audience might be thinking, you need to understand the core beliefs of the audience. Strictly defined, beliefs are the facts, ideas, and opinions that the audience holds to be true. Objectively, some of the beliefs of the audience may actually be untrue. However, you must take into account the sum total of the audience's beliefs in order to deliver an effective message. It may be that the purpose of your speech is to adjust the beliefs of the audience. If this is so, you'll need to appeal to either the reasoning skills or the emotions of the audience.

Facts versus opinions
When considering the convictions of an audience, it is good to distinguish between facts and opinions. Facts are those convictions which can be proven in an objective sense. Scientific assertions, for instance, are considered facts. Opinions, on the other hand, cannot necessarily be supported by hard data. Oftentimes, opinions are held for rather arbitrary individual reasons, like a personal experience. Communities hold collective opinions, which must be considered when making a speech. In general, it is easier for a speaker to adjust beliefs or convictions based on opinion than those based on fact.

Fixed versus variable beliefs
When describing the beliefs of audience, speech communication instructors will often distinguish between fixed and variable beliefs. The primary difference between the two is that fixed beliefs are harder to change. Typically, fixed beliefs have been held throughout an individual's life, and most likely reinforced by his or her experience. Variable beliefs, on the other hand, may have been recently acquired and therefore less established in the individual's mind. A speaker is more likely to change variable beliefs, and should therefore focus his or her attention on these. Variable beliefs are especially vulnerable to change when they are based on opinion rather than fact.

Speech preparation

Fundamentals
There is a basic set of activities that every individual must go through during the preparation of a speech. Learning this process beforehand allows one to organize material effectively and create an effective presentation. The first step in preparing a speech is to select a subject (sometimes, the subject will be predetermined). Next, one should articulate to oneself the most important ideas and arguments that will be made. As one begins to formulate these ideas and arguments, one should take into account the characteristics of the intended audience. At this point, one should begin gathering materials for the speech, whether through research or brainstorming. One should then make an outline of the speech contents, and finally, one should write a draft of the speech. It is always a good idea to practice delivering the speech and make adjustments where necessary.

Selecting a subject
Perhaps the most important component of an effective speech is an appropriate and interesting subject. When selecting a subject for a speech, one should take care to find a subject that is engaging to a general audience. While it is important for the speaker to have some familiarity with the subject, it is not necessarily a good idea for one to speak about

a subject on which one is an expert. Too often, an expert delivering a speech to a general audience dwells too much in details and specificities, which has a tendency to bore the audience. It is a good idea for the speaker to have a passing familiarity with the subject, so that he or she will be able to find good research materials and judge what will be interesting to a general audience. However, the speaker should also make sure to emphasize the aspects of the subject that are relevant to the lives of the audience members.

Using creativity to select a speech topic: Sometimes, it can be difficult to come up with a topic for a speech. It may seem as if all the good topics have already been covered, or as if there is no one single subject on which you have enough information to be effective. Effective speakers develop creative ways to come up with new speech topics. Being creative, however, does not mean sitting back and waiting for the muse of speech topics to visit. Creative speakers proactively work on developing new topics. They make lists of areas of interest, and are constantly considering everything they see and read in terms of how it would play as a speech. Most creative speakers discard more ideas for speeches than they ever use.

The creative analysis of a speech topic: After a speaker has decided upon the topic of his speech, his next move is to perform what is called a creative analysis on the topic. This sounds complicated, but it is just a detailed exploration of the topic. To begin with, the speaker assembles as much information as he or she can within the amount of time available. This may include interviews, books, and old periodicals. Experienced speakers will have a good working knowledge of the public or school library, and will be able to acquire diverse basic materials in a short period of time. After all this information has been assembled, the speaker will sort through it, looking perhaps for an entry point for his exploration. An interesting narrative, a point of local interest, or a previously overlooked

angle on the subject may all be ways for the speaker to engage the interest of the audience on a given subject.

Topic preparation phases
- *Preparation phase:* During the preparation phase of speech composition, a speaker will begin to organize his or her research material. Once the speaker has decided upon the basic angle and structure of his speech, he may need to acquire more research materials for elaboration and support. Of course, it may take the speaker a while to find the appropriate thrust of his speech. Speakers should not be discouraged by numerous blind alleys or false starts during the preparation phase. Even when it seems that progress is not being made, the speaker should remember that each false start eliminates a possible point of entry, and gets him closer to his ultimate goal.
- *Incubation phase:* During the incubation phase of creative speech analysis, the speaker actually does not perform any direct work on the speech. Instead, he allows his subconscious to mull over the content of the speech. Even though it seems like no work is being done during this period, the incubation phase is actually very important, as it is during this period that the speaker will do his most creative thinking on the subject. Also, the incubation phase gives the speaker a chance to freely imagine the speech, associate various ideas, and try unique combinations. Many speakers say that their most unique and powerful ideas often occurred to them when they are doing something totally different than speech preparation.
- *Illumination phase:* After the incubation phase, the speaker should have a solid structure as well as a

- 64 -

number of creative ideas for his speech. In the succeeding illumination phase, the speaker will apply the ideas gains during the incubation phase to the basic outline constructed during the preparation phase. It is very common for a speaker to feel a burst of enthusiasm during the illumination phase, as he discovers the unique ways in which his original ideas will elaborate and improve upon the original structure. The illumination phase is still basically a brainstorming phase. Speakers are still experimenting with new ideas and combinations of materials.

- *Verification phase:* The fourth and final part of the creative analysis of a speech topic is the verification phase. During this phase, the speaker looks over his notes carefully. Occasionally, some of the ideas which seemed so brilliant during the incubation and illumination phases turn out to be inappropriate or implausible. Other times, a careful examination of the speech will discover holes in the reasoning of the argument, or the necessity of adding or removing a particular part of the speech. The verification phase of creative speech analysis can be seen as a final polishing of the materials gathered and organized during the first three phases.

Title of the speech
It is very important to settle on a clear and appropriate title for a speech early on during the preparation process. The title should make explicit the central idea or concept to be discussed in the speech. The title should also indicate the intention of the speech. For instance, if the intent of the speech is to inform the audience about a particular subject, the title should clearly state the name of the subject. If the intention of a speech is to persuade the audience, the title should indicate the main arguments to be made by

the speech. In order to be effective, a title should be succinct, clear, and, if possible, engaging.

Managing creativity during development
In order for the process of creative speech analysis to be effective, a certain amount of discipline needs to be brought to bear on the creative instinct. This is one reason why the process of creative speech analysis is divided into four distinct phases. By adhering to a set pattern of procedure, the speaker will limit the amount of time spent in any one area and will move along towards completion at a predictable pace. Also, the organization of the creative analysis process helps to forestall procrastination, which is a common companion of the creative process. As much as possible, a speaker should try to work at specific times without interruption to allow the creative subconscious to do its work.

Basic message units
In every speech, the content is divided into what are called basic message units. A basic message unit has two parts: the point the speaker is trying to make and the evidence or supporting material he or she has assembled. In order to be complete, a message unit needs to have both components. Otherwise, the speaker will be making points without offering any reasoning or evidence, or he will be giving factual information and argumentation without connecting the dots to make a larger point. The point stated by the speaker needs to be a complete and discrete thought. The supporting material needs to be pertinent to the point and sufficient to convince a reasonable person.

Logic and ethics

Importance of ethics
In order to be effective as a public speaker, one needs to maintain a high degree of ethical rectitude. This is true not only because of the inherent virtues of ethical behavior, but because an audience will not trust a speaker whom they believe to be unethical. In order

to promote good ethics as a public speaker, one should always be as honest as possible. One should also try to promote the interests of the audience whenever appropriate. Is important to give the audience responsibility for making up their minds, rather than attempting to brow beat them into submission with one's argument.

Logical analysis

A speaker should always perform what is known as a logical analysis before presenting his speech. This is simply an analysis of the message units that make up the speech, as well as the connections between these message units. In order to be considered effective, the logic of a speech needs to progress in a systematic and discernible manner, and needs to be supported with ample evidence and supporting materials. Many times, speakers will compose a brief outline for their speech, in which they sketch the basic structure of the speech's logic, leaving out the supplementary material. In any case, it is essential to make sure that the logical skeleton of a speech is sturdy before focusing on other aspects.

Assessing the logic of a speech topic

As the speaker goes through his prepared speech and performs a logical analysis, he needs to be constantly asking himself whether each point and piece of supporting material is essential. There needs to be a clear and explicit reason to include everything that is in the speech, or else it must be considered superfluous. The speaker must also ascertain that all of the evidence clearly and directly supports the points it is intended to support. Finally, the speaker needs to make sure that the points made in his or her speech are made in the proper order, that they progress in an orderly fashion, and that they climax with his or her ultimate conclusion.

Errors of reasoning

Faulty attribution of causation: One of the most common errors of logic made in a speech is a faulty analysis of causation. This occurs

when the speaker erroneously assumes that just because one thing followed another, the second thing was caused by the first. For instance, I may grab my umbrella on the way out the door before it starts raining, but if I later use my umbrella I cannot say that bringing my umbrella made it rain. When the speaker is describing large historical or social events, it is almost always a faulty attribution of causation to suggest that there is only one cause. Major social and historical movements are simply too complex to be attributed to only one cause. At the very least, a speaker will need to provide detailed substantiation for any assertions of causation.

Circular reasoning: A common logical error in speeches is circular reasoning. A chain of logic is described as circular when the assumptions made at the beginning of the argument depend on the conclusion of the argument being true. For instance, imagine a speaker declaring that the Tigers baseball team will certainly lose their playoff series. As evidence for this claim, the speaker declares that the Tigers always lose their playoff series. As you can see, this reasoning does not hold up: in order to believe that the Tigers will lose their playoff series, we have to assume that they always lose their playoff series, which we do not really know yet, and which depends on their performance in the upcoming playoffs series. In other words, the claims made by the speaker depend for their support on the assumptions made by the speaker.

Contradictory argument: Occasionally, a speaker will fall victim to the logical error known as the contradictory argument. A contradictory argument is one in which the speaker introduces information that directly contradicts his main argument. For the most part, this error should be easy to avoid. After all, a speaker will be careful not to include information that undermines his main point. However, the inclusion of inconsistent arguments in a speech does happen, and can be highly detrimental. Contradictory argument is especially problematic in a persuasive speech, in which the speaker is attempting to alienate the audience from their pre-existing opinions, and to sell them on the merits of an alternative view.

Supporting material

Expository supporting material
For the most part, speakers use expository supporting material. The word expository comes from the same root as expose, and describes information that seeks to shine a light on areas which may be unknown to the audience. Some of the common forms of expository information are examples, analogies, and narratives. Expository supporting material is distinguished from argumentative supporting material in that it strives to remain as objective as possible. When a speaker claims to be using objective and impartial information, he or she will be held to that standard by the audience. For this reason, it is especially important for speakers who use expository supporting material to verify their sources.

Examples
Successful speakers are likely to use both real and hypothetical examples in the course of a speech. Real examples are appropriate in speeches describing a particular historical or social topic that is grounded in reality. It would not do, for instance, to use a hypothetical example in an argument about the Revolutionary War. After all, we have plenty of real examples to illustrate points about that conflict. In more general speeches, however, it may be necessary to use a hypothetical situation as an example. For instance, when describing the possible results of some decision, a speaker might invoke the case of some hypothetical person as a means of dramatizing his argument. In general, real examples are treated with more respect by an audience, and should be used whenever possible.

A good speaker knows that examples can be effective because they provide concrete case studies through which the audience can assess the arguments of the speech. Examples are also good at humanizing in an abstract speech; for instance, an audience may have a hard time listening to a speech about water conservation, but if the speaker introduces examples of how drought can affect individual people, they will be more likely to stay engaged. A good speaker includes examples that are appropriate and interesting, but which do not distract from his main points. Also, examples should not dominate a speech; they should simply add interest to the body of the speaker's message.

Analogies
An effective speaker will often elaborate and clarify his ideas with analogies. An analogy is simply an extended comparison between two things. For instance, a speech on economics might describe a current downturn in the economy as it relates to the Great Depression. In other words, the speaker is drawing an analogy between a current problem and a known historical event. The important thing about an analogy is to remember that the two things being compared will probably not be identical in all respects. The speaker should take care to indicate this, and should not make claims which suggest the analogy is perfect. On the other hand, an effective analogy can be a useful predictive tool, and can give the audience a way of engaging with the subject.

Narratives
Speakers often incorporate narratives into their speeches as a way of engaging interest and indirectly making a point. The narrative is simply a story. Narratives can be either fiction or nonfiction. As with examples, narratives tend to have more impact on an audience when they are true. However, an artfully told fictitious narrative can also captivate an audience. Recent scientific research suggests that audience members are mentally programmed to pay attention to information when it is presented as a story.

- 67 -

That is, the human mind is naturally receptive to a narrative. Good speakers take advantage of this tendency by delivering information in the context of a narrative.

Statistics
Speakers often use statistics to provide numerical evidence for their assertions. Basically, a loose definition of statistics is any information that contains numbers. In order to be effective, statistics need to be clear and accurate. Statistics can have a great deal of sway over an audience, since they carry with them the impression of objectivity and mathematical truth. That being said, audience members should keep in mind that statistics are often highly objective. For instance, by manipulating sample size, information taken into consideration, and scope of a statistical survey, a speaker can present information to support his point no matter how incorrect it is. Audience members should always be wary of statistics, and should press the speaker to provide more information on the origin and methodology behind any statistics that are used.

Uses of numbers
There are a few different ways to use numbers in a speech. For one thing, numbers can be used as markers of evaluation. When we say that a person weighs 120 pounds, for instance, we are using numbers to evaluate their weight. In a similar way, numbers can be used as a basis for comparison. By comparing the prices of two dishwashers, for instance, we obtain an important piece of information we can use in making a consumer decision. Numbers can use to make illustrative points. For instance, a speaker will often cite various statistics in support of his or her argument. It should be stressed that, although numbers suggest impartiality, they are calculated by highly subjective human beings whose agenda should be rigorously questioned.

Eyewitness testimony
Many speakers will incorporate eyewitness testimony into their speeches to great effect. Of course, this kind of supporting material is only appropriate for certain kinds of speeches. For instance, when delivering a speech about the Battle of the Bulge, it might be very useful to quote some soldiers who fought in the battle. A speech about global warming, on the other hand, seems less appropriate for eyewitness testimony, since this is such a widespread phenomenon as to be incapable of being viewed by any one person. When using eyewitness testimony, it is important to establish the credentials of the person being quoted. Also, a speaker should take care to indicate the particular vantage point of the eyewitness, so that the audience can consider his or her testimony in the light of that point of view.

Expert testimony
Whenever possible, speakers attempt to incorporate expert testimony into their speeches. Obviously, any time a speaker can quote a well-known authority who agrees with their point of view, they will be eager to do so. Most of the members of an audience will probably feel relatively uninformed compared to the speaker, and will be ready to listen to anyone who may consider to be an expert. Of course, expert testimony is only appropriate when the testimony is being given on the subject of expertise. That is, people are less likely to take seriously the political views of a person who is known as an expert in basketball than another person who is a respected public servant. Nevertheless, the members of an audience showed remain skeptical about persuasive arguments, even when they are made by experts. The same requirements of logic that apply to experts also apply to normal people.

Speech boundaries
Location: When preparing a speech, one should always keep in mind the occasion on which the speech will be given. In order to determine what kind of speech will be

appropriate, one needs to know the occasion on which the speech will be given. Individuals who have gathered together for a summer picnic, for instance, will not be interested in hearing a long and complicated speech. A short, humorous address would be more appropriate for this setting. A convention of professors, on the other hand, will want to hear a speech full of substance and technical information. On rare occasions, a speaker will decide it is necessary to deliver a speech that is not entirely appropriate for the setting; this should only be done, however, when it is absolutely necessary.

Time limits: When preparing a speech, one needs to know and keep in mind the time limits that will be set for the speech. Obviously, the subject matter to be tackled in the speech will be dependent upon the amount of time available. It will not be possible to effectively discuss a complicated subject in a short period of time, nor will it be possible to hold an audience's interest over a long period of time without having a wealth of information and ideas. Also, a persuasive speech will require a minimum amount of time in order to be effective. This is especially true when one is trying to convert an audience's opinion on a subject with which they are unfamiliar or on which they already have firm opinions. It generally will take a strong argument elaborated through a number of points to alter an opinion already agreed upon by most members of the audience.

Many speakers handicap themselves from the start by selecting a subject which is either too expansive or too narrow for their needs. In order to be effective, a speech subject needs to be appropriate for the amount of time in which the speech will be delivered. Obviously, a half-hour speech can go into much more detail and tackle a wider range of issues than can a five-minute speech. In a very short speech, there should be only one main idea, whereas in a longer speech the speaker may have time to deliver several

important points and give supporting information for each. Although the best way to determine the appropriate subject size is to gain experience as a public speaker, beginning speakers can still help themselves by considering the parameters of a speech as they begin to select a subject.

Tailoring the subject of a speech: When deciding on the subject of the speech, the speaker needs to take into account the characteristics and ability level of the audience. The speaker should be aware of the audience's expectations. That is, whether they expect to be informed, entertained, or persuaded. Audience members may be annoyed if a speech has a drastically different tone from the one that they expected. For instance, an audience expecting a serious speech will be impatient with a speaker who spends a great deal of time trying to make them laugh. In some cases, it may be necessary to thwart the expectations of the audience, as for instance when a serious moral point must be made instead of providing sheer entertainment.

When deciding upon the subject matter of a speech, the speaker should take into account the intelligence and subject-related knowledge possessed by the audience. A speech will be ineffective if it is either too elementary or too advanced for the audience. If the speaker is unfamiliar with the knowledge base of the proposed audience, he or she should take steps to inquire about this knowledge before preparing the speech. For an unschooled audience, it is a good idea to focus on the most basic and important principles of a given subject. For an audience of experts in a given field, however, it is important to provide information that will be stimulating and informative.

Setting: When preparing a speech, a speaker should take into account any idiosyncrasies of the speech format or setting. For instance, in some situations a speaker will have specific guidelines and rules for his or her speech.

When giving an address to the members of a particular religious or cultural group, for instance, one might need to abide by specific rules. Another thing to consider is the placement of the speech in the overall event. For instance, if other speakers are to follow one's speech, one might want to make sure there will be no overlap in speech content. Also, if one is going to be speaking directly after a dinner, one should be aware that audience members will be less likely to pay close attention to the details of the speech. Finally, a good speaker will find out the physical setting for speech: that is, will he or she standing or sitting, will there be a podium, etc.

Speaker issues

Practicing: Excellent speech delivery does not just happen; it is the result of extensive practice. After the speech has been outlined and drafted, you need to practice delivering it. Practicing a speech serves a number of purposes. For one thing, weak points in the speech may not be apparent to you until you actually say the words aloud. In addition, you can record yourself practicing and play back the tape to identify weaknesses in your delivery. It is often a good idea to practice delivering a speech in front of friends or family, and then have them critique your performance. Perhaps most importantly, practicing the delivery of the speech will further familiarize you with the material and increase your level of comfort and fluency in delivery.

Cultivating self-confidence: Most people struggle with some degree of anxiety when they are required to speak in public. One of the best things a person can do to reduce speech anxiety is present a confident image. For one thing, one should always practice delivering a speech several times beforehand. Through repetition, one becomes familiar with the rhythms and appropriate gestures in the speech, and feels increasingly confident in one's ability to deliver. Another good way to build confidence is to make eye contact with the audience during speech delivery. A forthright, steady gaze from the speaker connotes a feeling of confidence. Finally, confidence can be communicated through posture and body language. Standing up straight and emphasizing key points with hand gestures is a great way to communicate self-confidence.

Attributes of a speaker: In order to be an effective speaker, one must have a clear intention, a good attitude, and extensive knowledge of the subject of the speech, and a degree of credibility with the audience. The intention of the speech should be fully understood by the speaker, even if it is not directly expressed in the speech; sometimes, a speaker will have a hidden motive, or a long-term goal that cannot be expressed in the speech. In order to establish credibility, the speaker should possess a solid working knowledge of the subject of the speech. When the speaker is fluent in the subject he or she is discussing, the speech will flow more naturally, and the speaker will be able to tailor his or her message to the understanding of the audience. When we refer to the speaker's attitude, we are basically referring to the speaker's self-conception; that is, the image the speaker has of him or herself. If a speaker has a positive self-image, he or she is more likely to deliver an effective speech.

Speech evaluation

There are a few essential characteristics of a quality speech. An effective speech will have a good introduction that engages the audience and introduces the main idea or argument of the speech. The introduction will also establish the tone of the rest of the speech. The body of the speech should include clear exposition of ideas and appropriate supporting material. The conclusion of the speech should reinforce the main idea or claim and solidify audience understanding. The presentation of the speech should be appropriate to the audience and setting, and should be fluent in its delivery.

Speechmaking process

The speechmaking process has a few basic elements, which must be understood in order to master the subject. The central figure is the speaker; that is, the one delivering the speech. The speaker will have a self-conception and a conception of the identity of the audience. In the study of speechmaking, the audience is sometimes referred to as the receiver. Like the speaker, the audience will have a self-image as well as an impression of the speaker. The setting in which the speech is delivered is known as the situation. The speaker uses various channels of communication, including words and gestures, to communicate his or her message. The audience will deliver its response both through its body language and verbal responses to the speech. This response to the speech is called feedback.

Basic elements of the message: The message of a speech is communicated not only with the words that are spoken, but with the self-presentation of the speaker. In other words, the quality of the speaker's voice and his or her body language also contribute to the message. The message of the speech is generally considered to have three basic elements: structure, content, and presentation. The structure of the speech is the order in which information is delivered. In order to be effective, a speech must have a logical and coherent structure. The content of the speech is the information it contains; even an entertaining or persuasive speech must have good content. Finally, the presentation of a speech is the style in which it is delivered to the audience. Various presentation styles are used for different kinds of speeches. The most important thing is to match the presentation to the intention of the speech.

Research: In order to adequately prepare to deliver a speech, one needs to assemble all pertinent information and create a complete outline. One of the reasons why it is a good idea to select a familiar speech topic is so that the burden of performing research will be somewhat lightened. At the very least, one should know where to look to find the information necessary to deliver an informative and comprehensive speech. Speakers may need to consult with expert individuals, or peruse newspapers, magazines, and books for extra information. Many local and school libraries have extensive databases for performing research.

Speech outline: Before you can complete a first draft of a speech, you need to complete a detailed, comprehensive speech outline. After you have assembled all of the necessary material and information for your speech, you should organize the main points and the arguments and evidence supporting your ideas and claims. It is important that all of your secondary ideas and claims support your main idea or claim. You should always introduce your most important claim, or thesis, at the beginning of the speech. You can then spend the rest of the speech building a case for this thesis and elaborating other related points. When composing an outline, remember that the finished speech will likely be much more colorful and engaging. An outline is not meant to entertain, but rather to clearly and succinctly indicate the organization of the speech.

Fundamental qualities of a well-organized speech: There are certain qualities that all well-organized speeches have in common. For instance, a well-organized speech is comprehensible, meaning that it can be understood by all members of the audience. A well-organized speech also has a formal unity, which means that all of its parts contribute to its main idea. A unified speech has no extraneous parts. A well-organized speech is comprehensive; meaning that it covers all of the issues which an audience member would expect to be treated by a speech on the given subject. Finally, a well-organized speech does not have any repetition. Every major point should be covered in its entirety, but no points need to be repeated once they have been clearly delivered.

Process of speech organization: The process of speech organization entails selecting the elements that will make a speech, placing them into a coherent order, and arranging the supporting material for each message unit. During the organization process, a speaker will often summarize each message unit in a simple sentence. This gives the speaker simple building blocks that can be easily rearranged. In general, a speech is to have a coherent introduction, body, and conclusion. Introduction should engage the interest of the audience and summarize the main points to be made. The body should contain the central points of the speaker's argument, as well as the supporting evidence. The conclusion should summarize the argument and give the audience food for thought.

Effects of dialect: A dialect is simply the unique way of speaking held by a particular segment of a community. All Americans have a dialect of one sort or another. Individuals who have spent their entire lives within a given community, however, may not be aware that their mode of speech or of understanding language is different from that of any other American. To an extent, the spread of television and radio have minimized the differences among American dialects. Nevertheless, a speaker needs to be aware of the dialects of the members of his audience. Within certain dialects, common words may have unique connotative meanings which can confuse or even pervert a speaker's message. At the same time, the effective use of local dialect is a great way to endear oneself to the audience, and to establish a firm channel of communication.

Avoiding distractions: As much as possible, an effective speaker will minimize distractions during a speech. Distractions can be things that are done by the audience as well as by the speaker himself. Of course, it will not be possible for a speaker to exercise control over the behavior of the audience, but he can exercise control over himself. Too many speakers challenge the patience of the audience by hemming and hawing over their words, making distracting gestures, or engaging in frequent vocal tics. For many speakers, making noises like "uh" and "er" while searching for the right word is natural and unconscious. It can be very distracting to an audience, however, so a speaker would do well to practice delivering his message without incorporating these filler sounds.

Speaking appropriate to the topic and setting of the speech: With experience, a speaker should develop the ability to deliver his message in a manner that is appropriate to the topic, the audience, and the setting. For instance, when speaking to a group of five or six people, it is inappropriate to use a booming voice and wild, dramatic gestures. Likewise, it takes a very sophisticated speaker to deliver an intimate, informal lecture to a group of two or three hundred. One of the best ways to develop a sense of what is appropriate for a given setting is to study effective speakers in various settings. Notice how they vary their vocal quality and nonverbal communication repertoire in different environments. In order to obtain the attention and respect of the audience, the speaker needs to deliver his or her message in a manner that will meet their expectations.

Nonverbal communication in establishing the credibility: Many speakers underestimate the positive effects that nonverbal communication can have on their success in delivering a message. By making assertive and forceful gestures, a speaker can create an image of credibility and confidence. Similarly, by making easy gestures, a speaker can promote an image of relaxation and expansiveness. The trick is to know which gestures are appropriate in which situations. Furthermore, an effective speaker will be able to modulate the volume and pitch of his voice in accordance with the requirements of the speech. A bombastic tone is not appropriate to an academic discourse, nor is a dry delivery appropriate for a political rally. A speaker needs to be aware of the expectations of the audience, and only challenge them when such a challenge is necessary.

Improving voice and articulation problems: For many people, delivering an effective public speech is an uphill battle because they have never mastered the basics of vocal presentation. For instance, many people have not learned the proper manner of articulating complex sounds in English. Also, many people have not received enough exposure to effective oratory, and therefore do not understand the essential rhythms of speech delivery. There are a few common ways to improve voice and articulation problems. Some articulation problems are the result of physiological issues, and can only be treated by a doctor. Other issues, however, are behavioral, and can be resolved with therapy and training. Increasingly, schools are staffing speech clinicians to help students resolve problems with articulation.

Improving one's own public speech: The process of improving public speech technique will vary depending on the particular problems of the individual. However, there are a few common remedies that can be generally helpful. For one thing, a person can record themselves and listen to the way they speak. Oftentimes, one is not conscious of the articulation problems during the act of speech, but they become clear upon review. After a while, the individual can train himself to diagnose the problem and can subsequently learn to self-correct it. Practicing the production of the improved sound every day should result in an almost immediate progress. After a while, the corrections will become habitual and will no longer need review or practice.

Posture: Many speakers fail to recognize the significance of proper posture in the delivery of a speech. As much as words or gestures, a speaker's posture transmits information about his attitude, credibility, and confidence. In order to present a message effectively, a speaker needs to stand up straight and as tall as possible. Slouching toward or bending over one's notes indicates a lack of interest and preparation. This kind of advice may seem trivial, but an audience will subconsciously pay closer attention to an individual whose posture indicates command and authority. Effective speakers will pay close attention to their own posture and make sure that poor posture does not disrupt the transmission of their message.

Facial expression: The facial expressions made by a speaker can have a significant impact on the effectiveness of message delivery. The facial expressions of the speaker can either reinforce or contradict his words. If the words being spoken are amusing or colorful, it is appropriate for the speaker to be smiling and have a relaxed facial expression. However, if the speaker is attempting to describe a serious subject with a grin on his face, he can expect the audience to discount what he is saying. A speaker needs to match his facial expressions to the subject matter and to the expectations of the audience. A large audience can expect for the facial expressions of the speaker to be slightly exaggerated, while a small audience may be put off by what seems like a leering or grimacing speaker.

Eye contact: Speakers should never underestimate the importance of eye contact during message delivery. For one thing, it is very difficult for an audience member who is making eye contact with the speaker to lose interest. An effective speaker will often shift his gaze around the room, making eye contact with as many people as possible. Under no circumstances should a speaker look up in the air, stare at his notes, or fix his eyes on some point in the distance. At the same time, the speaker should not constantly move his eyes around the room, as this may be perceived as anxious behavior. Eye movements should be calm, regular, and smooth.

Gestures: A public speaker should make sure that his gestures are in harmony with the subject matter of the speech and the expectations of the audience. Many people are in the habit of either moving their hands frequently during speech or keeping their hands stationary. Both of these approaches are only appropriate in certain circumstances. When delivering a speech to a large audience, or delivering a speech with a high emotional content, a speaker may be advised to incorporate wide, energetic gestures. These kinds of motions are not appropriate for a more somber subject, however. And, although gestures can amplify the meaning of the speaker's words, they should never become a distraction from the message of the speech.

Using notes: Many speakers will require notes, but they should rely on these notes as little as possible during delivery of the speech. For one thing, notes tend to prevent the speaker from making effective eye contact and using his hands expressively while speaking. Also, a speaker may become reliant on his notes and may not be able to orient himself in a speech if something goes wrong with the notes. Notes should only be used as a reference point of last resort. They should be kept down in front of the speaker, preferably out of view of the audience. They should not be held and should be on as few pieces of paper as possible, to prevent excessive shuffling during a speech. Finally, a speaker who requires notes should carefully look over them before a speech to make sure they are understandable and arranged properly.

Basic skills required for making a speech: In order to deliver a successful speech, an individual needs to have acquired certain skills. For one thing, the individual needs to understand in depth the topic about which he or she is speaking. The individual needs to be able to address the topic from a number of different points of view, and to answer any questions the audience might have after the speech. More generally, a successful speaker needs to have an air of authority, so that the audience will pay attention and trust his or her words. A speaker also needs to have what

is known as rhetorical sensitivity, or the ability to adapt his or her message to different audiences. Successful speakers know that a given style of speaking may be very effective with one audience and ineffective with another. A successful speaker will be able to modulate his or her voice and gestures appropriately.

Intercultural contact: An effective speaker always needs to keep in mind the cultural characteristics of his or her audience. When a speaker is delivering a message to an audience whose culture is different from his or her own, he or she needs to be especially sensitive to the cultural mores observed by the group. For instance, excessive familiarity may be a sign of friendliness to the speaker, but it may demonstrate disrespect in the eyes of the audience. It is a good idea to familiarize oneself with the basic manners appropriate to the intended audience. A failure to observe the customs of the group may prevent a message from being heard.

Basic channels of public communication: Normally, when we think of speech delivery, we think of it as a simple transmission of words by one person to a group. However, this is only one of the channels through which information is delivered during a speech. In the technical language of speech communication, the words spoken by the speaker are said to pass through the verbal channel. At the same time, the speaker's tone of voice indicates his or her attitude through the aural channel. Some speakers will use visual aids, which transmit information through the pictorial channel. Finally, a speaker will transmit information about his or her attitude and self-image through gestures and facial expressions. This transmission is said to pass through the visual channel.

Physical setting: The physical setting in which a speech is delivered exerts significant influence over the expectations of the audience, and should therefore be taken into account by the speaker beforehand. For instance, an audience that is required to stand during a speech will have less patience for a long-winded and complex oration. On the other hand, if the audience is seated in soft, plush chairs, they may be too relaxed to pay attention to a serious lecture. When the subject of a speech requires a fair amount of technical detail, it is a good idea for the audience to be seated in upright chairs and for the room to have sufficient light. In any case, the speaker should consider how physical setting will influence the mood of the audience and should adjust his or her speech accordingly.

Social context: When speakers consider the characteristics of the environment in which their speech will be delivered, they sometimes neglect to consider the social context. The social context is the set of relationships between the members of the audience and the speaker, and between the members of the audience themselves. The speaker should know beforehand how he or she stands in relation to the audience. For instance, a speaker may be recognized as an expert, an entertainer, or an intriguing fraud. Also, the speaker should understand how the members of the audience stand in relation to one another; whether they are friends, colleagues, or strangers, for instance. The information obtained from this consideration of social context should inform the construction and delivery of the speech.

Communication rules: Sometimes, a speech will be delivered in a particular environment or to a particular group that is governed by specific communication rules. For instance, a speech delivered in church is unlikely to be followed by a question-and-answer period. As another example, some debating societies have strict rules for the presentation and critique of a speech. More informally, some groups will have different expectations for speaker behavior. For instance, a gathering of senior citizens is unlikely to respond well to coarse humor. So, communication rules may be explicit or implicit. During the preparation of a speech, the speaker needs to consider the formal considerations that will influence his or her message.

Feedback: Feedback is the response of the audience to the message delivered by the speaker. Although we typically conceive of feedback as verbal responses to the message, feedback also consists of body language, attention or inattention, and participation in dialogue after the speech. In order to be effective, a speaker needs to be attuned to all these kinds of feedback. In other words, he or she needs to be examining the audience during the speech to identify signs of boredom or engagement. The feedback a speaker receives while delivering his speech is called immediate feedback. The feedback the speaker receives after delivering the speech is called delayed feedback. Delayed feedback usually takes the form of critical comments, praise, or questions. A practiced speaker will use feedback to improve subsequent speeches.

Ideas and meaning

Ideas versus claims
A speech may try to disseminate information or persuade the audience. Another way of putting it is to say that a speaker will either deliver ideas or make claims. A speaker who is delivering ideas is expressing information and opinions for their own sake, and not necessarily to change the minds of the audience. Informative speeches are usually on subjects about which the audience is not expected to know very much. The purpose of the speech is to increase the knowledge of the audience, and not necessarily to convert them to any particular viewpoint. When a speaker makes claims, on the other hand, he or she is introducing opinions which may or may not be held by the members of the audience. The intention of the speech will be to provide arguments and evidence to support the claims made by the speaker.

Phrasing the main idea

It is important when giving an informative speech to lay out the main idea in a manner comprehensible to the audience. The main idea of an informative speech should be presented near the beginning of the address, and therefore should not require understanding of any concepts which will be explained later in the speech. The audience should be able to understand the gist of the main idea before the speaker goes on to elaborate. In the preparation of a speech, the speaker should define the main idea early on, so that he or she can procure evidence and supporting arguments appropriate to that main idea. Too often, speakers introduce evidence and arguments which are not directly supportive of the main idea of the speech. The effect of this is that it confuses the audience and waters down the effect of the speech.

Phrasing the main claim

When a speech is designed to present or advance a particular viewpoint, the speaker will need to pay special attention to the phrasing of the speech's main claim. The main claim should be phrased in such a way that it will be comprehensible to a general audience, and will not offend casual listeners with a harsh or controversial tone. The degree of intensity appropriate to the claim will depend on the audience. A more strident tone can be used with an audience of like-minded individuals, while a diverse group of uncommitted listeners requires a more evenhanded tone. When constructing the main claim of a speech, the speaker should be sure to only present ideas which can be supported by available evidence and reasonable argument. If the main claim of a speech is far-fetched or unsupportable, even the more rational elements of the speech may be dismissed by a skeptical audience.

Denotative meaning

Denotative meaning is the way in which a word indicates something else. The word table, for instance, denotes a flat surface with three or more legs. A speaker must always be conscious of the denotative meaning of the words he uses. The denotative meaning is not decided on an individual basis; rather it is the product of unconscious agreements on meaning made by the members of a community. In other words, the speaker must have a familiarity with the denotative meanings that will be known to the members of the audience in order to ensure that he communicates with them effectively. Effective speakers continually refer to a dictionary during speech composition in order to solidify their understanding of denotative meanings.

Connotative meaning

Connotative meaning is any implication or a suggestion connected to a word that extends beyond the denotative meaning of the word. The connotative meaning of the word, then, is not strictly the definition of the word. Connotative meanings are often quite emotional in character. For instance, the denotative meaning of the word whale is a large mammal that lives in the ocean. When the word is used in a certain way, however, whale can acquire the connotative meaning as a human being who is overweight. Speakers need to be aware of both the connotative and the denotative meanings of the words they use. Otherwise, the speaker runs the risk of confusing or even offending members of the audience. A detailed dictionary will often have explanations of the various connotative meanings of common words.

Many times, the members of a particular cultural group have special connotative meanings for words. Because connotative meanings can carry such emotional power, it is especially important for a speaker to understand the connotative meanings shared by his audience before delivering a speech. The best way to acquire a sense of connotative meaning is to spend time with the members of the community. Developing a feeling for what is appropriate language for a given audience is as much a matter of intuition as the acquisition of particular

- 76 -

definitions. When in doubt, a speaker should avoid using any language that may have unpleasant or hostile connotative meaning to his audience.

Role of definitions
In order to be an effective speaker, a person needs to know the basic definitions of the words they are using. Furthermore, the speaker needs to share his definition of words with the members of the audience. If the members of the audience understand different things by the words used by the speaker, there will be no possibility of communication. At all times, speakers should strive for clarity and precision in their words. By clarity, we mean choosing words that are directly tied to the intended meanings of the speaker. Clear language admits no confusion about the subject matter or intent. By precise, we mean words which do the best jobs of denoting the precise meaning intended by the speaker. When the language of a speech is precise, the audience should not have to guess what is denoted by each word.

Abstract terms
It is easy to discover the denotative meanings of simple nouns like table, turkey, and television. It is more difficult to determine the denotative meanings of abstract nouns. That is, nouns which describe feelings, ideas, and concepts. Some examples of abstract terms are freedom, jealousy, and capitalism. For the definitions of these words, a speaker must rely on a dictionary and on his own sense of how the word is used in a given community. For the most part, speakers who wish to present themselves as objective will try to make the denotative meanings of his words precise and minimize the connotative meanings as much as possible. Not only are connotative meanings more subjective for an audience, but they tend to introduce some emotional content. In other words, they compromise the objectivity of the speaker.

Effective naming
As much as possible, an effective speaker will try to choose the right words to describe their subject. In some cases, there may be several names for the same thing. For instance, we might refer to the same car as a sedan, an auto, or a jalopy. These three names all carry with them different connotations. Furthermore, whereas a word like auto suggests a certain objectivity or seriousness on the part of the speaker, a word like jalopy is more appropriate for a humorous or colorful speech. In order to maintain the right tone, then, a speaker will need to be able to select the appropriate names. The only way to do this consistently is to develop a keen ear for language by reading widely and listening to people in the community.

Effective descriptions
An effective speaker will be able to compose descriptions which clarify and illuminate his subject matter. For instance, consider the difference between describing a person as a "good man" and describing him as a "heroic, courageous inspiration to his community." Obviously, the second description is more colorful and paints a more comprehensive picture of the person. Indeed, it includes the information that the described person was valued for his effect on his fellow citizens. As much as possible, a speaker wants to include descriptions that combine engaging detail and vivid language, without being so colorful as to distract from the main point of the speech. A facility for effective description can be encouraged by paying attention to the way description is handled by great authors and speakers.

Speech anxiety

Apprehension
To some extent, all individuals grapple with speech anxiety. The fear of embarrassment or public disclosure can be overcome only with significant practice at Speaking and Listening in Different Contexts. There are a couple of different kinds of speech anxiety. State

apprehension is defined as speech anxiety that is only felt in specific situations. For instance, an individual who is comfortable talking in class but becomes anxious when required to speak informally with peers is experiencing state apprehension. Many people experience state apprehension in relation to delivering formal speeches in front of a group. State apprehension has both physical and mental symptoms, including vocal tics, sweaty palms, and a trembling voice.

Trait apprehension
Some individuals experience speech anxiety to a greater degree than others. The aspects of speech anxiety that are unique to an individual are known as trait apprehensions. For instance, an individual might have an aversion to Speaking and Listening in Different Contexts because of an experience in their past. People who have an unnaturally high level of trait apprehension tend to avoid situations in which they will be required to speak to a large group. The good news for these individuals is that trait apprehension can be overcome with experience. Unfortunately, however, this means practicing Speaking and Listening in Different Contexts until it becomes natural.

Interpretation of speech anxiety
Speech anxiety is a common malady, but not one which should cause an individual to lose heart. Even the most successful speakers have a bit of anxiety when delivering a message. In a way, this anxiety is a positive thing, because it focuses the attention and encourages concentration. Speech anxiety is a natural response to confronting an uncertain and unfamiliar situation. Research suggests that individuals who suffer from severe speech anxiety are often the most effective public speakers. Also, most speakers report that the anxiety they feel before delivering a speech is much greater than the anxiety they feel when actually in the process of speaking.

Using speech anxiety productively
The abundance of nervous energy felt before delivering a speech can be used to the speaker's advantage. For one thing, many people find that speech anxiety sharpens their senses and focuses their concentration on the task at hand. Human beings are naturally disposed to focus their attention when they perceive a threat. The good thing about speech anxiety is that the attention is sharpened even though the threat is not significant. Many accomplished speakers use speech anxiety to increase their level of excitement and dynamism while delivering a speech. Indeed, many speakers say that without speech anxiety, they would not be able to achieve the rhetorical effects that have made them successful speakers.

Note-taking

Benefits
One of the best things an audience member can do to organize his or her thoughts about a speech is to take notes. Taking notes during a speech allows the audience member to organize the message of the speaker and mark down any questions or concerns without becoming entangled in a long digressive thought. Taking notes during a speech is a skill that every college student has to use on a daily basis. It is important for students to begin practicing these skills early in their academic careers. Many people believe that they can accurately recall a speech in great detail, but few people actually can. Making notes helps to refresh the memory so that an individual can accurately consider the message of the speech long after it has been given.

Basic process
The importance of taking clear and accurate notes during a speech cannot be overstated. Most individuals acquire a personal note-taking style over time. This style may be highly idiosyncratic, but it usually includes a few core features. For one thing, good note-takers usually develop a style of organization,

so that they can look back over their notes
and discern the general structure of a speech.
Indentations, margins, and numbers/letters
are common ways of organizing a set of notes.
It is always a good idea to leave some room on
the margins of one's notes, so that one can fill
in any weak areas later on. Remember that
notes are meant to be reviewed. After all, the
primary goal of note-taking is to preserve an
accurate record of the speech, so that it can be
recalled later.

Advanced techniques
Over many years of study, most students
develop an efficient and organized way of
taking notes. There are a number of common
systems of organization that have proven
beneficial for top students. For instance,
many students use abbreviations and
shorthand so that they can condense a great
deal of information into a relatively small
space. There are a number of symbols for
common expressions that can save time
during note-taking. Other students color code
their notes. That is, they use a different color
pen depending on the type of notes they are
taking. Still other students create elaborate
outline procedures to organize the main idea
and supporting ideas in a speech or lecture.
While all of these methods can be effective, it
falls to the individual student to experiment
and decide which method of note organization
best promotes his or her own understanding.

Speech Education

Teaching Concepts

Curriculum components

The following are components of curriculum:
- *Scope and sequence:* Effective instruction focusing on the essential skills and concepts commonly found on standardized tests.
- *Curricular materials:* Equipment and materials needed to teach a subject
- *Learner objectives:* The establishing of objectives, types and levels of objectives, of what will be taught.

Reciprocal teaching

Reciprocal teaching is in many ways the aggregation of four separate comprehension strategies, which is summarizing, questioning, clarifying and predicting. Summarizing presents the ability to identify and integrate the information that is most important in a text. Text can be summarized across sentences and paragraphs and across passages. When students start the reciprocal teaching procedures they are usually focused at sentence and paragraphs. Questioning reinforces the strategy of summarizing. When students identify questions they identify a kind of information that is important enough to provides substance for a question then post the information in question form. Clarifying is important for students with comprehension difficulty. They are taught to be alert to the effects of comprehension impediments and take the measures to restore meaning. Predicting is when student predict what the author will discuss next in the text.

The order of the four stages of reciprocal teaching is not of great importance. A teacher will want to try out various ways to employ the strategy in order to see if a particular sequence fits a teaching style and the students' learning style. One also wants to carefully choose text selections so that they all fit in with the four stages of reciprocal teaching. Before successfully implementing reciprocal teaching, the students need to have been taught the four strategies as well as had ample opportunities to use them. One approach could be having students work from a chart with four columns. Each column will be headed by the different comprehension activity that is involved. Then put students in groups of four. Distribute one note card to each group member that tells the member's unique role of: summarizer, questioner, clarifier, or predictor.

Example: How a reciprocal teaching exercise would operate using four-column charts, groups of four students with each playing a specific part of summarizer, questioner, clarifier and predictor: The students would have their defined role on a note card. The students then could read several paragraphs of the assigned text passage. They should be encouraged to use note-taking strategies such as selective underlining or sticky notes in helping for their role in the discourse. At a given stopping point, the summarizer will give the key ideas up to this particular point in the text. The questioner will then ask questions about the text such as unclear parts, puzzling information, connections to concepts that have already been learned or motivations of the characters or actors. The clarifier will try to clear up the confusing parts and answer questions that were asked. The predictor may make guesses about what the author might tell next. The roles then switch one person to the right and another selection is read.

Rationale
Most important in reading education is turning out readers who can understand the meaning in texts. Reciprocal teaching is a scaffolded discussion technique built upon for ways that good readers can comprehend text

through questioning, clarifying, summarizing and predicting. Teaching the students the four strategies helps give the student tools that great readers use in meeting their text-reading goals. Thus, the four strategies are what are taught rather than reading skills. These multiple strategies help students to read by giving them a choice of strategies that they can use in reading. The scaffolding gives support to help the students connect what they know and can do with what they need to do in order to be successful at learning a particular lesson. This also helps give the students a chance to support each other and foster a sense of community among classmates.

Goals

The word "reciprocal" in reciprocal teaching is somewhat misleading in that it does not entail students doing the teaching. But the students do get to use a set of four strategies -- summarizing, clarifying, predict and questioning -- to better improve reading comprehension. That improvement is the ultimate goal. The other goals include:

- The teacher scaffolds instruction of the strategy by guiding, modeling and applying the strategies.
- It guides students to become metacognitive and reflective in the use of strategies.
- It helps students monitor their comprehension of reading.
- It uses the social nature of learning in order to improve and scaffold the comprehension of reading.
- The instruction is presented through different classroom settings including whole group, guided reading groups and literature circles.

Perspective

Social

A rich resource for students' of literature is their own developing social knowledge. For adolescent students', social relationships are of primary importance. It is common for younger students' to impose their own social attitudes on a text, which is fertile ground for exploring how the understanding of texts is colored by social attitudes and experiences. Student's attitudes can help them reflect on the characters in a work, and can determine their relationship with the text itself.

Social perspectives can shed light on a number of important ways which can effect a reader's engagement with the text. A skillful teacher may probe these attitudes and experiences and make students' more aware of the impact of social attitudes to reading and studying a work of literature. This knowledge can become cumulative and promote more careful understanding of a literature over a period of time.

Cultural and historical context

The cultural knowledge and background of readers affects their response to texts. They can relate the works in a context of subcultures such as peer group, mass media, school, religion, and politics, social and historical communities. Engaging with the texts, readers can better understand how characters and authors are shaped by cultural influences. Cultural elements influence reader's reactions to events, including their responses to literature.

Cultural and historical context is important in understanding the roles of women and minorities in literature. Placing works of literature in their proper cultural setting can make a work more understandable and provoke reader interest in the milieu of the day. These factors can stimulate a reader's interest in how their own cultural background impacts the engagement with the text. Thus, the cultural aspects of literature become an opportunity for the reader to gain insight into their own attitudes.

Topical

In using a topical perspective, students apply their background in a variety of different fields, for instance sports, science, politics or cooking, to the literary work they are studying. Students may then engage the text in a holistic manner, bringing all their knowledge to bear on a work. It is useful to encourage students to determine how their own information pool relates to the work. There are an infinite number of fields or topics that relate to literature.

Students are most likely to integrate topics they are currently studying into their engagement with a text. These topics would include history, science, art, and music among others. Thinking about literature from these other topical point-of-view can help students ' understand that what they are learning in other courses enhances their experience of both literature and life.

Complementary learning

History and literature
When students employ topical knowledge of history in their study of literature, they may do much more than remember date, events, and historical figures in relation to a text. They may well apply what they know about a historical period to better understand the attitudes and relationships in a work of literature. Students learn to think historically, considering different explanations for events, or cause and effect relationships in tracing a sequence of events. For example in reading Steinbeck's novels, students may draw on what they know about the historical period of the depression. Hemingway's "Farewell To Arms" may evoke a historical picture of Europe embroiled in World War I.

Literature offers an opportunity to apply historical knowledge in the context of a work. Students understand that both literary and historical accounts of an event or character may differ significantly, and that one may illuminate the other.

Scientific knowledge and literature
Students can apply their knowledge of science when reading literature. Their description of carefully observed phenomena can be used to describe a piece of writing. After reading essays by science writers, students' may be encouraged to transpose this knowledge into reading other texts. Understanding the scientific method gives readers' an opportunity to impose this process on events narrated in literature. The validity of events may be tested in the students' mind to assess the "reality" of the text.

There are many texts that take as their subject the role of the scientist in society. *Frankenstein* or *Dr. Faustus* raise many issues about the responsibilities of scientists in conducting experiments. The blending of science and literature is particularly compelling to some students' when they read science fiction or futuristic texts. An example would be "1984" which posits an authoritarian government controlling the lives of people.

Art, music and literature
Art and music contain many opportunities for interacting with literature for the enrichment of all. Students could apply their knowledge of art and music by creating illustrations for a work, or creating a musical score for a text. Students' could discuss the meanings of texts and decide on their illustrations or score could amplify the meaning of the text.

Understanding the art and music of a period can make the experience of literature a richer, more rewarding experience. Students should be encouraged to use the knowledge of art and music to illuminate the text. Examining examples of dress, architecture, music, and dance of a period may be helpful in a fuller engagement of the text. Much of period literature lend itself to the analysis of the prevailing taste in art and music of an era, which helps place the literary work in a more meaningful context.

Grouping

Between-class ability grouping

Between-class ability grouping is not a strategy in which all students can learn. Students at the top level seem to benefit but middle and lower students may not. It is nonetheless a popular practice in American education. The problem may lie more with the method of grouping than with the concept. Ability groups are mostly determined by standardized test or basic skills tests. But students may not have uniform knowledge and aptitude of the content areas. Another problem found in research is that teachers' expectations and the quality of instruction are often lower for lower-track groups in between-class grouping. Students may also lower their own expectations when placed in a lower-level group. This may affect self-concept in academic achievement, and thus, affect the teacher's expectations.

Within-class ability grouping

Research tends to support within-class ability grouping, grouping those with like abilities, as helping most students learn. It is generally flexible and not as stigmatizing as other groups. If such groups are considered then teachers might want only two such groups to help make management of the grouping process easier.

Cooperative learning

Cooperative learning is an instructional strategy in which students are put into heterogeneous groups. It is perhaps one of the best researched innovations in recent times and can have dramatic student achievement effects when implemented properly.

Individualized instruction

Individualized instruction or one-on-one instruction is the best way to deal with individual student difference but it is very difficult to accomplish. Computer-assisted instruction may change that.

Combined grouping formats

Small group reading instruction has been shown in a number of studies to be more effective than instruction of the class as a whole. Most of these studies did not include students who were disabled. Teacher-led groups of between three to 10 students help them learn much more than when they are taught using instruction of the whole class. Smaller groups of three to four are usually more efficient than larger groups in terms of time, peer interaction and improved skills. Combinations of formats also produce reading benefits that are measurable especially for those children with disabilities. For instance, students who work in pairs for two days in small and in small groups for two days can be combined with whole-class instruction for a part of a period.

Nongraded or upgraded grouping

Nongraded and ungraded grouping usually refers to grouping children in classes without designation of grade levels and with age spans of more than one year. The original rationale was to increase the heterogeneity of class compositions and liberate children and teachers from rigid achievement expectations that are based on the age of a student. But research later found that implementing these classes tended to result in homogeneous grouping of children for children based on ability and achievement level despite age. In many instances of nongraded groups, children in classes are put in regular or temporary groups for specific instruction regardless of age. In such approaches, the main goal is to increase homogeneity of ability of groups rather than interaction across ability group lines.

Combined grade classes

Combined classes are those which include more than one grade level in a classroom. These classes are sometimes referred to split classes, blended classes or double-year classes. These classes usually will include the required curriculum for each of the two grades that are represented. But some class activities may take place with children who are from both of the combined grades. This type of grouping takes place more frequently in smaller schools as well as on occasion in larger schools when the number of children in different age cohorts tend to have fluctuated. The main purpose of such classes appears to be the maximization of personnel and space resources instead of capitalizing on the diversity of ability and experience within the groups of mixed ages.

Continuous progress

Continuous progress generally means that children remain with their classroom peers in an age cohort despite having met or surpassed specific grade-level achievement expectations. This term is usually associated with the emphasis on the individualized curriculum so that teaching and learning tasks are responsive to previous experience and the rates of progress of the child despite age. This practice is sometimes referred to as social promotion. The main reason for the practice is that there might be a stigmatizing effect on children if removed from one's age cohort. The programs that are focused on continuous progress, like ungraded approaches, are not aimed at maximizing the educational benefits of children of different abilities and ages being together. Instead it is to let the children progress without being made to meet expectations of achievement.

Mixed-age or multi-age grouping

Mixed age or multi-age grouping refers to grouping children so that the age span of the class is greater than one year, as in the nongraded approach. Mixed-age and multi-age grouping emphasize the goal of teaching and curriculum practice use that makes maximum benefit of the cooperation and interaction of the children of various ages. In multi-age classes, teachers encourage the children with different ages of development and experience to help each other with all classroom activities including application and mastery of basic literacy and mathematical skills. But, teachers use small temporary subgroupings in mixed-age classes for children who require the same types of instruction that will help them get basic skills.

Implications of different age grouping schemes

Grouping practices might seem to have slight distinctions but there are significant implications in practice. Ungraded or nongraded approaches indicate that age is not a good indicator of what children are ready to learn. It emphasizes regrouping children for class based on perceived readiness to acquire skills and knowledge instead of age. Its main goal is of homogenizing children for instruction for achievement rather than age even though this was not the original reasoning for the term. Groupings of combined grades and continuous progress practices do not intend to increase a sense of family within class or to encourage children to share knowledge and experience. But mixed-age grouping does take advantage of heterogeneity of experience and skills in a group of children.

Learning centers

Learning centers should be established one at a time. Clear rules and routines for using each center should be understood. A chart should be posted at each center that indicates the rules such as how many children should be in the center or what materials and equipment may be used. The center should be closely supervised at first. Teachers can determine when children are able to work both independently or cooperatively. Possible centers include a writing center, an alphabet center, a science center, a writing center or other centers. These can be changed throughout the year. Learning centers help play an important part in classroom management. Effective classrooms have a combination of direct instruction, cooperative learning, independent practice and learning center activities.

Writing centers are found in secondary schools, colleges and universities. They provide students with help on their papers, projects and reports from a variety of personnel including both professional and peer tutors. Such services help with purpose, structure and organization of writing and are geared accordingly to setting. Writing centers may offer individual conferences where feedback is offered on the piece of writing. Discussions may be made on how to make the writing clearer and more grammatically correct. An elementary writing center may have a white eraser board, rubber stamps for "date," "first draft" and "complete." There might be a variety of colors with pencil, markers, pictures and crayons as ways to start stories. One goal of such a center is to get children to continue to investigate the many functions of print in communicating.

Paired summarizing

Paired summarizing is a cooperative learning strategy in which students work together to elaborate on the retelling of their passages or stories that they have read. The students should complete an individual retelling before pairing off to do their work. This step will help avoid much of the wasted time and confusion that can take place when students attempt to coordinate work before being individually ready for the task. The procedure focuses on individual preparation and the value of a collaborative participation. Just after reading the selection, the student immediately writes a retelling. The students cannot write any of the retelling while looking at their text. The students might compete with their partner for the most complete retelling. Students should be told not to worry about grammar or other mechanical aspects. When finished the students exchange papers and each writes a retelling of the other's paper.

Student peer training

Students have long had informal, untrained peer helping networks. Students share their concerns with each other naturally while at lunch, after school and while talking on the phone at home. The seriousness of the problems discussed have changed somewhat in today's world. Students may likely know someone who was pregnant or suicidal, who had a drug problem, was being abused or who had an eating disorder. But many of these students with such problems do not seek adult help for their problems. This results in a crisis where a student's coping mechanisms are not effective and many students end up getting little or no help from professionals. Peer programs offer the ability to increase the student's skill in responding and helping friends, and train students to know when there is a crisis and where the peer may be referred.

The peer helper and adult resource connection is not often understood by educators who are unfamiliar with the concept. But that linkage is a bedrock of the program. Young people with serious worries can be helped by their peers and adults. Help can come early and can take place where there is trust. Students can build a circle of support around them with such programs. It is a challenge, however, because students do feel rejected or neglected by their peers. Research shows that the best way to keep stress away is being part of a stable, tight-knit group. Peer helpers can be trained to help with continued needs that help foster more well-rounded communities within schools.

Computers and classroom management

A classroom which is equipped with computers for all students might resemble a computer lab to some students so teachers should make attendance rules well known to get the class off to a better beginning. A routine also may need to be established for students who are put off by the non-traditional roles that computer technology has them assume. Pacing is also a concern in a classroom with computers. Fewer activities exist for students to work on at their own pace than those that are carefully-timed activities during class periods. Teachers who set goals and activities for a class at the beginning of a class and then let students work at their own pace usually are more comfortable with computers in the classroom.

Since businesses use computers to their advantage in making their companies more efficient, teachers also can use computers in managing their classrooms. Teachers can use the computer to do traditional paperwork and help free them from a number of tasks that are classified as noninstructional. A computer will not make a business a success by itself. And a teacher must know, like the business manager, what programs will do and how they are used. Teachers can use computers to:

- Keep student progress records, test, cumulative and average scores.
- Prepare notes to individual students.
- Keep records of attendance.
- Keep inventory of supplies that include what quantities are available and where they are located.
- Generate tests and worksheets. They sometimes can help score tests. Students may also be able to take the test on the computer.
- Produce posters and calendars.
- Send parents notes.

Students and homework

Students may have difficulties with homework because parents come home tired after a hectic day and are unable to properly monitor the students' assignments. The personal difficulties students have and priorities that compete with classwork also are some of the obstacles for studying work at home. Often times the parents do not realize that there is a problem. Some parents are too tired and busy with homemaking chores that finding time to check their children's assignments carefully becomes difficult. Students also have many more extracurricular activities in which to participate and other options such as jobs, sports, activities, television and the Internet. Students also

have personal difficulties such as an unstable home life, a lack of adult role models or drug problems.

Teachers should make known their expectations early in the school year before the first homework is assigned. The teacher should go over the ground rules with the students. An explanation of expectations that is written down helps to increase the chances for students successfully completing homework. Students should know:

- Homework is important and has meaning.
- Doing assignments or not doing them has consequences such as lower grades if the assignments are not done.
- Students need to be held to a high standard. Research has shown that students make better gains academically when teachers set high expectations and tell the students of their expectations. Students also should know how much and when homework will be assigned.

Creating assignments with a purpose
Assignments that are made for work to be done outside of class should be done so with a purpose rather than to provide busy work. Good from the homework helps contribute to the class and is much like finishing a project. Among the major purposes of homework are:

- Review and practice of what the students have learned.
- To get ready for the next day's class.
- Improving overall study skills by learning to use resources such as the library, reference material, encyclopedias, or the Internet.
- Exploring subjects more deeply than time allows while in class. In elementary school, as well as to a certain extent in junior high and high school, homework can: teach the children the fundamentals of working independently and encourage self-

- 86 -

discipline through time management and meeting deadlines.

While students may appreciate understanding an assignment's purpose, the purpose might now become clear until students are mid-way through the assignment or have completed it. Students need to know what it is that is expected of them. There should be clear communication or scant confusion over what is the value of the assignment. The teacher should not just tell a student to read something or answer questions without knowing why they are doing it. Students should be given the bigger picture of just how their assignments fit in the realm of what they study. This is even though the student may not entirely appreciate the project's significance until it is finished or partially finished.

Focusing assignments

Assignments that are focused are less difficult for students to complete and to understand. Assignments that try to reinforce an overabundant number of ideas is not likely to help a student learn. This is especially the case for students who have not yet developed abstract thinking to the point where they can successfully integrate many of the concepts. Assignments need not be a large, overwhelming dissertation about what it is the teacher expects. The assignment should stick to one issue or concept. and it should ask for maybe four or five examples. A teacher can easily determine if the students are getting what is being sought and if not, help can be given in studying for the objective. Focus and the appropriate background information is also important in class discussions of assigned readings. Some children can be frustrated trying to get at the reading all at once.

Challenging assignments

Homework can give a student the ability to apply concepts that are beyond the controlled environment of a classroom. It can also help students collect and connect information from a variety of sources, subjects and places. The best assignments challenge students to expand or break away from how they normally think. Such an assignment might combine two unassociated ideas. Assignments can range from listing what one finds in a desk drawer to writing paragraphs about family members. In those assignments, students can break the punctuation or capitalization rules in order to better learn the rules. Integrating topics also helps the thinking process, such as putting together an art, writing and science class.

Varying assignments

If all assignments are alike, students will get bored. Mixing approaches and styles should be tried. All students will not be interested in a given assignment, but mixing it up creates better chances that some of the homework will be enjoyed by the students. Short-term assignments can help students practice and review material already covered in class. Long-term projects allow students to vary the pace of their work, get into subjects of interest to them and to manage time and deadlines. Variety may also help stimulate the teachers. Students are given more opportunities to better learn when the teacher is enthusiastic. The teachers might try not teaching the same topics or points year in and year out.

Personal assignments

Assignments that make learning personal are often very effective in helping students appreciate studying and completing those assignments. Such work often lets students look into their family, community and cultural experiences and learn a better appreciation of both their own and their peers' backgrounds. Family tree projects in social studies classes are an example because of the great diversity of most American schools. These projects or others such as historical ones in which family members are sought out may often bring out values that the students might otherwise not appreciate and can also foster close family relationships. Making assignments personal and with value give students a great incentive

- 87 -

to appreciate studying about a subject and find learning as a quest.

Tying assignments to the present
Students may often feel that they can relate to assignments about events from long ago in the past. It is hard to teach most types of history unless they are related somehow to the present. But assignments can draw comparisons between what is happening today and events years or centuries ago. For instance, students might approach an assignment on a Civil War battle by contrasting it with more modern battles. They might see the battle through the eyes of a television war correspondent who interviews the principal leaders and ask what they might do differently if they were to "do over" the battle. Students learn the specifics of such battles through these interviews and can appreciate the significance of the events that took place. This is a way of piquing interest in study.

Matching skills, interests and needs of students
The chances are greater that a student will complete his or her homework assignments if they:
- Are not too hard or too easy.
- Match children's preferred learning styles.
- Let students work on material that they really like. Assignments cannot be customized for every student. But teachers can give assignments to a heterogeneous class that varies in content, format and style. This will better the chance that all students will have some elements of the assignments that are of interest.
- Teachers can give the students choices. The student may be expected to master all the same material but it can be done in different ways. This helps student feel they control parts of their learning which encourages studying and helps them to enjoy an

assignment that they otherwise would not.

Art and writing skills

An art component can be added to writing activities that make such an activity fun as well as giving the student an outlet for expression. Many of the developmental stages of young children in terms of writing and art have almost interchangeable terms. Scribbling, for instance, takes place in both writing and art. A child learns to print a name in letters and learns to make symbols to represent objects in art. Both processes use the same type of thinking skills as well. Creative thinking that builds a storyline is the same thinking that puts a work of art together. Both processes ask: "Where do I go from here?" Preparation for any writing or art topic should be prefaced with a discussion on who, what, when, where, why and how.

Effects of television

Past studies have shown that American children watch more television than any other activity. But despite the negative aspects that have been linked with watching TV, studies also have indicated that it can be a valuable tool in literacy instruction. Studies suggest there may be some overlap between pre-reading and television viewing for very young children with respect to their later skills in reading. Research indicated those children who were good at comprehending content on television were also good at aural comprehension. Certain Public Broadcasting Service programs aimed at educating and entertaining produced research results that showed those youngsters watching the shows performed better on some reading tasks. It has also been suggested by research that incorporating reading instruction and TV may help motivate readers who are reluctant and improve fluency.

Drama activities

Dramatic activities as a language arts instructional tool is based on a principle that the child is directly involved through drama and that an involved child would be more interested in learning. Drama has been found to be effective in literacy in a number of areas.

- Students develop affect through drama. Motivation is stimulated through drama by student participation and helps students respond in reading instruction.
- Drama is a source of scaffolding for emergent readers in that it provides valuable background experiences for reading that is done in the future.
- Dramatization helps students develop symbolic representation which is required for children in understanding the alphabetic principle.
- Drama provides students an environment where they can repeatedly practice oral reading to develop fluency.
- New vocabularies from drama give students opportunities to get meanings visually, kinesthetically and aurally.

Elementary and English as a Second Language classes can receive scaffolding for effective literacy teaching from dramatic activities. Researchers have found that scaffolded play with students of elementary age allow them to participate in language learning in an active way. Students may also be more motivated to discuss, organize, rewrite and perform in the dramatic presentation. Students have also become more engaged in which there was interwoven activities involving literature, drama, music and movement, even for at-risk students in grades K-3. Activities involving bilingual children in which their own cultural experiences are called upon and valued. This also helps motivate and support literacy and meaningful learning environments.

Management and motivation

Various instructional approaches to classroom management and student motivation:

- Model-based classroom management
- Concise and efficient instructions
- Developmentally and age appropriate instruction
- Large (whole) group instruction
- Small group instruction
- Be able to create and maintain an atmosphere that encourages questions, conjectures, problem solving, and experimentation

Other helpful approaches include:

- *Organization:* The state or manner of being organized
- *Discipline:* Training expected to produce a specific character or pattern of behavior, especially training that produces moral or mental improvement.
- *Procedures:* A set of established forms or methods for conducting the affairs of an organized body
- *Learner responsibility:* The student must have responsibility for their actions or non-action
- *Interventions:* Interference so as to modify a process or situation.

IEP and curriculum standards

Individualized Education Program is a written document that's developed for each public school child who's eligible for special education. The IEP is created through a team effort and reviewed at least once a year.

Standards focus on developing coherency across grade levels, teaching for understanding, and relevancy of subject matter, helping courses to build upon each other in age appropriate ways. This farsighted statement sets an excellent vision for what students should be learning. The standards are broken into ten areas within two broader categories. Process Standards, the first category, define how students should "do" the content and how they should be able to use their knowledge. The second category, the Content Standards, deal with the content that students should learn.

Home and school socialization

Student success appears to be related to congruence between home and school socialization. Studies show that high achievers have a home environment that is congruent with a school environment. High achievers learned how to independently and obediently complete tasks at home. Such behaviors are important to school success as well. A dissonance between home and school may be caused by cultural differences in some cases. Some studies have indicated black children prefer and do better in communal learning settings while white students like and do better in those settings that are competitive. Cultural dissonance may also lead to wrong interpretations of parent behaviors that create misunderstandings between school and home.

Culturally responsive teaching

One goal of effective teaching is making learning a meaningful endeavor for children. Children must see connections between what they know and what they experience in schools and other settings in order to comprehend their experience. Increasing the congruence and continuity between children's home and school environments is a crucial aspect in achievement for children who come from diverse cultures and varied social classes. Recognizing and fostering the cultural knowledge of children from culturally and linguistically diverse backgrounds can help bridge the gap between home and school. Creating a culturally responsive learning situation takes a lot of work. This includes effective partnerships between schools and

families where each a treated as a full partner in attaining a successful outcome.

Effects of parents

Expectations
Research has found that parental expectations are significant to school performance as well as critical to achievement in academics. The high expectations from parents are usually found in association with levels of educational attainment that are higher. Parenting practices that are effective and associated with high levels of academic achievement include expectations that children receive high numerical grades of their schoolwork. Additionally, research indicates that child rearing beliefs, ways to academically enrich home environments and standards of behavior that are acceptable both in and out of school are likewise important to achieving academically. Insofar as behavior is concerned, the children who succeed have the adaptability to conforming with behavioral standards at school, something many have already learned through parental expectations.

Parental education and socioeconomic status
The exact nature of the impact parental education and social economic status has on student achievement although it does have an impact. Studies have found that parental education and family socioeconomic status alone are not necessarily predictors of how students will achieve academically. Studies have found that parental education accounts for about a quarter of the variance in student test scores while socioeconomic status accounts for slightly more than a quarter. Other research indicates that dysfunctional home environments, low expectations from parents, parenting that is ineffective, differences in language and high mobility levels may account for the low achievement levels among those students that come from lower socioeconomic levels.

Helping with technology

Children of this age will be barraged with more electronic media than ever before. Children's curiosity will naturally draw them into video games or interactive television as well as the Internet. Children also are a target consumer base for a number of businesses such as cable operators, video game publishers and television networks. But the students who read the best spend their non-school hours reading and writing. And households that value literacy will push children to read will have children who exceed in this area. Studies have shown connections between television and the affect it has on reading and writing skills. Other electronic media such as videos, movies, tapes and to some extent computer use can also have a detrimental affect. Literacy will thus be needed to succeed successfully and to process these different media for the consumer's best use.

Conjoint behavioral consultation

Conjoint behavioral consultation (CBC) is a partnership model of service delivery in which parents, educators, other primary caregivers and service providers all work in collaboration to meet the developmental needs of children, address their concerns and to achieve success by promoting the competencies of all parties concerned. CBC creates an opportunity for families and schools to work together for a common interest and to build upon and promote the capabilities and strengths of the family members and school personnel. Individual needs are identified and acted upon using an organized approach that is data-based and that has mutual and collaborative interactions between parents and children along with guidance and assistance of consultants such as school psychologists.

Conjoint behavioral consultant partnerships (CBC) can be implemented through four stages: needs identification, needs analysis, plan development and plan evaluation. Three of these stages use interviews to structure the decisions to be made. Overall, the goal is to effectively address needs and desires of parents and teachers for children. Specific objectives include:

- Addressing concerns as they happen across rather than only within settings.
- Enhancing home-school partnerships to helps student learning and performance.
- Establishing joint responsibility for solving problems.
- Improving communications between children, family and school personnel.
- Assessing needs in a comprehensive and functional way.
- Promoting continuity and consistency among agents of change and across various settings.
- Providing opportunities for powers to become empowered using strength-based orientation.

Reading

Grades three through six

Young children should be exposed to all types of stories such as folk tales, funny tales, tales of the wondrous and stories about everyday life. Reading aloud to children is an essential step in learning. Parents who read aloud to children teach them literacy concepts just by sharing the books. Encourage listening, comments and asking questions about the books by the children. Be flexible enough to abandon a book that is not appealing after a reasonable try at reading it. No one enjoys every book and children should not have to listen to or be forced to read a boring book. Children still enjoy hearing stories read aloud even after they have outgrown picture books. If a child hears a good story that is well read and perhaps a bit beyond the child's capabilities, it could encourage independent reading.

First grade reading comprehension

The process of learning to read is not a linear one. Students need not learn decoding before they learn to comprehend. Both skills should be taught at the same time beginning at the earliest stages of instruction for reading. Comprehension strategies can be taught using material that is read to children and the material that they read for themselves. Before reading, teachers can delineate the reason for the reading: vocabulary review, encouraging children to predict what stories are about or activating background knowledge. Teachers can direct children's attention to subtle or difficult portions of the text during reading, point out difficult words and ideas and ask children to find problems and solutions. After reading, children can be taught particular metacognitive strategies such as asking themselves regularly whether what is being read makes sense.

Second grade and beyond

Instruction for those in the second grade and beyond should be focused on:

- *Literature.* Children should read quality literature that is appropriate to their reading levels at this point. Basal program, novels, anthologies, student readers and other material can be good sources for reading. The children should increasingly develop a joy of reading that makes them want to frequently and widely read.
- *Expository text (content knowledge):* Reading instruction in most schools traditionally focused on narratives. But children need as well strong comprehension strategies for content areas such as science, geography and history.
- *Reading comprehension:* All that teachers do in reading class and beyond should be aimed at building the child's ability to understand complex content of all sorts on an increased pace.

- *Vocabulary:* Children's vocabularies can be aided by teaching specific words in students' texts.

Early proficiency

There is strong evidence that young people who are not fluent readers and writers by the end of the third grade may never catch up with their peers. One study found that first graders who were not on grade level by the end of the year stood a 1-in-10 chance of ever having proficiency at grade level in reading. A governor of Indiana indicated that the determination of how many new prison beds to build was based, in part, on the number of second graders who do not read at second grade level. The number of future prison beds in California depends on numbers of children who do not go past the fourth grade reading level.

Influence of writing

Specific instruction in writing for different reasons and audiences as well as instruction in strategies to help clarify and enrich language expression is crucial. Language mechanical skills such as usage, capitalization and grammar can be taught and integrated into the students' own writing through the process of editing. Students might study, for instance, the use of adjectives and adverbs and then write descriptive compositions. Cooperative learning can be a very effective upper elementary reading and writing instruction if used properly. Students should generally work in groups of from four to five members that stay together for six-to-eight weeks. The group might be presented a lesson on main idea and the students can work in groups to practice such a skill.

Contextual cues

The knowledge a reader has in how the language works is a factor in how successful that reader will comprehend a text. For example, readers may comprehend more thoroughly if they know the position of words in a sentence, punctuation marks and word relationships within sentences. This is all done through the contextual cue systems -- graphophonic, syntactic, semantic and pragmatic -- in order to make sense out of what they have read. Proficient readers are the most concerned with meaning. They use a continuous formulation of meaning in order to figure out how much attention should be paid to the text in confirming or correcting predictions, as well as in making other predictions. Middle-level students must continue to balance the use of interacting language cuing systems in order to extract meaning from texts.

Cubing

Cubing is a literacy strategy in which students are able to explore topics from six separate dimensions or viewpoints. The student can:

- Provide a description of the particular topic.
- Compare the topic to a different topic.
- Associate the topic with something else and provide specific reasons for the choice.
- Analyzing the topic and telling how the topic came about.
- Give an explanation of what the topic is composed after analysis.
- Providing an argument for or against the topic.
- The teacher chooses a topic related to the thematic unit. Students are divided into six groups. Students brainstorm about their dimension ideas and then use a quick write or quick draw. These are shared with the class and are attached to the sides of a cube box. This strategy can be applicable to subjects such as social studies.

History frames/story maps

A history frames/story map strategy is used in helping a student think on the major points of a history story by:

- Identifying the important individuals who are a part of the story.
- Summarizing in a succinct manner the story by highlighting its main events.
- Putting the story into context and realizing the problem that was to be overcome or the goal to be achieved.
- Explaining the outcome.

When relating the story to history, four graphic organizers are used: the history frame, story map, story pyramid and framed character. The history frame can be used by students who choose main events from a chapter and fill in varying sections for participants, goals, summary and resolution. The story map can be used for individual articles or for excerpts from oral histories, biographies or to help understand motives of key historical players.

Using newspapers

Students learn when they are motivated in the topics they study have interest and relevance to their lives. Many classrooms are using newspapers as a source for some very good motivational and timely resources. It is a concept that dates back to 1795 when the Portland Eastern Herald in Maine published an editorial that put forth the role that newspapers can play in helping to deliver, extend and enrich the curriculum. Classrooms around the world are using newspapers to compliment text books and other relevant resources for a variety of disciplines. Newspaper feature articles, editorial and advertising help students apply literacy and numeracy skills as well as to appreciate the importance of studying history and current affairs. Studies have shown that students who use newspapers score higher on reading comprehension tests and develop stronger critical thinking skills.

Speeches and Debates

Extemporaneous speaking

In an extemporaneous speaking event, students select one of three questions, and then prepare and deliver a speech within 30 minutes. During the 30 minute interval, students are given a selection of articles from magazines and newspapers. The extemporaneous speech usually is required to be approximately 7 minutes long. It must be delivered without notes or other visual aids. Speakers are expected to deliver their message in a way that is informative to the audience as well as entertaining. Moreover, an extemporaneous speech needs to have a discernible structure: that is, an introduction, body, and conclusion.

There are two common types of extemporaneous speaking events: foreign extemporaneous speaking and domestic extemporaneous speaking. The only real difference between these two events is that foreign extemporaneous speaking takes foreign issues as its subject, while domestic extemporaneous speaking concentrates on issues particular to the United States. Both of these events have a similar format: students are required to prepare and deliver a speech within a short amount of time, typically 30 minutes. Each round of competition contains between five and eight students. Judges rank the performances in order from first to last.

In order to be effective, an extemporaneous speech needs to follow a discernible structure. At the beginning of the speech, the speaker will try to engage the attention of the audience with a memorable quotes or statistic. Then, the speaker will show how this interesting piece of data relates to his larger point. At this point, the speaker will fully introduce his topic. The speaker may need to define any words which may be unknown to the audience. After clarifying his thesis statement, the speaker will continue to support this point with supporting arguments and evidence. Extemporaneous speaking competitions typically require the speaker to use a certain number of sources. In the conclusion of an extemporaneous speech, a speaker will be sure to restate his thesis and create a memorable or intriguing image or anecdote for the audience.

Debates

Formal debate
A debate is simply an organized communication event, in which two or more parties offer opposing views on the same subject. A debate is not a synonym for an argument; debates are meant to be civil and constructive. A typical debate format has two sides: affirmative and negative. A statement (known as a proposition) is read, and the affirmative side argues in favor of it. The negative side then argues against it. It should be noted that the hosting sides of the debate are not trying to persuade one another, but rather are trying to convince some third party, whether it is a judge or the audience. The terms of the debate are usually set ahead of time. These may include time limits and order of speaking.

Good proposition characteristics
In the debate, the statement which is to be discussed is called the proposition. Some propositions are better than others at inspiring good debate. A proposition which has an obvious answer, for instance, will not be very good for debate, because one side of the argument will be much stronger than the other. A proposition should limit itself to a reasonable scope of application, so that the debaters can focus on a few key issues. Also, the wording of the debate should be simple and clear. The debate should be centered on the topic indicated by the proposition, and not on the meaning of the words in the proposition.

Propositions of value in formal debates: In a formal debate, propositions begin with the words "resolved that" followed by the statement. There are three basic kinds of proposition: propositions of value, propositions of judgment, and propositions of policy. A proposition of value makes a statement about the correctness or practical utility of something. For instance, a proposition of value might state that eliminating summer vacation in favor of year-round schooling is a good idea. The affirmative position will then argue in favor of this proposition, and the negative position will argue against it. Propositions of value usually require statistical evidence to be supported or opposed effectively.

Propositions of judgment in formal debates: In a formal debate, propositions begin with the words "resolved that" followed by the statement. There are three basic kinds of proposition: propositions of value, propositions of judgment, and propositions of policy. A proposition of judgment states that something is true or exists. For this reason, propositions of judgment are often referred to as propositions of fact. For instance, a proposition of judgment might state that men earn more money for the same labor than do women. This is an unfortunate fact, and it will be up to the affirmative position to provide the argument proving it to be so.

Propositions of policy in formal debates: In a formal debate, propositions begin with the words "resolved that" followed by the statement. There are three basic kinds of proposition: propositions of value, propositions of judgment, and propositions of policy. A proposition of policy and declares that a particular course of action should be taken. Propositions of policy usually include the words "ought" or "should." For instance, a proposition of policy might read: "resolved, that teachers should be required to eat lunch with their classes." Propositions of policy often make for the liveliest debate, because there is no way of absolutely knowing whether a proposed policy will be effective.

Debate topic selections
The first step in the planning of a debate is to find an appropriate issue. The best issues are those which are controversial without being potentially offensive, and which provide equal opportunity for both sides to make a convincing case. Of course, the responsibility of proving a proposition is borne by the affirmative side. Debate instructors have isolated three common issues in a policy proposition debate. To begin with, the debaters will need to determine whether there is a pressing need for immediate change. They will also have to decide whether there is a plan that provides the appropriate change. Finally, the affirmative side will have to prove that the proposed plan is the best available plan. The negative side is not required to win all three of these issues, but the affirmative side is required to win all three in order to hold sway.

Defining terms
In order for a debate to be successful, any unclear or abstract terms must be defined at the appropriate time. Debates are not meant to be inquiries into the meaning of the words in the proposition. Rather, the propositions should be clear enough to be understood without complication by both the affirmative and negative sides. If there is any troublesome language in the proposition, it is usually the responsibility of the first speaker in the debate to define the terms. Since the affirmative speaker is the one who has the responsibility of proving his case, it makes sense for him to define the terms of the proposition.

Constructing debate cases
The process of constructing a debate case is very similar to constructing an outline for a speech. It is common for both sides in the debate to compose what is known as a debate brief, in which their case is outlined point by point. These debate briefs are prepared ahead of time; as the debate proceeds, each side will outline the argument made by the other side in what is known as a flow sheet. A

- 95 -

debate brief usually begins with a thesis statement and, if necessary, definitions for any problematic terms in the proposition. It then goes on to list the major points to be made, as well as rebuttals to potential counter arguments made by the other side.

Higher order thinking skills
- *Evaluation:* Appraise, choose, compare, conclude, decide, defend, evaluate, give your opinion, judge, justify, prioritize, rank, rate, select, support, value
- *Synthesis:* Change, combine, compose, construct, create, design, find an unusual way, formulate, generate, invent, originate, plan, predict, pretend, produce, rearrange, reconstruct, reorganize, revise, suggest, suppose, visualize, write
- *Analysis:* Analyze, categorize, classify, compare, contrast, debate, deduct, determine the factors, diagnose, diagram, differentiate, dissect, distinguish, examine, infer, specify
- *Application:* Apply, compute, conclude, construct, demonstrate determine, draw, find out, give an example, illustrate, make, operate, show, solve, state a rule or principle, use
- *Comprehension:* Convert, describe, explain, interpret, paraphrase, put in order, restate, retell in your own words, rewrite, summarize, trace, translate
- *Knowledge:* Define, fill in the blank, identify, label, list, locate, match, memorize, name, recall, spell, state, tell, underline

Finding proof
Obviously, the ability of each side in the debate to claim victory will depend on their ability to produce adequate proof. In a debate, proof consists of two basic components: evidence and reasoning. Evidence is factual information. Reasoning, on the other hand, is the set of inferences or judgments that are drawn from evidence. In order to provide adequate proof, then, a debater will need to have both evidence and reasoning. Also, the debater will have to have this information organized so that it can be used to greatest effect during the course of the debate, and so it can be produced in direct contrast to the argument made by the opposing side.

Evidence
In a debate, evidence is the factual information used to support an argument. In order to be successful, a debater will need to have substantial evidence to support his case. It is a good idea to record this information on paper before the beginning of the debate. The most important pieces of evidence should be used in the first speech made by each side, known as the constructive speech. As a debate progresses, minor pieces of evidence can be used in the various rebuttal speeches. Also, a debater should recognize which evidence is appropriate for supporting his main case, and which evidence is better suited to rebut possible counterarguments by his opponent. Debaters should be able to identify the sources of their evidence.

During preparation for a debate, each side will gather as much evidence as possible to support their case. They will need to apply strict guidelines in their evidence gathering, so that they make sure to only select evidence which will stand up to scrutiny from their opponent. The four most important qualities of good evidence are as follows: relevance, consistency, timeliness, and the ability to be verified. A piece of evidence needs to pertain directly to the argument that is being made. It needs to hold up in a number of different conditions and be the same from different sources. It needs to have been produced recently enough to remain believable. Finally, it needs to be susceptible to verification, so that the debate judge does not have to depend on the word of the debater.

There are a few different kinds of evidence that are commonly used in debates. Perhaps the most common form of evidence is documented statistics. Statistics can be obtained from a variety of books, trade journals, and other publications. Sometimes, debaters will introduce the testimony or writings of acknowledged authorities on the subject. It is important to establish the credentials of the authority when this kind of evidence is used. Finally, debaters will often rely upon what they believe to be commonly accepted facts. These are matters of truth which are generally accepted by a reasonable audience, and therefore do not need further support.

Inductive reasoning
Debaters rely upon inductive reasoning frequently in making their points. Inductive reasoning is the process of beginning with a group of specifics and gradually working towards a general idea. In other words, inductive reasoning begins by looking at the trees, and eventually broadened its scope to take in the whole forest. For instance, in a debate, the affirmative view might begin by citing a number of statistics. He could then make a general point which is supported by all of those statistics. Inductive reasoning is a good way to utilize pieces of evidence which can stand alone on their own merit.

Deductive reasoning
In a process of deductive reasoning, a debater transitions from a general rule to a specific instance of the rule. To begin with, the debater offers what is known as a premise. For example, a premise might be "all teachers love summer vacation." The debater will then offer an example of this premise in what is known as the minor premise: "we are all teachers." The debater will then give the conclusion that stems from the information so far provided: "we love summer vacation." This process is known as a logical syllogism. In order for a syllogism to be logically correct, all of the premises must be true. This example of deductive reasoning, then, would be easy to

argue against, since there are probably teachers who do not love summer vacation.

Process of refutation
The negative side in the debate will be primarily responsible for refutation, which is the act of damaging the opponent's case. The process of refutation has a few general components. To begin with, the argument that is going to be refuted is defined. Next, the importance that this argument has to the opponent is emphasized. The debater then presents his counterargument, along with evidence in support of it. Finally, the debater summarizes his refutation, and makes any clarification necessary. Refutation does not necessarily need to constitute a direct attack on the position of the opponent. Instead, it is possible to refute and opponents argument by simply offering a stronger argument for one's own side.

Process of rebuttal
The process of rebuttal is a formal element in a debate. A rebuttal gives the debater an opportunity to counter any refutation of his argument that has just been made. During a rebuttal, the debater is allowed to introduce new evidence, but may not make a new argument. To begin a rebuttal, the debater will restate the arguments that have been made so far. The debater will then restate the refutation offered by the other side. Then, the debater will attempt to demonstrate problems with his opponent's arguments. He will then give any additional information to strengthen his position, and will conclude by summarizing his original argument.

Forms of debate
- *Traditional:* In a traditional debate (also known as a standard debate), there are two sides composed of two individuals. The affirmative side speaks first, and the negative side speaks second. A traditional debate generally lasts for about an hour, and begins with a 10 minute speech by the first affirmative speaker. This is

followed by a five-minute rebuttal from the first negative speaker. The first negative speaker is then given 10 minutes to make a constructive speech, followed by a five-minute rebuttal from the first affirmative speaker. This arrangement is then duplicated with the second members of each team.

- In a traditional debate, the *first affirmative constructive speech* should be the only one that can be fully organized ahead of time. It is during the speech that the main argument of the affirmative side is advanced. The speaker will also want to clear up any problems with language that may exist in the proposition, and deliver important background information that is required to understand the topic. The speaker will then outline the major points of the affirmative case, and will give as much evidence as possible within the time constraints. At the conclusion of the first affirmative constructive speech, the speaker will summarize his main argument.

- After the first affirmative constructive speech has been made in a traditional debate, *the first negative constructive speech* will be given. In this speech, the negative speaker issues his basic response to the arguments advanced by the affirmative side. He may call into question the definitions offered by the affirmative side. For the most part though, the first negative constructive speaker is likely to attack the premises and evidence given by the first affirmative speaker. If appropriate, the first negative constructive speaker may want to advance an alternative to the argument proposed by the first speaker.

- In a traditional debate, the *second affirmative constructive speech* follows the first negative constructive speech.

In this speech, the affirmative speaker directly addresses the counter arguments made by the first negative constructive speaker. The affirmative speaker may wish to clarify any problems that have been raised about the language in the proposition. The affirmative speaker will want to address all of the counter arguments made by the first negative constructive speaker. It is best to address these points in a systematic manner. The second negative constructive speaker will want to simultaneously strengthen his own case and attack the alternative proposed by his opponent.

- In a traditional debate, the *second negative constructive speech* follows the second affirmative constructive speech. The second negative constructive speech is a brief period in which the negative speaker can summarize the debate to this point, and then attacked the major arguments of the second affirmative speech. This is the final constructive speech in the debate, and so the second negative speaker will want to make every argument he or she has at his disposal (new arguments will not be allowed in the rebuttal sections). It is a good idea to conclude the second negative constructive speech with a simple but forceful counter argument to the affirmative case.

- The *second negative constructive speech* is the final constructive speech in a traditional debate. At this point, the rebuttal speeches begin. For starters, the first negative rebuttal speech serves as a reminder of the major weaknesses in the affirmative case. The first negative rebuttal speaker will also take this opportunity to re-state the arguments made by the negative side. Next, the *first affirmative rebuttal* will the high points of the affirmative case, and will

- 98 -

attempt to counter any arguments that were made during the first negative rebuttal. The first affirmative rebuttal speech will also include the response to the second negative constructive speech.

- The arguments made by the negative side in a traditional debate will conclude with the *second negative rebuttal speech*. In this speech, the negative side will conclude their argument, resolving any questions about their side, and pleading with the debate judges to agree with their point of view. A traditional debate concludes with the *second affirmative rebuttal speech*. In this speech, the affirmative side summarizes their argument and response to the previous rebuttal speech. Finally, the affirmative side delivers their own plea for the support of the debate judges. These judges may be specially chosen, or may simply be the audience at the event.

- *Cross-examination:* In a cross-examination debate, the affirmative side and the negative side both have two members. Unlike in a traditional debate, where debaters are given lengthy amounts of time in which to make their cases and counter arguments, a cross-examination debate encourages each side to directly question the other. It begins with a constructive speech by the first affirmative speaker, followed by a few minutes in which the second negative speaker can question the first speaker. The first negative speaker then makes a constructive speech, followed by a few minutes of questioning from the first affirmative speaker. The second affirmative speaker then delivers a message, followed by questioning from the first negative speaker. The second negative speaker delivers a message and is then questioned by the second affirmative speaker. The first

negative speaker issues a rebuttal speech, followed by a rebuttal speech from the first affirmative speaker. Finally, the second negative speaker issues a rebuttal, concluding with a rebuttal from the second affirmative speaker.

- *Lincoln-Douglas:* The common format for two-person debate is typically referred to as a Lincoln-Douglas debate in reference to the celebrated debates between Abraham Lincoln and Stephen A. Douglas in Illinois in 1858. In the typical arrangement, the debate begins with a topic being introduced by the moderator. The affirmative speaker than has 10 minutes to deliver his argument, followed by a 15 minute period for the negative speaker. The affirmative speaker is then given five minutes in which to issue a rebuttal. Lincoln Douglas debates often end with the floor being opened to questions from the audience.

High school competitions

High school policy debate competitions are a great opportunity for beginning debaters to get some experience in a tournament setting. It is typical for these debates to be held over two days. On the first day, the preliminary rounds of the policy debate competition are held. All of those students who qualify will participate in what are known as "out rounds" on the second day of the tournament. In these out rounds, debaters are judged against one another by a set of official judges, who eliminate one debater in each round. Eventually, the two best debaters will be pitted against one another in the final.

National and Debate Tournament
Every year in early June, the National Forensic League hosts the National and Debate Tournament. It is a weeklong tournament held in a different city every year. Only the best high school debaters are invited to

compete in the national tournament; every year, only about 3000 students participate. The tournament contains the following events: domestic extemporaneous speaking, duo interpretation, foreign extemporaneous speaking, humorous interpretation, dramatic interpretation, Lincoln-Douglas debate, original oratory, policy debate, public forum debate, and student congress.

The National Forensic League
The National Forensic League administrates hundreds of high school competitive speech events. This group also coordinates changes to the rules of speech and debate competition. Every state has a subsidiary organization that pledges to abide by the rules changes made by the National Forensic League. Perhaps the most important function of the organization is to host the annual National Speech and Debate Tournament, which includes over 3000 high school students. The NFL also publishes a monthly magazine, the Rostrum, on the subject of debate education. High school students who participate in speech and debate competitions are awarded points by the NFL.

A school forensics program has a number of objectives. Perhaps most importantly, it aims to provide students and ability to develop their public speaking and oral interpretation skills. In order to be effective, a school forensics program needs to offer frequent opportunities for all student members to practice these skills. Teachers should aim to develop both verbal and nonverbal communication skills. Also they should teach their students how to apply critical reasoning skills to the arguments and ideas of others. Students should learn how to effectively organize their own ideas. Finally, students should be able to dramatically interpret the literary works of others.

Students can expect to receive a number of benefits from participation in a forensics program. To begin with, students will develop their skills in oral and nonverbal

communication. Students will also learn to effectively present an argument to a group. In order to construct a clear argument, students will develop research skills. Students will also build relationships among themselves and with students from other schools in debate and speech competitions. Finally, many students will use participation in a forensics program as a springboard to other leadership opportunities.

Perhaps the most overlooked benefit of school forensics programs is the strong relationships between schools that are developed. During speech and debate competitions, students from various schools will get to know one another through their shared interest in forensics. Many schools travel overnight to participate in forensics competitions, and find that this experience encourages them to make friends with people from different parts of the state and country. The National Forensics League is the umbrella organization under which all school forensics programs work. This organization strives to cultivate relationships between schools through speech and debate.

Parliamentary procedure

Procedures

Purpose
Parliamentary procedure is a system of administrating meetings. These rules were developed for formal situations, but they are often used by informal organizations to keep business on track and provide structure to professional interactions. One of the benefits of parliamentary procedure is that it gives every member of a group in opportunity to participate in making proposals and voting. Also, parliamentary procedure limits the control that can be exercised by any person or group of people, and therefore makes decision-making a more streamlined process.

Parliamentary procedure can be used by very large and very small organizations.

Parliamentary procedure terms:
- *Abstain:* To opt not to vote on a particular proposal
- *Amend:* To change the words in a particular proposal
- *Chair:* The person who is designated to preside over the activities of the group
- *Floor:* The authority to speak
- *Majority:* The position that is supported by a larger group of people; in parliamentary procedure, the majority holds more influence than the minority
- *Minority:* The position that is supported by a smaller group of people; certain rights of the minority are guaranteed by parliamentary procedure
- *Minutes:* The written report of the happenings at the previous meeting
- *Motion:* A proposal which the group will consider
- *Pending:* In the process of being considered, as in "the motion is pending"
- *Second:* Approve a motion publicly; in order to be introduced for discussion, a proposal must be seconded
- *Table:* Set aside a motion until a later time; this is done when more information is likely to be obtained and it will become more appropriate to discuss the given motion

Majority rules principle
In parliamentary procedure, decisions are made on a democratic basis. In other words, the will of the majority drives the decision-making process. The success of an organization relies on the ability of the minority to accept the decisions of the majority. In parliamentary procedure, a simple majority is defined as any more than one half of the voting individuals. Individuals who do not vote (that is, who abstain from voting) are not counted in the calculation of simple majority. For important decisions, an organization might require a two thirds majority vote, as this means that the decision will require a greater consensus in order to be made.

Rights of the minority
Although the decisions that are made within the framework of parliamentary procedure favor the majority, the minority is accorded certain rights. Within parliamentary procedure, there are numerous opportunities for the members of the minority to make their voices heard an attempt to persuade other members of the group. Even after a decision has been made, the minority is given a chance to declare its sentiments. Moreover, the chairperson is responsible for not favoring or showing undue influence on behalf of the majority. One of the resulting benefits of parliamentary procedure is that no one becomes alienated or feels excluded from the process.

Equal rights and responsibilities
In parliamentary procedure, all of the members of the organization are given equal rights in all responsibilities. Certain members of the organization may be designated as leaders, or may be given other special roles, but this is only done with the consent of all the members. Within a parliamentary organization, every member is given the right to vote and the right to speak his or her mind. It should be noted, however, that parliamentary procedure frames these actions as responsibilities as well as rights. That is, in order for an organization to be healthy, all of the members need to participate by voting and making their opinions known.

Discussing one problem at a time
One of the things that parliamentary procedure stresses is that discussion should be organized, to minimize digressions and confusion. It is the job of the chairperson to introduce issues to the group, and to make

clear transitions between discussion topics. The most important issues before the group should always be discussed first. Usually, an issue will be discussed for a limited amount of time, at which point the group will decide whether to vote on it. It is only after a vote has been held or the issue has been tabled that the group can move on to the next issue. The best chairpersons are those who limit discussion to the matter at hand and efficiently move through the agenda of the group.

Maintaining focus
In order for a parliamentary organization to function effectively, the members need to limit their discussion to the issues that are currently on the floor. In part, this is the responsibility of the chairperson, but each member needs to be careful to limit his speech to the issues at hand. Every motion requires a second in order to be discussed. If some members of the group feel that discussion has gone on too long, they may call for a two thirds vote to end discussion and hold a vote. If they do not achieve the two thirds majority, discussion may go on. A chairperson can cut off members if they begin to speak on subjects other than those on the floor.

Chair's objectivity
In order to administer and a parliamentary organization in a fair manner, a chairperson must remain objective at all times. A chairperson cannot be seen to favor either side in the debate. This is especially important because the opinions of the chairperson have the ability to sway the opinion of the members. The important consideration for members, however, should be the quality of the arguments on either side and not the opinions of the chairperson. In order to be viewed as objective, a chairperson needs to allow equal time to both sides.

Order of business
Parliamentary procedure outlines a specific order of business. To begin with, a certain number of members must be in attendance before business can be introduced. This minimum number of members, which is usually one more than half of the total members, is referred to as a quorum. Once a quorum has been reached, the chair will call the meeting to order. At this point, the meeting has begun. The secretary will then read the minutes from the last meeting. After the minutes have been read, the chair will ask if any members of the group have any additions or corrections to make to the minutes. If not, the minutes will be approved.

After the minutes have been approved, the group may hear from various officers in the heads of committees. For instance, the treasurer often makes a report at this point in the meeting. An organization may have standing committees, which exists in perpetuity, or special committees, which are created to accomplish specific purposes and disbanded after the purpose is accomplished. Once the committees have reported, the chair will ask if there is any unfinished business in front of the group. If there is, it must be resolved before moving on. Once unfinished business is complete, the chair will open the floor to new business.

As the chair opens the floor to new business, he or she may describe in brief the agenda for the current meeting. The chair may also ask if any member of the group has items to be added to the agenda. At this point, members of the group can propose motions. It is during the introduction of new business that elections for new officers in the group are held. The chair will call for nominations and seconds, and then votes will be held. After new business is complete, the chair may ask the group if they have any particular announcements to make. After all business is complete, the chair may ask if there is a motion to adjourn. If so, the group can vote on whether to end the meeting.

Voting

There are a number of different ways for votes to be held according to parliamentary procedure. The most common form of vote is a voice vote, in which all those in favor of the motion say "aye" and all those opposed to the motion say "nay." Votes can also be held by having members stand up or raise their hands to indicate their approval or disapproval of a motion. In a roll call vote, the names of the members of a group are called out loud one by one, and each member indicates his vote. Finally, a secret ballot can be held when members may want anonymity.

Motions

Main motions, subsidiary motions: There are a number of different ways to make a motion according to parliamentary procedure. A main motion is use to introduce the topic for discussion. If a main motion gets a second, it will be discussed and will require a majority vote for passage. A subsidiary motion, on the other hand, is introduced to alter or eliminate some other motion. Subsidiary motions are issued after a main motion. They must be voted on before the attention of the group can return to the main motion. Subsidiary motions include the motion to table, to postpone debate, or to amend the main motion.

Privileged motions, incidental motions, and unclassified motions: There are a number of different ways to make a motion according to parliamentary procedure a privileged motion has to do with the requirements of the members. A privileged motion, for instance, may be made to adjourn at a certain time or to set a date for a future meeting. An incidental motion has to do with the way business is conducted in the meeting. For instance, an incidental motion may be made to withdraw a motion, or to object to a certain idea. Incidental motions refine motions that have already been made. Finally, an unclassified motion attempts to recall issues that have been tabled or dismissed earlier.

Motion to fix time to reassemble: A motion to fix time to reassemble is a privileged motion. Indeed, in the table of motions used in parliamentary procedure, it is the most privileged motion, meaning that it is more important than any other motion. This motion is typically made directly after a motion to adjourn has been seconded. It is made, however, before the motion to adjourn has been voted on. This is because the motion to adjourn will then be voted on taking into account the proposed time for future meetings. There is no debate on a motion to fix time to reassemble, though the motion may be amended. A simple majority is required to pass this motion.

Motion to adjourn: A motion to adjourn is the privileged motion which usually ends a meeting. If some members of a group feel that debate has gone on too long, or they do not like the way the debate is tending, they may call a motion to adjourn as a way of stopping discussion. If the motion is seconded, it must be voted on immediately. A motion to adjourn requires a simple majority; it is not debatable or amendable. It should be noted that a motion to adjourn does not eliminate the subject under discussion for good; on the contrary, because the issue under discussion was not resolved, it will be taken up again at the next meeting.

Motion to recess: A motion to recess is a privileged motion in which one member moves to suspend a meeting for a brief period of time without fully ending it. For instance, a member might make a motion to recess for lunch. One of the advantages of going into recess rather than adjourning a meeting is that after a recess, the regular order of business does not need to be repeated. This can save a great deal of time. A motion to recess requires a second, and is debatable and amendable. It requires a simple majority for passage.

Motion to rise to a question of privilege: A motion to rise to a question of privilege is a privileged motion in which a member asks permission to make a request regarding the safety, comfort, and convenience of the group. In other words, this is a motion which briefly interrupts discussion to take care of some environmental distraction. For instance, a member might make a motion for a question of privilege if he or she wants to adjust the air-conditioning in the meeting room. The passage of this kind of motion simply depends on the will of the chairperson. A motion to rise to a question of privilege does not require a second, and is neither debatable nor amendable.

Motion to call for the orders of the day: A motion to call for the orders of the day is a privileged motion in which a member asks that attention be paid to the predetermined order of business in a meeting. This kind of motion is typically made when a member feels that the agreed-upon order has been abandoned, or that the group has forgotten their original intent in a discussion. A motion to call for the orders of the day can interrupt a speaker, and does not require a second. It is neither debatable nor amendable. The chairperson decides whether or not this motion will be passed.

Motion to appeal a decision: A motion to appeal the decision in parliamentary procedure is an incidental motion, in which a member disagrees with the decision made by the chair and asks for a vote of all the members. This motion is typically made after a motion decided solely by the chairperson. It is debatable, but is not amendable. Before voting on this motion, both sides are allowed to briefly state their cases. It is acceptable to interrupt a speaker with this motion, but in order to be voted on this motion requires a second. For passage, this motion requires a simple majority.

Motion to rise to a point of order: A motion to rise to a point of order is an incidental motion in which a member seeks to indicate that an error has been made in procedure. A member

might make this motion if he feels that discussion has wandered off-topic or that the order of business has not been followed. A member may interrupt discussion to make this motion, and it does not require a second. A motion to rise to a point of order is neither debatable nor amendable. Its passage depends on the will of the chairperson.

Motion to call for a division of the assembly: A motion to call for a division of the assembly is an incidental motion in which a member declares that a voice vote has been too close to call, and then a more precise and vote should be taken. Specifically, a motion for a division of the assembly calls for a vote by show of hands or by standing. This motion may be made as an interruption to current discussion, and does not require a second. It is neither debatable nor amendable. A motion to call for a division of the assembly requires a simple majority for passage.

Motion to object to a consideration of a question: A motion to object to a consideration of a question is an incidental motion used to stop discussion of a particular topic. This motion may be made for any number of reasons. In some cases, a member may feel that discussion is fruitless, or that discussion has wandered too far away from the original topic. A member might also feel that the meeting has run on too long. A motion to object to consideration of a question can be made as an interruption to discussion, and does not require a second. It is not debatable or amendable. Because it is such an important motion (in that it has the ability to stop discussion) it requires a two thirds majority.

Motion to ask permission to withdraw a motion: A motion to ask permission to withdraw a motion is an incidental motion in which a member tries to remove a motion which has been previously made. For instance, a motion might seem like a good idea at the time, but after subsequent discussion may be discovered to be weak or wrongheaded. In such a case, a member who made the motion may ask permission to withdraw it. A motion to ask permission to withdraw a motion cannot interrupt a speaker, and does not require a second. It is neither debatable nor amendable. It requires a simple majority for passage.

Motion to suspend a rule: A motion to suspend a rule is an incidental motion used when a group wants to temporarily remove the restrictions placed on them by a certain rule. For instance, in some cases it might be appropriate to alter the normal order of business in order to obtain an important piece of information from a committee report. A member could then move to suspend that rule in this particular case. This motion cannot be made as an interruption to a speaker, and it requires a second. It is neither debatable nor amendable. Because it calls for a fundamental change in the rules of the group, it requires a two thirds majority for passage.

Motion to table a motion: A motion to table a motion is a subsidiary motion which is made when a member seeks to postpone further discussion of the topic. This motion is often made when a member of the group feels that more and better information about a subject will be available in the near future, and that it is not incumbent upon the group to make a decision immediately. This motion does not stop discussion, but rather postpones it to a later date. This motion cannot be used to interrupt a speaker, and requires a second. It is neither debatable nor amendable. It requires a simple majority for passage.

Motion to move the previous question: A motion to move the previous question is a subsidiary motion which is meant to conclude discussion on a particular topic. This motion is often made when a member of the group feels that the group has fully discussed a topic and is only repeating previously made arguments. If this motion is passed, the chairperson will then have the right to cease discussion on anything other than new points

on the designated topic. This motion is neither debatable nor amendable. It cannot interrupt a speaker, and requires a second. It requires a two thirds majority for passage.

Motion to limit or extend debate: A motion to limit or extended debate is a subsidiary motion which has made it to outline the length of time which will be allowed for discussion of the topic. This motion is made when a group is under particular time constraints, or when the members of the group feel that discussion has the potential to extend for an impractically long time. This motion may limit the number of speeches, may designate a time limit for each speech, or may limit the total amount of time to be spent in discussion. A speaker may not be interrupted with this motion. This motion requires a second, and is both debatable and amendable. It requires a two thirds majority for passage.

Motion to postpone to a definite time: A motion to postpone to a definite time is a subsidiary motion which is made when a speaker wants to table discussion until a designated point in the future. This motion is slightly different from the motion to table, in that it specifies when discussion will be resumed. It is typically made when a member feels the meeting has gone on too long, or that discussion has become unprofitable at present. The motion to postpone to a definite time cannot interrupt a speaker, and requires a second. It is both debatable and amendable. It requires a simple majority for passage.

Motion to refer to a committee: A motion to refer to a committee is a subsidiary motion in which a special committee designated by the group is asked to study a particular problem and report back to the group at large at a later date. This motion often contains a recommendation for the people who should be on the committee, as well as the designated time at which the committee will report to the group. This motion is often made to prevent a regular meeting from running on too long. It may not be used to interrupt a speaker, and does require a second. It is both debatable and amendable. It requires a simple majority for passage.

Motion to amend: The motion to amend is a subsidiary motion that is made to alter a previously made motion. It may amend the previous motion in the following ways: adding more language; subtracting language; substituting language; or substituting an entirely new motion. It is okay to amend main, subsidiary, and privileged motions. A motion to amend must be discussed and voted on immediately, before any other business is handled. These motions cannot be used to interrupt a speaker, and to require a second. They are both debatable and amendable. They require a simple majority for passage.

Motion to postpone indefinitely: A motion to postpone indefinitely is a subsidiary motion made in order to prevent a vote on a pending main motion. If this motion is passed, discussion on the topic in question must be ceased for the rest of the current meeting. Also, the passage of a motion to postpone indefinitely suggests that most of the members of a group are not really interested in passing the main motion. A motion to postpone indefinitely cannot be used to interrupt a speaker, and does require a second. It is both debatable and amendable. It only requires a simple majority for passage.

Assessment and Evaluation Issues

NAEP

The National Assessment of Education and Progress (NAEP) was created to determine what the nation's students know and are doing in today's classroom. By focusing on the arts, the NAEP has developed standards to use for students to include music and arts education as an integral part of their schooling. Discussion has occurred regarding what arts education is appropriate and how much is necessary for students to understand and master for a well-rounded education. Some researchers believe that arts education should also include theater, dance, and media and design. By agreeing that art education is fundamental to a child's education, the NAEP views arts education as the foundation for children who learn other skills and ideas as they get older.

Interpreting recent immigrants

Immigrant students are often under a great deal of anxiety and stress as they learn English and cope with new surroundings. The pressure can result in feelings of being overwhelmed, confused or frustrated. If this is so, support services such as counselors or social workers may be needed to help relieve this stress. At other times, the way a student responds to a perplexing situation may be misinterpreted by educators. Humans tend to use behaviors that have worked for them before. And students are likely to use behaviors reinforced by the home and home culture. These misunderstandings have sometimes resulted in immigrant children being labeled as emotionally disturbed and are placed in special programs.

Questioning strategy

Good readers will, throughout the process of reading, ask questions. Students first identify the kind of information significant enough for the substance of a question when those questions are first generated. They then ask this information in the form of a question and test themselves to find out if they might answer their own questions. The generation of questions is a flexible strategy insofar as students can be taught and encouraged to ask questions on a number of different levels. When students know before reading that they need to think of questions about the text, they then read while aware of the important ideas in that text. This helps increase comprehension, process the meaning and make inferences and connections to prior information before forming a question.

Progress monitoring

Progress monitoring is a classroom-based assessment for instruction that evaluates how a child is learning based on a systematic review by teachers of children who are performing academic tasks that are a part of the daily classroom instruction. Unlike a one-time test for proficiency, this type of ongoing assessments helps to determine whether students are making sufficient progress or require more help in achieving grade-level reading outcomes. Progress monitoring should have certain benchmarks, reliability and validity. The progress monitoring can be assessed for the various components in the instruction of a student's reading such as in phonemic awareness, phonics, fluency, vocabulary and reading comprehension.

Socratic questioning

The following questioning is appropriate for high school:
- *Clarifying questions:* These questions that ask for more information, verification, clarifying a main idea or point, students building on an opinion, explaining a certain statement or rephrasing content.
- *Assumption-probing questions:* These questions ask for verification, explanation, reliability or clarification.
- *Probing evidence and reasons:* Such questions ask for more examples, reasons for statements, evidence, asking if reasons are adequate, asking how the process led to the belief and anything that might cause a change in the student's point of view.
- *Questions about perspectives and points of view:* These questions look for a particular viewpoint's alternatives, how others might respond, or compare differences and similarities among points of view.
- *Questions probing consequences and implications.* These questions describe implications of what is said, the cause and effect of actions and alternatives.
- *Questions about questions.* These break the question into smaller questions or concepts for added evaluation.

Socratic questioning is at the heart of critical thinking skills. It is more than just having a one-word answer or an agreement and disagreement from students. Socratic questions make students make assumptions, sort through points that are relevant and irrelevant as well as explain those points. This instruction can take many different forms including:
- Raising basic issues.
- Probing beneath the surface of matters.
- Pursing areas of thought fraught with problems.
- Helping students find the structure of their own thinking.
- Helping students develop clarity, accuracy and relevance.
- Helping students make judgments by reasoning on their own.
- It also helps students think about evidence, conclusions, assumptions, implications, points of view, concepts and interpretations.

Critical questioning

Critical thinking requires a systematic monitoring of thought. Critical thought must not be accepted at face value but should be analyzed for accuracy, clarity, breadth, logicalness, and depths. Critical thinking also requires that reasoning occur within various points of views and frames of reference and that all reasoning stems from goals and objectives and has an informational base. When data are used for reasoning it must be interpreted and the interpretation involves concepts that contain assumptions and that all inferences in thought have implication. The result of critical thought is that the basic questions of Socrates can be framed more focally and used, leading to question:

- Ends and objectives
- Wording of questions
- Sources of information and fact
- Method and quality of information collected
- Assumptions that are behind the concepts being used

Questioning techniques

Key questions should be planned to give direction and structure to the lesson. Spontaneous questions that come up are fine but the overall direction of the discussion has been mostly planned. Here are some simple guidelines to asking questions that will help teacher's questioning skills:

- Be sure the question is clear. Think about what it is required from the student before asking the question.
- Frame the question without calling on a particular student. Students are free to ignore the question when a student is called upon before the question is asked.
- After framing the question, pause while the students have a chance to think of an answer and then call on a student to respond. This pause, called wait time, is an important questioning skill. A wait time between a question and asking for response should be between 2-4 seconds.

Culture and evaluation

There are commonly differences found between cultures in how one prefers to learn some type of information and how that knowledge is displayed. A lack of understanding of different learning styles and the influence of one's cultural background can bring conflict, lack of achievement and confusion. It is common for a culturally

different student's preferred ways of learning to be in contrast with those ways that are used in American schools and are suggested for teacher training programs. It is important to discern the learning preferences for a recently arrived immigrant student and then teach to that style. Evaluation of the learning and teaching styles and process for acquiring a second culture and language may change how students are taught in America. Some studies suggest teachers understanding preferred learning styles of students allows them to adjust their style to maximize teaching.

Developing assessment strategies

Testing children before the third grade or approximately age eight is risky business. Children this age are notoriously poor test-takers because they don't understand the concept or why the person giving the test doesn't already know the answers. Studies have shown that the younger the child who takes a test, the more errors made in interpreting the results. When planning strategies to evaluate young children, teachers and parents should recognize the limitations of report cards and grades in general. Children develop at different rates so their performance is uneven, inconsistent and variable. Children should be assessed on general age-appropriate knowledge gained and skills attained, how much progress they have made learning to control their behavior and their overall improvement in social interactions. Children should also be encouraged to evaluate their own progress. Most children this age are realistic about their progress and will ask for help when they need it.

Assessing prediction skills

Teachers observing students will hear the language of prediction. Students might say "I think ..." or "I wonder if ... " By observing, the teachers can view certain reading behaviors that students show. When observing students making predictions about fiction text, the teacher should look out for these reading behaviors:

- Do students look at the text cover and make predictions that are based on the title or illustration?
- Do students stop prediction-making while he or she is reading?
- When reading the text, do the students make predictions based on clues from the illustration or text?

These behaviors should be observed for nonfiction text reading:

- Do students use headings or subheadings in order to make predictions?
- Doe students use charts, graphs, illustrations or maps to make predictions?
- Doe students predict what is likely to be learned based on clues from the illustration or text?

Test-taking strategies

A reason for test anxiety and poor performance on tests is often a lack of preparation. Children will often know about a test in advance. Some teachers also tell parents when tests will be given. Knowing when the test will be and what is to be covered can help give the child a study schedule to prepare for the test. One schedule is for the student to study nightly, for several nights before the test. Teachers may encourage parents to determine how long the child can be expected to concentrate at a given sitting. The parent should also be encouraged by the teacher to ask the child what material might be on the test and go over questions at the end of chapters and sections. Maps, charts and diagrams should receive special attention. A sample test can be developed from this information which can even make studying fun.

Before a test students should:

- Begin to study the material a few days before the test and take study breaks every 20-30 minutes.
- Take time to do some kind of physical activity that will help reduce tension and stress.
- Eat a good breakfast the morning of the test and get a good night's sleep during the night before the test.
- Skim the material and determine which parts are best understood and which ones are still difficult.
- Read a sentence or two and reread what you don't understand.
- Pick out main ideas or key terms. Think up by yourself possible test questions.
- Read aloud and study with a partner or parent. While reading the student should listen to himself.
- Think about what important points the teacher talked about during class.
- Remain motivated and positive.

Test-taking tips that might benefit intermediate students

When it is time to take a test, the student should:

- Think positively about doing the best that he or she can do.
- Take some deep breaths and relax. Breathe slowly. Clear the mind of worries and anxious thoughts.
- Push the feet down on the floor to the count of five. Push them harder and hard. Relax and then repeat.
- Visualize by closing the eyes and picturing oneself in a happy and peaceful place.
- Bring all materials needed for the test.
- Listen carefully to the directions and ask if they are not understood.
- Reread the directions carefully
- Look over the entire test to see what must be done before beginning.

- Determine how much time there is to spend on each question, allowing more time for essay questions.
- Skip difficult questions and go back later to answer those skipped.

Elementary students

Students should follow directions carefully. Have the student listen and read the directions to the test so they understand what is expected of them. Teachers need to make sure the students understand vocabulary words and concepts in the directions. Words appearing in the test directions that are common should be introduced to students as part of the process of test preparation. Ensure the students understand what they are to do. If they have questions they should be encouraged to ask the teacher before the test starts. Listening and reading activities can be incorporated into the classroom that will provide practice for following directions. Students need to know how to budget their time for the test. They should work fast but comfortably. Students can practice this.

Some students finish the test early and do not check their answers. This should be a habit that they develop. When they check their work, they need to ensure that the answers are correctly marked on the answer sheet. They should make sure the answers match the number of questions on the answer sheet. Students should have time to check and reconsider their work if time has been efficiently managed. Students should be encouraged to change answers when they think a better answer is appropriate. Students need reinforcement that their word should be checked daily. Teachers can do this by refusing to accept work until it is confirmed the work has been checked.

Students should not stop reading an item when they believe they have a right answer or that a better answer might be available to them. They should consider each possible option or alternative and then select the best answer. Students should be encouraged to very carefully go over each question and pay

particular attention to key terms. This information may be translated by the student into different forms, such as changing the question into their own words or substituting common words. They can use their knowledge to anticipate what an answer might be and to select an answer that appears similar to the one they predicted. These skills may be practiced in regular classroom activity.

Assessment systems

Assessment systems may include those that are norm-referenced, criterion-referenced, alternative assessments or classroom assessments, Criterion-referenced systems are those where an individual's performance is compared to a certain learning objective of performance standard and not based on the performance of other students. Norm-referenced systems are those where student performance is compared to a larger, "norm group," which may be a national sample that represents a diverse cross-section of students. These tests usually sort student and measure achievement towards some performance criterion. An individual assessment is one focusing on the individual student such as a portfolio assessment. This is a portfolio of the students' classroom work. Alternative assessments are those requiring students to respond to a question rather than a set of responses.

The Wide-Range Achievement Test

The Wide-Range Achievement Test is one of a number of standardized achievement assessments to determine a child's cognitive ability. It is for individuals ages 5-75. It contains scoring for reading, spelling and math. It provides up to 30 minutes for each of the three forms. The test uses a single-level format as well as alternative forms. These alternative forms may be used with one another in order to provide a more qualitative assessment of academic skills, or leaving the other form for testing at a later time. The reading subtest includes letter naming and word pronunciation out of context. The spelling subtest asks the student to write his or her own name and then write words as they are directed. The mathematical portion includes counting, reading problems, number symbols and written computation.

Group reporting

Group reporting is a fun way for students to show the teacher and their peers what they have learned. Small groups are used with students interacting with each other. The students also learn from each other and use social skills. Groups that work together consistently may create a portfolio of the group work. This could include self-assessments where the students can comment on what they have learned creating the portfolio. A group skit is a creative way to demonstrate almost anything the students have learned. A mini-fair is another activity where, after a small group project, the students can share it with booths in a location where other class members can see it.

Rubrics

Rubrics are a set of assessment criteria that specifies the characteristics, knowledge and competencies indicating a student's level of achievement. It is basically a list of characteristics that are used to assess a learning product's quality. Rubrics identify traits and components that indicate to what extent a learning outcome has been achieved. Rubrics are often used to attach authentic meaning to both letter and number grades. Rubrics also offer advantages such as:

- Rubrics allow students to document the grade they earned rather than the grade given or assigned.
- Tests and research papers may not offer a valid reflection of learning outcomes while rubrics are tied to learning outcomes.
- Grades alone offer limited reflections of a student's learning.

Informal assessment

Although there is no uniformly accepted definitions for formal and informal assessments, informal can mean techniques that are easily put into classroom routines and learning activities to measure a student's learning outcome. Informal assessment can be used without interfering with instructional time. The results can be an indicator of the skills or subjects that interest a student. They do not provide comparison to a broader group like standardized tests. Informal tests require clear understanding of the levels of a student's abilities. Informal assessments seek identification of a student's strength and weaknesses without a regard to norms or grades. Such assessments may be done in structured and unstructured manners. Structured ones include checklists or observations. Unstructured assessments are those such as student work samples or journals.

Surveys

Surveys help gather information of any type whether specific names need to be attached are do not need to be detached. Surveys are good in determining what a student feels about the instruction. They may be used in order to determine the level of knowledge on various issues related to the content that is being studied. This could help provide a baseline of where the students are. Surveys that are similar can then be given at later periods of time to determine what they have learned. Surveys are good in determining how the student feels about what he or she has learned in the class from their point of view. Rather than from a standardized test score that shows academic outcomes, surveys can provide a more personal level of knowledge that the student may have gained from the class.

Reasons for assessing children's academic growth

Parents and teachers want and need to know how children are progressing in learning age-appropriate tasks and acquiring age-appropriate skills. If problems are diagnosed early, they can be addressed, and many times, corrected before they become serious roadblocks in development. One cautionary note: be careful of attaching a good or bad label; they tend to follow a child throughout his entire educational experience. Determining children's progress helps make placement and promotion decisions, aids in the design of curriculum and other programs and can lead to improvements in instructional methods and classroom management. Assessments of young children, especially in first and second grades, should always consider four major areas: knowledge, skills, temperament and feelings. Adding observations made during informal work and play situations helps minimize possible errors inherent in evaluating young children. Assessments should include a balance between standardized evaluations and specific progress made by individual students.

Decisions regarding assessments
The following are ideas that might help when deciding appropriate testing:
- What students are doing correctly
- The concepts that your class is developing
- Point our your students misconceptions and errors
- Appropriate measures of scoring aptitude.
- Figure out appropriate methods of remediation and acceleration
- Know the appropriate uses of rubrics

Evaluating student writing
The evaluation of student writing should be structured to include three basic goals:
- To provide students a description of what they are doing when they respond.
- To provide a pathway for potential improvement.
- To help students learn to evaluate themselves.

To fulfill these goals it is necessary for the concept of evaluation be broadened beyond correcting or judging students. Any teacher response to a student's response should be considered part of the evaluation. In responding to student's responses, a teacher may use written or taped comments, dialogue with students, or conferencing between teachers and students to discuss classroom performance. Students may be asked to evaluate themselves and a teacher and student can review past progress and plan directions for potential improvement.

Formulating a response
There are seven basic components of teacher's responses to be considered:
- *Praise:* To provide positive reinforcement for the student. Praise should be specific enough to bolster student's confidence.
- *Describing:* Providing feedback on teacher's responses to student responses. This is best done in a conversational, non-judgmental mode.
- *Diagnosing:* Determining the student's unique set of strengths, attitudes, needs, and abilities. This evaluation should take into consideration all elements of the student.
- *Judging:* Evaluating the level, depth, insightfulness, completeness, and validity of a student's responses. This evaluation will depend on the criteria implied in the instructional approach.
- *Predicting:* Predicting the potential improvement of student's responses based on specific criteria.
- *Record-keeping:* The process of recording a student's reading interests, attitudes, and use of literary strategies, in order to chart student progress across time. Both qualitative and quantitative assessments may be used.
- *Recognition:* Giving students recognition for growth and progress.

Literary tests and assessments

Literary tests are measures of a student's individual performance. Literary assessments are measures of performance of a group of students without reference to individuals. Tests take into consideration what the teachers have taught the students, while assessments do not.

For either tests or assessments, the teacher needs a clear purpose on which to base their questions or activities. Students should be told of the purpose of the tests or assessments so they will know what to expect. Tests should be used sparingly as a one tool among many that can be used to evaluate students. Tests should encourage students on formulation of responses rather than rote answers. They should evaluate students on the basis of their responses rather than 'correct answers". Improvement over time may be noted and the student given praise for specific responses.

Standardized achievement tests

These multiple choice tests measure student's ability to understand text passages or apply literary concepts to texts. Although these tests are widely used, they have many limitations. They tend to be based on a simplistic model that ignores the complex nature of a reader's engagement with a text. These tests also do not measure student's articulation of responses. The purpose of these tests is to rank students in group norms, so that half the students are below the norm.

To accurately measure a student's abilities teachers should employ open ended written or oral response activities. In developing such tests, teachers must know what specific response patterns they wish to measure. The steps involved in measuring these response patterns must be clearly outlined. Teachers may wish to design questions that encourage personal expressions of responses. This would obviate the pitfall of testing primarily facts about literature rather than how students relate and use this information to engage texts.

Assessing attitudes toward literature

An important element in teaching literature is to understand the attitudes of students about reading and studying text. This may be done by group or individual interviews encouraging students to discuss their feelings about literature. Another way to measure attitudes is with a paper and pencil rating scale using six or eight point Liker scales. This type of assessment can be refined to explore preferences in form and genre. Another type of assessment is done by using semantic scales to indicate students interest (or lack thereof) in reading in general and favored forms and genres.

Questionnaires can be developed to learn more about student's habits regarding literature. Do they use the library regularly, read books or periodicals, and what types of reading is done. Comparisons before and after instruction can indicate the effect of instruction on habits and attitudes about literature.

Terms

The following terms used in scoring:
- *Mean:* A number that typifies a set of numbers, such as a geometric mean or an arithmetic mean. The average value of a set of numbers.
- *Mode:* The number or range of numbers in a set that occur most frequently.
- *Median:* The middle value in a distribution, above and below which lie an equal number of values.

Reteaching, Enrichment, and Extensions:
- Reteaching: The act of teaching over again
- Enrichment: Above and beyond the given
- Extensions: Small add-ons that help in teaching

Approaching Projects

General assignments

Understanding assignments

Many writing assignments address specific audiences (physicians, attorneys, and teachers) and have specific goals. These writers know for whom and why they are writing. This can clarify the writing significantly. Other assignments, particularly in academic settings, may appear with no specific subject, audience, or apparent purpose. Assignments may come with some variables; a specified audience, subject, or approach and leave the rest up to the writer. Because of these variables, it is useful to consider the following questions:

- What specifically is the assignment asking the writer to do?
- What information or knowledge in necessary to fulfill the assignment?
- Can the topic be broadened or limited to more effectively complete the project?
- Are there specific parameters or other requirements for the project?
- What is the purpose of third assignment?
- Who is the intended audience for the work?

These questions can clarify the writing task, and open avenues for exploration.

Encouraging metacognition

Metacognition is the process of thinking about thinking. As applied to reading, students can use metacognition to develop specific plans of action to enable a better understanding of the material. The three key elements of this process are: designing the plan of action, monitoring it and assessing its effectiveness. The process can be facilitated by encouraging students to ask a series of questions.

- *Developing a plan of action:* "Why am I reading this?"; "How much time do I have?"; "What should I read first?"
- *Monitoring the plan:* "What information is most important?"; "Am I on the right track?"; "What should I do if I don't understand?"; "Should I go in a different direction?"
- *Assessing the effectiveness of the plan:* "How did I do?"; "What could I have done differently?"; "How can I apply this process in other areas?"

Considering an audience

The careful consideration of the anticipated audience is a requisite for any project. Although much of this work is intuitive, some guidelines are helpful in the analysis of an audience.

- Specifically identify your audience. Are they eclectic or share common characteristics?
- Determine qualities of the audience such as age, education, sex, culture, and special interests.
- Understand what the audience values; brevity, humor, originality, honesty are examples.
- What is the audience's attitude toward the topic; skeptical, knowledgeable, pro or con?
- Understand the writer's relationship to the audience; peer, authority, advocate, or antagonist?

Understanding the qualities of an audience allows
the writer to form an organizational plan tailored to achieve the objectives of the writing with the audience in mind. It is essential to effective writing.

Understanding the topic

Easily overlooked is the basic question of ascertaining how knowledgeable the writer is about the subject. A careful evaluation should be made to determine what is known about the topic, and what information must be acquired to undertake the writing assignment.

Most people have a good sense of how to go about researching a subject, using the obvious available resources: libraries, the internet, journals, research papers and other sources. There are however some specific strategies that can help a writer learn more about a subject, and just as importantly, what is not known and must be learned. These strategies or techniques not only are useful in researching a subject, they can also be used when problems come up during the actual writing phase of the assignment. These strategies include brainstorming, free writing, looping, and questioning.

Brainstorming
Brainstorming is a technique used frequently in business, industry, science, and engineering. It is accomplished by tossing out ideas, usually with several other people, in order to find a fresh approach or a creative way to approach a subject. This can be accomplished by an individual by simply free-associating about a topic. Sitting with paper and pen, every thought about the subject is written down in a word or phrase. This is done without analytical thinking, just recording what arises in the mind about the topic. The list is then read over carefully several times. The writer looks for patterns, repetitions, clusters of ideas, or a recurring theme. Although brainstorming can be done individually, it works best when several people are involved. Three to five people is ideal. This allows an exchange of ideas, points of view, and often results in fresh ideas or approaches.

Prior knowledge
Prior knowledge is information that is already known that is brought to the awareness level in order for the reader to connect new information with the known. This allows students categories on which to hang their newly acquired knowledge. Research has found that what readers bring to a text is one of the best ways to predict how they will comprehend the text. When a student uses prior knowledge, he or she has the ability to

better focus on what is most important in the text. This also leads to inferences and elaboration as the text is read. Student may fill in the blanks if needed and store such information in memory by using this prior knowledge. Research has also shown that the use of predication to activate prior knowledge indicated students were more interested in what they were reading and remembered it better.

Looping
Looping is a variation of freewriting that focuses a topic in short five-minute stages, or loops. Looping is done as follows:
- With a subject in mind, spend five minutes freewriting without stopping. The results are the first loop.
- Evaluate what has been written in the first loop. Locate the strongest or most recurring thought which should be summarized in a single sentence. This is the "center of gravity," and is the starting point of the next loop.
- Using the summary sentence as a starting point, another five minute cycle of freewriting takes place. Evaluate the writing and locate the "center of gravity" for the second loop, and summarize it in a single sentence. This will be the start of the third loop.
- Continue this process until a clear new direction to the subject emerges. Usually this will yield a starting point for a whole new approach to a topic.

Looping can be very helpful when a writer is blocked or unable to generate new ideas on a subject.

Formal approach of questioning
Asking and answering questions provides a more structured approach to investigating a subject. Several types of questions may be used to illuminate an issue.
- *Questions to describe a topic:* Questions such as "What is It?", "What caused it?", "What is it like or unlike?", "What is it a part of"? What do people

- 115 -

say about it?" help explore a topic systematically.

- *Questions to explain a topic:* Examples include" Who, how, and what is it?", "Where does it end and begin?" What is at issue?", and "How is it done?"
- *Questions to persuade:* "What claims can be made about it?", "What evidence supports the claims?", "Can the claims be refuted?", and "What assumptions support the claims?"

Questioning can be a very effective device as it leads the writer through a process in a systematic manner in order to gain more information about a subject.

Thesis
A thesis states the main idea of the essay. A working or tentative thesis should be establisher early on in the writing process. This working thesis is subject to change and modification as writing progresses. It will serve to keep the writer focused as ideas develop.

The working thesis has two parts: a topic and a comment. The comment makes an important point about the topic. A working thesis should be interesting to an anticipated audience; it should be specific and limit the topic to a manageable scope. Theses three criteria are useful tools to measure the effectiveness of any working thesis. The writer applies these tools to ascertain:

- Is the topic of sufficient interest to hold an audience?
- Is the topic specific enough to generate interest?
- Is the topic manageable? Too broad? Too narrow? Can it be adequately researched?

It is most important that the thesis of the paper be clearly expounded and adequately supported by additional points. The thesis sentence should contain a clear statement of the major theme and a comment about the thesis. The writer has an opportunity here to state what is significant or noteworthy of this particular treatment of the subject. Each sentence and paragraph in turn, should build on the thesis and support it.

Particular attention should be paid to insuring the organization properly uses the thesis and supporting points. It can be useful to outline the draft after writing, to insure that each paragraph leads smoothly to the next, and that the thesis is continually supported. The outline may highlight a weakness in flow or ideation that can be repaired. It will also spatially illustrate the flow of the argument, and provide a visual representation of the thesis and its supporting points. Often things become clearer when outlined than with a block of writing.

Research
Many writing assignments require research. Research is basically the process of gathering information for the writer's use. There are two broad categories of research:

1. Library research should be started after a research plan is outlined. Topics that require research should be listed, and catalogues, bibliographies, periodical indexes checked for references. Librarians are usually an excellent source of ideas and information on researching a topic.
2. Field research is based on observations, interviews, and questionnaires. This can be done by an individual or a team, depending on the scope of the field research.

The specific type and amount of research will vary widely with the topic and the writing assignment. A simple essay or story may require only a few hours of research, while a major project can consume weeks or months.

Organizing information
Organizing information effectively is an important part of research. The data must be organized in a useful manner so that it can be

effectively used. Three basic ways to organize information are:

- *Spatial organization:* This is useful as it lets the user "see" the information, to fix it in space. This has benefits for those individuals who are visually adept at processing information.
- *Chronological organization:* This is the most common presentation of information. This method places information in the sequence with which it occurs. Chronological organization is very useful in explaining a process that occurs in a step-by-step pattern.
- *Logical organization:* This includes presenting material in a logical pattern that makes intuitive sense. Some patterns that are frequently used are illustrated, definition, compare/contrast, cause/effect, problem/solution, and division/classification. Each of these methods is discussed next.

There are six major types of logical organization that are frequently used:

1. Illustrations may be used to support the thesis. Examples are the most common form of this organization.
2. Definitions say what something is or is not is another way of organization. What are the characteristics of the topic?
3. Dividing or classifying information into separate items according to their similarities is a common and effective organizing method.
4. Comparing, focusing on the similarities of things, and contrasting, highlighting the differences between things is an excellent tool to use with certain kinds of information.
5. Cause and effect is a simple tool to logically understand relationships between things. A phenomenon may be traced to its causes for organizing a subject logically.
6. Problem and solution is a simple and effective manner of logically organizing material. It is very commonly used and lucidly presents information.

Initial plan

After information gathering has been completed and the fruits of the research organized effectively, the writer now has a rough or initial plan for the work. A rough plan may be informal, consisting of a few elements such as "Introduction, Body, and Conclusions," or a more formal outline. The rough plan may include multiple organizational strategies within the over-all piece, or it may isolate one or two that can be used exclusively. At this stage the plan is just that, a rough plan subject to change as new ideas appear, and the organization takes a new approach. In these cases, the need for more research sometimes becomes apparent, or existing information should be considered in a new way. A more formal outline leads to an easier transition to a draft, but it can also limit the new possibilities that may arise as the plan unfolds. Until the outlines of the piece become clear, it is usually best to remain open to possible shifts in approaching the subject.

Proofreading

As a proofreader, the goal is always to eliminate all errors. This includes typographical errors as well as any inconsistencies in spelling and punctuation. Begin by reading the prose aloud, calling out all punctuation marks and insuring that all sentences are complete and no words are left out. It is helpful to read the material again, backwards, so the focus is on each individual word, and the tendency to skip ahead is avoided.

A computer is a blessing to writers who have trouble proofreading their work. Spelling and grammar check programs may be utilized to reduce errors significantly. However it is still important for a writer to do the manual proofing necessary to insure errors of pattern

- 117 -

are not repeated. Computers are a wonderful tool for writers but they must be employed by the writer, rather than as the writer. Skillful use of computers should result in a finely polished manuscript free of errors.

Conducting classroom based research

Teacher's can conduct their own informal descriptive research to assess the effects of their teaching on student's responses. This allows teachers an opportunity to review and reflect on their instructional methods and results. This research can take many forms including:

- An analysis of student's perception of guided response- activities to determine which were most effective.
- An analysis of student's small and large group discussions.
- A teacher self analysis of their own taped, written, or conference feedback to students writing.
- Interviews with students about their responses and background experiences and attitudes.
- Evaluating student's responses to texts commonly used in their instruction.

These are only a few possibilities for effective classroom based research. Any research that provides insight into student needs and preferences can be a valuable tool.

Steps to conducting classroom research
1. Create a research question related to literature instruction or responses.
2. Summarize the theory and research related to the topic.
3. Describe the participants, setting, tasks, and methods of analysis.
4. Summarize the results of the research in a graph, table, or report.
5. Interpret or give reasons for the results.
6. Draw conclusions from the results that suggest ways to improve instruction and evaluation of students.

Teachers must always keep in mind the purposes driving the research. Evaluation itself is relatively easy, the challenge is using the evaluations to help both students and teachers to grow, and become better at what they are doing.

Student note-taking

Reading for certain information and then taking notes are perhaps the most challenging step in the process of solving information problems. Students in grades 3-8 require many developmentally-appropriate chances to locate information before the techniques are mastered. Note-taking consists of identifying keywords and related words, skimming and scanning, and extracting needed information. These steps start after students define and narrow the task as well as construct researchable questions then find the right sources. After students build researchable questions from the information needed to finish a task or solve an information problem, the questions can be transferred to graphic organizers or data charts. This can allow them to focus on the key words. Skimming and scanning will help them use text with less time and effort. Information may be extracted and recorded with different forms of note-taking including citation, summary, quotation and paraphrasing.

Outlining

Outlines are a blueprint for a final document. It gives the content of a body of work in brief, organizing topics and supporting details in the order they are to be discussed or used. An outline helps teachers demonstrate that the student understands the assignment, that the teachers has clearly focused the topic and that the content being taught is thorough and well organized. It also shows the teacher that the student was thinking about the paper before deadline. Outlining is organizing. Those elements organized might be ideas, activities, events or other matters. Outlines are a concept map, an overview of an idea set, and an organized terse summary of categories and idea. The ideas can be organized by using text, a drawing, a graphic or some combination.

Outlines may be done in text or on paper, in a computer or on a chalkboard. However they may be done certain concepts apply across each of these approaches. They can benefit by a standard sequence for outlining including brainstorming, cluster/sort, pruning and sequence. Brainstorming is coming up with a large amount of ideas then sorting through them. Cluster/sorting is to dragging ideas from the brainstorm session into sub-topics. Then ideas are sorted out and expanded upon. Pruning is deleting certain ideas that are in the outline such as ones that are redundant, off topic or not part of the primary focus. Sequence relates to placing the information into a sequence of events such as chronological order, spatial, topical or other forms.

Research and Writing Assignments

Basic research concepts

Research is a means of critical inquiry, investigations based on sources of knowledge. Research is the basis of scientific knowledge, of inventions, scholarly inquiry, and many personal and general decisions. Much of work consists of research or finding something out and reporting on it. We can list five basic precepts about research.

- Everyone does research. To buy a car, go to a film, to investigate anything is research. We all have experience in doing research.
- Good research draws a person into a "conversation" about a topic. Results are more knowledge about a subject, understanding different sides to

issues, and be able to discuss intelligently nuances of the topic.
- Research is always driven by a purpose. Reasons may vary from solving a problem to advocating a position, but research is almost always goal oriented.
- Research is shaped by purpose, and in turn the fruits of research refine the research further.
- Research is usually not a linear process; it is modified and changed by the results it yields.

Primary and secondary sources

Primary sources are the raw material of research. This can include results of experiments, notes, and surveys or interviews done by the researcher. Other primary sources are books, letters, diaries, eyewitness accounts, and performances attended by the researcher.

Secondary sources consist of oral and written accounts prepared by others. This includes reports, summaries, critical reviews, and other sources not developed by the researcher.

Most research writing uses both primary and secondary sources. Primary sources are from first-hand accounts and secondary sources are for background and supporting documentation. The research process calls for active reading and writing throughout. As research yields information, it often calls for more reading and research, and the cycle continues.

Analyzing an assigned topic

In academic settings, a teacher assigns many topics. The assignment should be carefully studied with special attention paid to the following elements:
- Determine the purpose of the assignment. It may be to compare, contrast, describe, or narrate. Key

- 119 -

words in the instructions will be a good guide.

- Identifying the audience, if it is to include someone besides the teacher. An analysis of the audience and their knowledge and expectations is always helpful.
- Note the length of the assignment. Does it limit or require a certain number of pages? If so, what are the parameters?
- It is important to note the deadline for an assignment. Sometimes preliminary materials are to be submitted before the main assignment. Considering these factors will give a writer information needed to set a schedule for the project.

When assignments are specifically understood the writing is smoother. Extra time spent in this understanding is rarely wasted.

Choosing a topic

The choice of a topic is a matter of understanding what potential subjects engage the writer. A writer may have a natural affinity for a number of subjects, any of which might be a good choice. A subject that provokes a strong reaction in a writer may be a good one. It is helpful if a writer discusses the potential topic or topics with peers and instructors. Feedback could include approaches to the subject, sources of information about the subject, and an opinion on the scope of the topic.

A common problem is limiting the scope of a writing assignment. Narrowing the scope is not always enough, because the new subject may itself be too broad. Focusing on an aspect of a topic often effectively results in a topic both interesting and manageable. For example narrowing a topic like the "Civil War" to the "Battle of Antietam" may still leave an unwieldy topic. To sharpen the focus, an aspect such as "The use of artillery by

Confederates at the battle of Antietam" could be selected.

Research question and hypothesis

The result of a focusing process is a research question, a question or problem that can be solved by through research data. A hypothesis is a tentative answer to the research question that must be supported by the research. A research question must be manageable, specific, and interesting. Additionally, it must be argumentative, capable of being proved or disproved by research.

It is helpful to explore a topic with background reading and notes before formulating a research question and a hypothesis. Create a data base where all the knowledge of a topic is written down to be utilized in approaching the task of identifying the research question. This background work will allow a narrowing to a specific question, and formulate a tentative answer, the hypothesis. The process of exploring a topic can include brainstorming, freewriting, and scanning your memory and experience for information.

Observing and recording data

Collecting data in the field begins with direct observation, noting phenomena in a totally objective manner, and recording it. This requires a systematic approach to observation and recording information. Prior to beginning the observation process, certain steps must be accomplished:

- Determine the purpose of the observation and review the research question and hypothesis to see that they relate to each other.
- Set a limited time period for the observations.
- Develop a system for recording information in a useful manner.
- Obtain proper materials for taking notes.

- Consider the use of cameras, video recorders, or audio tape recorders.
- Use the journalistic technique of asking "who, what, where, when, and why" to garner information.

Research interviews

After determining the exact purpose of the interview, check it against the research question and hypothesis. Set up the interview in advance, specifying the amount of time needed. Prepare a written list of questions for the interview, and try out questions on peers before the interview. Prepare a copy of your questions leaving room for notes. Insure that all the necessary equipment is on hand, and record the date, time, and subject of the interview. The interview should be businesslike, and take only the allotted time. A flexible attitude will allow for questions or comments that have not been planned for, but may prove helpful to the process. Follow-up questions should be asked whenever appropriate. A follow-up thank you note is always appreciated and may pave the way for further interviews. Be mindful at all times of the research question and hypothesis under consideration.

Survey of opinion

Surveys are usually in the form of questionnaires which have the advantage of speed and rapid compilation of data. Preparation of the questionnaire is of critical importance. Tie the questionnaire to the research question as closely as possible, and include questions which will bear on the hypothesis. Questions that can be answered "yes" or "no" can be easily tabulated. The following checklist may be helpful:

- Determine the audience for the questionnaire and how best to reach them.
- Draft questions that will provide short, specific answers.
- Test the questions on friends or peers.

- Remember to include a deadline for return of the questionnaire.
- Format the questionnaire so that it is clear and easily completed.
- Carefully proofread the questionnaire and insure that it is neatly reproduced.

Library as resource

After reviewing personal resources for information, the library is the next stop. Use index cards or notepads for documentation. Create a system for reviewing data. It is helpful to create "key words" to trigger responses from sources. Some valuable guidelines for conducting library research include:

- Consult the reference librarian for sources and ideas.
- Select appropriate general and specific reference books for examination. Encyclopedias are a good place to start. There are numerous specialized encyclopedias to assist in research.
- Survey biographical dictionaries and indexes for information.
- Review almanacs, yearbooks, and statistical data.
- Scan periodical indexes for articles on the research topic.
- Determine if there are specialized indexes and abstracts that may be helpful.
- Review the computer or card catalog for relevant references.

Drafting the research essay

Before beginning the research essay, revisit the purpose, audience, and scope of the essay. An explicit thesis statement should summarize major arguments and approaches to the subject. After determining the special format of the essay, a survey of the literature on the subject is helpful. If original or first-hand research is involved, a summary of the methods and conclusions should be prepared.

- 121 -

A clustering strategy assembles all pertinent information on a topic in one physical place. The preparation of an outline may be based on the clusters, or a first draft may be developed without an outline. Formal outlines use a format of "Thesis statement," "Main topic," and "Supporting ideas" to shape the information. Drafting the essay can vary considerably among researchers, but it is useful to use an outline or information clusters to get started. Drafts are usually done on a point-to-point basis.

Introduction

The introduction to a research essay is particularly important as it sets the context for the essay. It needs to draw the reader into the subject, and also provide necessary background to understand the subject. It is sometimes helpful to open with the research question, and explain how the question will be answered. The major points of the essay may be forecast or previewed to prepare readers for the coming arguments.

In a research essay it is a good idea to establish the writer's credibility by reviewing credentials and experience with the subject. Another useful opening involves quoting several sources that support the points of the essay, again to establish credibility. The tone should be appropriate to the audience and subject, maintaining a sense of careful authority while building the arguments. Jargon should be kept to a minimum, and language carefully chosen to reflect the appropriate tone.

Conclusion

The conclusion to a research essay helps readers' summarize what they have learned. Conclusions are not meant to convince, as this has been done in the body of the essay. It can be useful to leave the reader with a memorable phrase or example that supports the argument. Conclusions should be both

memorable but logical restatements of the arguments in the body of the essay.

A specific-to-general pattern can be helpful, opening with the thesis statement and expanding to more general observations. A good idea is to restate the main points in the body of the essay, leading to the conclusion. An ending that evokes a vivid image or asks a provocative question makes the essay memorable. The same effect can be achieved by a call for action, or a warning. Conclusions may be tailored to the audience's background, both in terms of language, tone, and style.

Review checklist

A quick checklist for reviewing a draft of a research essay includes:
1. *Introduction:* Is the reader's attention gained and held by the introduction?
2. *Thesis:* Does the essay fulfill the promise of the thesis? Is it strong enough?
3. *Main Points:* List the main points and rank them in order of importance.
4. *Organization:* What is the organizing principle of the essay? Does it work?
5. *Supporting Information:* Is the thesis adequately supported? Is the thesis convincing?
6. Source Material: Are there adequate sources and are they smoothly integrated into the essay?
7. *Conclusion:* Does the conclusion have sufficient power? Does it summarize the essay well?
8. *Paragraphs, Sentences, and Words:* Review all these for effectiveness in promoting the thesis.
9. *Overall Review:* Evaluate the essay's strengths and weaknesses. What revisions are needed?

MLA style

The Modern Language Association style is widely used in literature and languages as well as other fields. The MLA style calls for noting brief references to sources in parentheses in the text of an essay, and adding an alphabetical list of sources, called "Works Cited," at the end. Specific recommendations of the MLA include:

- *Works Cited:* Includes only works actually cited. List on a separate page with the author's name, title, and publication information, which must list the location of the publisher, the publishers' name, and the date of publication.
- *Parenthetical Citations:* MLA style uses parenthetical citations following each quotation, reference, paraphrase, or summary to a source. Each citation is made up of the author's last name and page reference, keyed to a reference in "Works Cited."
- *Explanatory Notes*: Explanatory notes are numbered consecutively, and identified by superscript numbers in the text. The full notes may appear as endnotes or as footnotes at the bottom of the page.

APA style

The American Psychological Association style is widely followed in the social sciences. The APA parenthetical citations within the text direct readers to a list of sources. In APA style this list is called "References." References are listed on a separate page, and each line includes the author's name, publication date, title, and publication information. Publication information includes the city where the publisher is located, and the publisher's name. Underline the titles of books and periodicals, but not articles.

APA parenthetical expressions citations include the author's last name, the date of publication, and the page number. APA style allows for content footnotes for information needed to be expanded or supplemented, marked in the text by superscript numbers in consecutive order. Footnotes are listed under a separate page, headed "Footnotes" after the last page of text. All entries should be double-spaced.

General writing assignments

An early assessment of the writing assignment is very helpful. Understanding the subject and your relationship to it is important. Determine if this subject is broad enough for the assignment, or perhaps it must be narrowed to be effectively addressed. If a choice of topics is offered, it is wise to select one of which you have significant prior knowledge or one that can be reasonably investigated in the time given for the work. An important part of assessing the topic will be to decide in how much detail to use in writing.

Where will the information from the project come from? Will field research be necessary or will secondary sources suffice? Is there a need to use personal interviews, questionnaires, or surveys to accumulate information? The amount of reading to be done should be considered, and the type of documentation planned. Answering these questions will help estimate the time needed for research.

Purposes of writing
Discovering a purpose is an important first step in writing. Here are some common purposes for writing: To inform, persuade, change attitudes, to analyze, argue, theorize, summarize, evaluate, recommend, to request, propose, provoke, to express feelings, to entertain, and to give pleasure are all legitimate purposes in writing.

It is a common error to misjudge the purpose of a writing assignment. A writer would do well to ask "Why am I communicating with my readers?" before undertaking a specific assignment. Another important question that follows is "Just who are those readers?" Audience analysis can sometimes suggest an effective strategy for reaching the readers. Sometimes audiences do not fall into a neat category, but are mixed in interest and purpose. This presents additional challenges to the writer.

Controlling length and design
Writers seldom have control over length and document design. Usually a academic assignment has a specified length, while journalists work within tight word count parameters. Document design often follows the purpose of a writing project. Specific formats are required for lab reports, research papers, and abstracts. The business world operates within fairly narrow format styles, the business letter, memo, and report allowing only a small departure from the standard format.

There are some assignments that allow the writer to choose the specific format for the work. The increased flourishes provided by computers allow a great deal of creativity in designing a visually stimulating and functional document. Improving readability is always a worthwhile goal for any project, and this is becoming much easier with available software.

Three types of people who review writing
Many professional and business writers work with editors who provide advice and support throughout the writing process. In academic situations, the use of reviewers is increasing, either by instructors or perhaps at an academic writing center. Peer review sessions are sometimes scheduled for class, and afford an opportunity to hear what other students feel about a piece of writing. This gives a writer a chance to serve as a reviewer.

Deadlines
Deadlines are a critical element in any writing assignment. They help a writer budget their time to complete the assignment on schedule. For elaborate or complex writing projects, it is useful to create a working schedule that includes time for research, writing, revising, and editing. Breaking the process down into more workable parts with their own deadlines, helps keep a writer aware of the progress being made.

Determining focus
As the topic of the writing assignment is explored, various possibilities will emerge as to focusing the material. This is an ideal time to settle on a tentative central idea. This tentative idea may change during the course of the assignment. Often a central idea may be stated in one sentence, which is called a thesis sentence. The thesis prepares the reader for the supporting points in the work. The thesis will usually appear in the opening paragraph of the text. The thesis contains a key word or phrase that provides the focus of the writing. This is usually a limiting or narrowing of the main subject.

After determining a thesis, the writer may proceed to an informal outline. This can be as simple as writing the thesis followed by a list of major supporting ideas. Clustering diagrams may also be used to formulate informal outlines.

Preparing formal outlines
A formal outline may be useful if the subject is complex, and includes many elements. Here is a guide to preparing formal outlines:
- Always put the thesis at the top so it may be referred to as often as necessary during the outlining.
- Make subjects similar in generality as parallel as possible in the formal outline.
- Use complete sentences rather than phrases or sentence fragments in the outline.
- Use the conventional system of letters and numbers to designate levels of generality.
- There should be at least two subdivisions for each category in the formal outline.
- Limit the number of major sections in the outline. If there are too many major sections, combine some of them

- and supplement with additional sub-categories.
- Remember the formal outline is still subject to change; remain flexible throughout the process.

Introduction

An introduction announces the main point of the work. It will usually be a paragraph of 50 to 150 words, opening with a few sentences to engage the reader, and conclude with the essay's main point. The sentence stating the main point is called the thesis. If possible, the sentences leading to the thesis should attract the reader's attention with a provocative question, vivid image, description, paradoxical statement, quotation, anecdote, or a question. The thesis could also appear at the beginning of the introduction. There are some types of writing that do not lend themselves to stating a thesis in one sentence. Personal narratives and some types of business writing may be better served by conveying an overriding purpose of the text, which may or may not be stated directly. The important point is to impress the audience with the rationale for the writing.

Effective thesis

Creating an effective thesis is an art. The thesis should be a generalization rather than a fact, and should be neither too broad nor narrow in scope. A thesis prepares readers for facts and details, so it may not be a fact itself. It is a generalization that requires further proof or supporting points. Any thesis too broad may be an unwieldy topic and must be narrowed. The thesis should have a sharp focus, and avoid vague, ambivalent language. The process of bringing the thesis into sharp focus may help in outlining major sections of the work. This process is known as blueprinting, and helps the writer control the shape and sequence of the paper. Blueprinting outlines major points and supporting arguments that are used in elaborating on the thesis. A completed blueprint often leads to a development of an accurate first draft of a work. Once the thesis

and opening are complete, it is time to address the body of the work.

Body and conclusion

The body of the essay should fulfill the promise of the introduction and thesis. If an informal outline has not been done, now is the time for a more formal one. Constructing the formal outline will create a "skeleton" of the paper. Using this skeleton, it is much easier to fill out the body of an essay. It is useful to block out paragraphs based on the outline, to insure they contain all the supporting points, and are in the appropriate sequence.

The conclusion of the essay should remind readers of the main point, without belaboring it. It may be relatively short, as the body of the text has already "made the case" for the thesis. A conclusion can summarize the main points, and offer advice or ask a question. Never introduce new ideas in a conclusion. Avoid vague and desultory endings, instead closing with a crisp, often positive, note. A dramatic or rhetorical flourish can end a piece colorfully.

Global revisions

Global revisions address the larger elements of writing. They usually affect paragraphs or sections, and may involve condensing or merging sections of text to improve meaning and flow. Sometimes material may be rearranged to better present the arguments of the essay. It is usually better for the writer to get some distance from the work before starting a global revision. Reviewers and editors can be usefully employed to make suggestions for revision. If reviewers are utilized, it is helpful to emphasize the focus on the larger themes of the work, rather than the finer points. When undertaking a global review, the writer might wish to position himself as the audience, rather than the writer. This provides some additional objectivity, and can result in a more honest appraisal of the writing and revisions that should be made. Global revisions are the last major changes a writer will make in the text. seal to persuade, inform, or entertain them.

Following is a checklist for global revisions
- *Purpose:* Does the draft accomplish its purpose? Is the material and tone appropriate for the intended audience? Does it account for the audience's knowledge of the subject? Does it seek to persuade, inform, or entertain them?
- *Focus:* Does the introduction and the conclusion focus on the main point? Are all supporting arguments focused on the thesis?
- *Organization and Paragraphing:* Are there enough organizational cues to guide the reader? Are any paragraphs too long or too short?
- *Content:* Is the supporting material persuasive? Are all ideas adequately developed? Is there any material that could be deleted?
- *Point -of-view:* Is the draft free of distracting sifts in point-of-view? Is the point-of-view appropriate for the subject and intended audience?

Answering these questions as objectively as possible will allow for a useful global revision.

Sentence revision
Revising sentences is done to make writing more effective. Editing sentences is done to correct any errors. Revising sentences is usually best done on a computer, where it is possible to try several versions easily. Some writers prefer to print out a hard copy and work with this for revisions. Each works equally well and depends on the individual preference.

Spelling and grammar checks on software are a great aid to a writer but not a panacea. Many grammatical problems, such as faulty parallelism, mixed constructions, and misplaced modifiers can slip past the programs. Even if errors are caught, the writing still must be evaluated for effectiveness. A combination of software programs and writer awareness is necessary to insure an error free manuscript.

Paragraphs
A paragraph should be unified around a main point. A good topic sentence summarizes the main point of the paragraph. A topic sentence is more general than subsequent supporting sentences. Sometime the topic sentence will be used to close the paragraph if earlier sentences give a clear indication of the direction of the paragraph. Sticking to the main point means deleting or omitting unnecessary sentences that do not advance the main point.

The main point of a paragraph deserves adequate development, which usually means a substantial paragraph. A paragraph of two or three sentences often does not develop a point well enough, particularly if the point is a strong supporting argument of the thesis. An occasional short paragraph is fine, particularly it is used as a transitional device. A choppy appearance should be avoided.

Using examples
Examples are a common method of development and may be effectively used when a reader may ask "For Example?" Examples are selected instances, not an inclusive catalog. They may be used to suggest the validity of topic sentences. Illustrations are extended examples, sometimes presented in story form for interest. They usually require several sentences each, so they are used sparingly. Well selected illustrations can be a colorful and vivid way of developing a point. Stories that command reader interest, developed in a story form, can be powerful methods of emphasizing key points in a essay. Stories and illustrations should be very specific and relate directly to a point or points being made in the text. They allow more colorful language and instill a sense of human interest in a subject. Used judiciously, illustrations and stories are an excellent device.

Literacy Issues

Sociocultural theory approach

Sociocultural approaches to literacy developed out of more general sociocultural theory which came from theories of Soviet psychologist L.S. Vygotsky. The three central planks of sociocultural theory have contributed to a new interpretation of literacy: The concept of genetic analysis, social learning and mediation. Genetic or developmental analysis suggests it is possible to understand mental functional aspects by understanding their origin and transitions. From genetic analysis it is understood the futility of seeing literacy as something that is isolated. Rather, a proper understanding of the emergence of literacy has to take into account the broad cultural, social and historic factors that relate to the significance of reading and writing for human communication and cognition.

Along with genetic analysis, social learning and mediation are the three major components of a sociocultural approach to literacy. Social learning refers to the social origin of mental functioning. Vygotsky said that every function in the child's cultural development appears on the social level and later on the individual level. The first development is between people and the second is inside the child. Vygotsky also believed the development occurred through means as apprenticeship learning, or interaction with teachers and peers. This view looks at learning not as an isolated act of cognition but rather a process of gaining entry to a discourse of practitioners. Mediation is the notion that all human activity is mediated through signs or tools. It is not so much the tools such as computers or writing by themselves as it is how they transform human action in a fundamental way.

Discourse theory

Discourse theory includes the view that language is either an abstract system of linguistic forms or an individual form of activity, that language is a continuous generative process that is used in a social and verbal interaction of speakers. Such views espouse more focused and increased interaction leading to higher forms of learning. It is an intense social interaction where creative energies are found through the partial or total restructuring of ideological systems. Such interactions are seen by some as most beneficial when crossing cultural boundaries. Other discourse theorists posited that it is not isolated words that learners assimilate through dialogic interaction but rather discourses and genres.

Workforce-related approaches

Dislocated workers have grappled with marginal literacy in their own language as well as with limited English proficiency for years. A number of literacy opportunities have taken place with often successful but different approaches:

- The English as Second Language (ESL) approach is usually a pre-employment activity that focuses on learning for an employment or vocational context. Instruction would largely be job related.
- Vocational ESL approach includes programs in a vocational setting, offering training in specific occupations and language skill related to a particular occupation.
- The ESL work experience approach combines workplace experience with classwork in vocational ESL and in combination with vocational skills training.
- The workplace ESL approach gives customized training for employer for particular jobs and stresses language skills related to particular job areas.

- The bilingual vocational approach uses the learners' native language to facilitate ESL instruction and/or vocational training.

Volunteer literacy programs

A number of different approaches can be used for volunteer literacy programs that will benefit both adults and children. Many operate under the premise that well-supported and well-trained volunteers can be effective tutors and that mobilizing the talents of large numbers of diverse types of people can make significant impacts on the problem of illiteracy. Some volunteer groups use learner-centered approaches and whole language philosophies in individualized reading and writing tutoring. This is done both in one-on-one and in small group settings. Approaches may be promoted that let learners practice with materials from different formats such as moving from controlled activities and responses to more spontaneous situations which allow real communication and self-expression.

Teacher expectations

The original Pygmalion study gave teachers false information about the learning potential of certain students in the 1-6 grades in a San Francisco elementary school. Teachers were told student had been tested and found to be on the edge of a period of rapid intellectual growth but the student had actually been selected at random. At the end of the experimental period, some of the targeted student exhibited superior scores on IQ tests compared to those of similar abilities. The results led researchers to claim that inflated expectations of teachers for target students actually caused accelerated intellectual growth in the students. A numbers of studies have since taken place and some found technical defects serious enough to cast doubt on the original findings. Whether one accepts or doubts the Pygmalion study, educators and the public are very interested in the power of expectations and how they affect the outcomes of students.

Self-fulfilling prophecies such as those argued as the outcome of the Pygmalion study on teacher expectations are the most dramatic form of teacher expectation effects because they involve changes in the behavior of children. Sustaining expectations are situations in which teachers fail to see student potential and do not respond by encouraging the student to fulfill their potential. But both actually involve change. High expectations may not be the magic trick needed to close achievement gaps. But raising expectations can make a difference when the effort is accompanied by a relevant and rigorous curriculum, adequate materials and current textbooks. This, along with effective teaching strategies, good classroom management, tutoring programs, uncrowded classrooms and involved parents just to name a few.

Most teachers have high hopes for their students. Some may be better than others at communicating those expectations. Others might unconsciously expect less of students who show little interest in learning or who have significant barriers to hurdle. But by holding all students to high standards most teacher believe they can help students achieve their full potential. Studies do show that students tend to internalize beliefs teachers have about their ability. When students are not expected to make a lot of progress, they may tend to take on a defeatist outlook. Some student may think their teachers believe they are not capable of handling demanding assignments. Teachers must see themselves as responsible for finding ways to raise performance despite whatever circumstances the students face.

Researchers have found certain ways that school may let students know the school's expectations of them are high:
- Establishing policies that emphasize how important it is to achieve academically. Parents can be notified

if students are not meeting the academic expectations or setting minimally acceptable achievement levels for students to participate in sports or extracurricular activities.

- Use slogans that communicate high expectations for the students such as "Yes we can."
- Protect instructional time and discourage tardiness, absenteeism and interruptions.
- Provide insistent coaching to students who experience difficulty with learning tasks. Researchers say that excusing children from trying hard to succeed in academics because it is not fair or hopeless to expect any more, or trying to protect them from failure does not really help students in learning. It detracts from academic skills and can also lower motivation and self-esteem.

Literacy learned everywhere

Literacy does not just come from going to school. It is learned everywhere including the reading of bus stop signs and boxes of cereal to listening to family stories in the language of the home and on the Internet. Caregivers as well as parents have a profound impact of their children's readiness upon entering school. The influence grows and changes each year. The positive influence of the family continues in importance as the children develop through elementary, junior high and high school. It can be helped by meaningful involvement by engaging parents, having parents and children participate in literacy activities together and helping adults help children with adult education. Likewise, peers and community members will all play a significant part as well in developing literacy among each other.

Most of the differences in academic achievement can be explained by the quantity and quality of reading materials in the home, the number of pages read for homework, the number of days absent from schools, the number of hours in which TV is watched and the presence of two parents in the home. There are other factors within these factors as well. One factor is the activities in which children engage at home such as reading storybooks, visiting libraries or playing word games. Another factor is the potential difference between the home and school cultures. Culture is used in this sense as a broad sense to include the behavior and attitudes of parents. If there is a wide gap between the home culture and school culture, children may perceive tasks such as reading as devaluing their identity.

Peer influence

Peer influence on children's behavior as well as on learning is well recognized in psychological literature. Peer influence can operate both ways, positive and negative. Teachers exploit the positive influence on peers and promote many of the learning experiences the children may have by organizing them into small groups in which they can become involved in learning. The negative aspects of peer influence are obvious when parents of children expect him and her to show interest in school work and spend time on homework but many of the children's peers do not have the same goals on their agendas. It is under such circumstances that it might become necessary to have the child discontinue his or her association with those peers who are negative influences.

Students, teenagers specifically, look to each other to learn and this sometimes brings about problems. Teenagers are growing and learning and through this development the students look toward each other to acquire what their peers deem to be acceptable. In many instances this may lead to inaccurate understandings. Teenagers purposely acquire knowledge sometimes that is unmistakably wrong and continue to use it in everyday situations. Some students are so influenced by their culture that, even though they are capable of speaking properly, they will not do so for fear they will not fit in with their peers. These students who are properly taught will acknowledge to adults they are speaking in slang yet still do so because their culture has shaped them to do so.

Black-white achievement gap

The black-white achievement gap refers to a general difficulty African-American students experience with academic achievement. They consistently perform below non-minority peers in reading, science and mathematics. The gap has had negative economic and social effects. Some studies have suggested the difference may be caused by cultural linguistic or cultural differences. Good language skills are necessary for reading. Vocabulary skills support reading development in both younger and older readers. African-American children have been shown to have receptive and expressive skills in vocabularies that are below those of their age levels. But vocabulary breadth can be increased by direct teaching methods. Such teaching methods may act as a start in improving reading for young African-American children and may hopefully narrow the so-called gap.

Dr. John Ogbu has argued for years that blacks have developed an oppositional cultural identity because of discrimination developed by their own culture. This stems in part from the times when blacks were asked to have the same behavior and speech as whites such as after emancipation. With the Black Power Movement of the 1960s, an oppositional cultural identity was in place where racial pride was expressed. Still, Ogbu believed that blacks still try to enter white culture. A resulting behavior derided by some, especially younger blacks, called "acting white" can be stressful for blacks. They get accused of being an Uncle Tom or disloyal to the black community. Speaking is one way in particular blacks are labeled as talking white.

Dialect

Dialect is a regionally or socially distinctive variety of language that is characterized by particular accents, sets of words and grammar. Even though it is easy to distinguish between a dialect and a language the difference often turns out to be a matter of degree. People are said to speak different languages when they do not understand what they other is saying. They are said to speak dialects if they can understand each other, even though not perfectly. There are exceptions. A single dialect spoken usually by a majority of people and that comes to predominate as the official standard form of the language is one exception. It is also the written form of that language. Hence, the English dialect spoken by a majority of the people becomes standard English, not that it has singular linguistic features but because most people speak it that way.

School system literacy problems

A big problem behind high rates of illiteracy in America is that students are not always taught properly in their educational environments. Within school systems, education is not giving the youth what it needs to achieve later goals in life. Goals are also not set high because the goals they are trying to reach reflect what the students have learned up to that point in life and not what they should have learned. In order for these students to achieve higher education levels, they will need to be encouraged to want to learn and set higher goals that they one day reach. Some say that to accomplish this, the teaching methods and disciplines in schools will have to be altered to suit all students and their needs, despite their backgrounds.

Lower socioeconomic classes

There are disagreements among scholars as to the direct correlation between a child's socioeconomic level and comprehension levels in school. Some see a direct correlation others say the correlation is more in degrees. Despite the socioeconomic status, the students still need to learn and that the most important time for students to learn language, according to some academics, is before they enter the education system. Children from a low socioeconomic black or Hispanic family may have worse phonemic awareness that Anglo children and experts have suggested that teachers adjust their styles of teaching to meet the children with those needs. Certain reasons exist for certain social groups having a difficult time reaching the top. In order to reach the top one needs to have a good foundation and that foundation is being able to read and to communicate.

Multiliteracies

A great deal of interest has risen around the world in the future of literacy teaching through so-called "multiliteracies." The multiliteracies argument is that our personal, public and working lives are changing these days in some very significant ways and these changes have the effect of transforming cultures and the way we communicate. The ramification of this is that way literacy is now taught is obsolete and what counts for literacy must also change. Multiliteracies have at its hear two major and closely related changes. First is the growing significance of cultural and linguistic diversity. This is reinforced every day by modern media. And it is becoming necessary to negotiate differences each day in our local communities as well as globally that are interconnected with our working and community lives. As this happens, English is becoming a world language. The second major shift is the influence of new communications technologies.

Model family literacy program

Family literacy programs focusing on both parent and child can follow different basic types:

- *Direct adult-direct children:* This is a highly structured model that allows the most intensive formal literacy instruction for both children and adults and has a high amount of parent-child interaction.
- *Indirect adult-indirect child:* These programs include voluntary attendance, short-term commitment and less formal learning through events such as storytelling: Usually, reading skills are not taught although adults may get tutoring in literacy.
- *Direct adult-indirect children:* Adults are given literacy instruction in these programs and may get coaching on reading with their children as well as other activities.
- *Indirect adults-direct children:* This includes in-school, preschool or after-school programs that help parents with their children's reading and other literacy matters.

Program designs should recognize multiple literacies and literacy behaviors in both the home and community and attempt to integrate both communities. Programs should build their strengths on the parents and their culture such as language, tradition and native language literacy as well as setting a literacy education in a meaning cultural context. Instruction in parental skills should be sensitive to cultural differences in child raising and dynamics of the family. Parents should be helped in being advocates for the education of their children. Family literacy programs need holistic approaches through collaboration of different agencies and staff. Parents must also be a partner. Program evaluation should use a broad literacy definition that guides programs and the informal and ethnographic techniques that may be most needed for the community.

Improving school literacy levels

Schools found to be low-performing from assessments sometimes have to adjust their entire curriculum. When such changes takes place there are many aims that are incorporated, much more than just a single program or a single type of instruction. These aims may include helping students' lifelong skills, improving the quality of teaching, learning to make sure all teachers recognize the role that language plays in learning. Among possible strands in a strategy for an entire school, that students in years 7 and 8 read in their form period time or that all year 7 pupils have a literacy hour each week. The focus might include having staff mark all children's books for spelling and grammar as well as content, that all departments provide a glossary of subject-specific words for pupils and that all departments would use a writing frame to provide writing structure for children in each subject.

A culture capsule is a biliteracy activity that is usually prepared outside class by students but presented during class for about five or 10 minutes. It contains of a paragraph or two and explains one minimal difference between an American custom and that of another culture's custom. It also includes several photos and other information that is relevant. These capsules can be used in addition by role playing. Students may act out a part of another culture. Essentially the capsule is a brief description of some aspect of the target culture followed by contrasting information from the students' native language culture. These are done orally with teachers giving a brief talk on the chosen cultural point and then leading a discussion on cultures.

Recent immigrant students

American schools have been a major agent for helping those children and youth who recently arrived in this country with adapting to the civic and social demands of their new homes. Classroom lessons and socialization on the school yard takes place. But sometimes the home culture teachings and expectations are contrasted with those of American schools. This can lead to labeling children as disabled when none actually

exists. These students do have issues with psychosocial stress as they attempt to adapt. A transition that is successful to one's new country requires a secure cross-cultural identity. How much of each culture forms this identity depends on the person's needs, skills, experience, education and support. Recognition of these transitioning needs and support are among the strategic help that can be given to these children.

A sample reading lesson for elementary students that incorporates the Hispanic culture: Children can be find places on the map of the United States with names that come from the Spanish language such as San Francisco, Los Angeles, and Pueblo. An activity can be done that invites students to use the library, class or Internet to find Hispanic Americans in history. Students can be invited to design a postage stamp of the Hispanic Heritage stamp series that might show a famous Hispanic American or some aspect of the Hispanic-American culture or history. Students can be given a list of Spanish words and be invited to find the English equivalent such as "ensalada" -- "salad." Invite students to create books to help them learn the Spanish words for the numbers one to 10 and for the common colors. For example, 1 -- uno, yellow -- amarillo.

Goals
The following are goals that should be attained in teaching culture:

- *Interest:* The student shows a curiosity about the target culture and also shows empathy toward its people.
- *Who:* The student understands that effective communication requires the discovery of the culturally conditioned images that are seen in the minds of people when they think, act and react to the world that is around them.
- *When and where:* The student recognizes that situational variables and convention mold behavior in

- 132 -

significant manners. He or she should know how people in the target culture act in both normal situations and crisis situations.

- *Why:* The student knows that people generally act how the do because they are using options for satisfying basic physical and psychological needs and that cultural patterns are interrelated and tend mutually to support the satisfactions of needs.

A framework for teaching and learning culture

- *Knowing about getting information:* The nature of content and getting information. Facts about the United States and what are important facets of its culture?
- *Learning objectives:* Demonstrating a mastery of information.
- *Techniques and activities:* Cultural readings, films, videotapes, cultural artifacts, personal anecdotes.
- *Note how culture is traditionally taught:* Are students given information and are they asked to show that they know it.
- *Knowing how to develop behaviors:* Knowing about what facts you learned and acting upon them.
- *Learning objectives:* Demonstrating an ability, a fluency, an expertise, confidence and ease.
- *Techniques:* Dialogs, role playing, simulations and field experiences.
- *Knowing where communicative competence in the language occurs.* Students know both what to say and how to do it in an appropriate manner.

Objectives for students learning culture

Students learning culture should react appropriately in social situations. They should describe a pattern in the culture. They should recognize a pattern when it is illustrated. They should be able to explain patterns. They should predict how a pattern is likely to apply in a given situation. They

should describe or manifest an attitude that is important for making oneself acceptable in a foreign society. They should evaluate the form of a statement concerning a culture pattern. They should describe or demonstrate defensible methods of analyzing a sociocultural whole. They should identify basic human purposes that make significant that what being taught is understood. There are other of these steps that can be made with similar goals.

Measuring changes in attitudes over foreign cultures

Ways to measure the change in attitudes about foreign cultures include:

- *Social distance scales:* This is to measure the degree to which one separates oneself socially from members of another culture. For instance: Would you marry, have someone as a close friend, have as an acquaintance, work with or have as a close friend?
- Semantic differential scales: This is to judge the defined culture group in terms of a number of traits that are bipolar. For instance, are people from this culture clean, are they dirty, are they good, and are they bad?
- *Statements:* This is to put a check in front of statements the student agrees with. Is the person you know envious of others, self-indulgent, quick to understand, tactless?
- *Self-esteem change:* This is to measure self-esteem changes in the primary grades. For instance, am I happy with myself?

Benefits to teacher learning about cultures

Students may display behaviors in their cultures but are different that those in the American mainstream thus they are at risk for being labeled by uniformed educators as having behaviors that are "wrong." Teachers should familiarize themselves with a student's home culture's values and practices. There should be an awareness of differences that

- 133 -

promote understanding and tolerance, acceptance, celebration of others and their ways and acceptance. Information on other cultures can be found in many textbooks, travel books and on various Web sites. Another way to develop familiarity with a student's cultural background is the use of a "cultural informant." This is someone who might be familiar with the group and their ways such as teachers or other successful members of that cultural group.

Keeping expectations high for recent immigrant students
It is common for some teachers to become frustrated when they see themselves as unable to reach one or more of their students. Becoming more culturally informed can help enhance the teaching repertoire. The information can also help teachers realize that these student may have trouble under the teaching of any skilled instructor. But the belief that is expressed in a student helps to create persistence and motivation on their part. Linguistic achievements as well as academic ones in the United States is often because of the patience, tolerance and encouragement that American teachers display. Effort is promoted by teachers who are supportive and who create a valuing, welcoming and accepting educational setting.

Obtaining and supplying support services
Schools can help recent immigrants feel welcome and supported while developing positive identities that are cross-cultural. Schools have many ways to assist their student in learning the curriculum and adapting to the American ways. A recent arrival can be partnered with another student who speaks his or her language or dialect, even if they are not from the home region or heritage of the new student. Cross-age tutoring is also an option that might be considered. Perhaps the tutor could be someone from that culture or region of the world, is a recent immigrant as well, or is an accepting and helpful American youngster.

Hiring paraprofessionals who speak the student's language can also be helpful.
Developing personal relationships with newly arrived immigrants
Students need to feel welcomed and valued by their teacher. A direct verbal communication may not be feasible but there are other methods of showing acceptance and personal warmth toward students. This will help relieve anxiety and can promote an enthusiasm to learn academics and American patterns of behavior. Smiles are a good way to reach different cultural, ethnic and linguistic groups. Also, teachers should take time to talk with the youngster, even through an interpreter. Having students talk about their prior life will help the teacher become more familiar with their concerns and will also help in emotionally supporting the new student. The teacher may also answer questions about schools and what is needed to live here in America. The teacher may also ask how he or she can help make the transition easier.

Professional issues

The following issues related to professional growth:
- *Reflective teaching:* Looking at what you do in the classroom, thinking about why you do the things you do.
- *Collaboration:* The act of working jointly
- Partnerships with colleagues and the community
- Interactions with parents

Efficiency
Especially with special education, teachers cannot get to each classroom and paraprofessionals are often sent into classrooms to help students with special needs. Regardless of the use, the roles and routines in which the paraprofessional is used needs to be carefully and clearly laid out. An educator might want to keep notes after discussing the use of a paraprofessional with colleagues. Say the paraprofessional is in the

classroom for reading a half-hour each day. No guidance has been given the teacher. One might consider the routines that could be put into place for that time period. Ensure that it would not take up too much time for the teacher and be within what is expected in the skills of a paraprofessional. One might discuss the benefits of the paraprofessional helping with readers who struggle. Also one might plot the progress of students that are being helped by the paraprofessional.

Teacher planning and preparation

Despite the status of the teacher's knowledge on instructional matters, he or she does select certain curricular content, makes decisions about groupings and allocates specific time periods for activities. These are at the crux of teacher preparation and planning. Teachers must turn curricular goals and related content into a plan that works. This includes textbook and material selection, content strategies, learning assessments for particular pupils, scheduling lessons and detailing instruction for particular days. The planning may be informal or it may be formal and explicit. A skillful teacher plans his or her school day. Teachers have perceptions of the students' needs in different subject areas. Teachers have a central portion of what defines education taken away if they become hindered in actualizing their plans.

Assessing instructional methods

Assessing instructional methods within a school, district, or state can help determine instructional goals and techniques relative to overall system goals. Results can indicate needed changes in the curriculum and can help an accreditation process measure the quality of an English or literature program.

An effective assessment usually includes interviews, questionnaires, and class-room observation. Trained observers rate the general type of instruction being provided, (lectures, modeling, small groups, and so on), the focus of instruction (novels, poetry, drama, and so on), the critical approach used, the response strategies used, and the response activities employed. Observers may also analyze the statements of goals and objectives in a curriculum, as well as the scope and sequence of the curriculum. Interviews of both students and teachers are helpful in getting first hand accounts of instruction and results.

Practice Test

Multiple Choice Questions

1. Which of the following are effective listening techniques?
   a. Interrupt to ask questions; paraphrase
   b. Focus; don't form opinions too soon
   c. Lean forward; tap on the table
   d. Make eye contact; avoid being defensive
   e. a, b, and d

2. Which of the following series lists the elements of effective communication?
   a. Sender, receiver, message, channel, feedback
   b. Sender, receiver, message, direction, response
   c. Speaker, listener, point, medium, reaction
   d. Speaker, respondent, purpose, route, organization
   e. To, from, directionality, reason, accomplishment

3. Broadly speaking, in our culture personal space is typically ____, while social space is ____. Of these types of spaces, ____ is more likely to affect how communication is shaped.
   a. 0-3 feet; 4-12 feet; social space
   b. 1 ½-4 feet; 4-12 feet; personal space
   c. 1 ½-4 feet; 4-12 feet; social space
   d. 0-3 feet; 4-12 feet; personal space
   e. 1 ½-4 feet; 3-7 feet; personal space

4. Which type of nonverbal message deals with belonging, control, respect, or disapproval?
   a. Emotive messages
   b. Relational messages
   c. Relationship messages
   d. Interpersonal messages
   e. Intrapersonal messages

5. What is involved in language comprehension?
   a. Hearing sounds, processing words and organizing them, understanding abstract components, interpreting meaning
   b. Hearing sounds and understanding their meanings
   c. Speaking the same language as the sender
   d. Identifying word units, knowing their meanings, understanding their syntactical use, processing abstractions, interpreting meaning
   e. All of the above

6. To what degree is effective listening natural to all people?
   a. An innate ability to listen effectively is inborn.
   b. An innate ability to listen effectively is inborn for some people.
   c. An innate ability to listen effectively is inborn, but is quickly lost if not nurtured.
   d. An innate ability to listen effectively is inborn for some people, but will be lost if not nurtured by age three.
   e. An innate ability to listen effectively is not a natural skill.

7. Expressive language competency requires:
   a. Oral language
   b. Gesture
   c. Tone
   d. Context
   e. All of the above

8. The best way to emphasize an important point in a public presentation is:
   a. Prepare the audience by telling them you are about to reveal a key point.
   b. Speak more quickly to attract the audience's attention.
   c. Speak more slowly to give the audience time to consider what is being said.
   d. Pause for a long moment before delivering the point.
   e. Speak loudly to alert those whose minds are drifting.

9. Within a classroom setting, the reason for a debate is:
   a. To determine which side has the most correct answers
   b. To teach students to research, collaborate, argue, and listen
   c. To demonstrate to students that there is no ultimate truth
   d. To cast doubt on the other side's position
   e. All of the above

10. The earliest known writing on dramatic theory was:
   a. Plato's poetics
   b. Aristotle's poetics
   c. Virgil's poetics
   d. Virgil's dramatica
   e. Plato's allegories

11. Another word for "tragic flaw" is
   a. Hamartia
   b. Peripeteia
   c. Catharsis
   d. Character fault
   e. The unraveling

12. The study of aesthetics in literature and drama is <u>not</u> concerned with which of the following?
   a. Practical concerns
   b. Moral concerns
   c. Political concerns
   d. Ethical concerns
   e. All of the above

13. A good storyteller relates a story using:
   a. Sensory images
   b. A moral
   c. A thesis statement
   d. Rhyme
   e. All of the above

14. A teacher with an inattentive class can use which of the following dramatic techniques to gain their attention?
   a. Raise her voice above theirs.
   b. Make her voice commanding by speaking loudly at a low register.
   c. Drop a book or slam a drawer, lean forward on her desk, and speak slowly and deliberately in a low voice.
   d. Drop a book or slam a drawer, march forward, and speak in a loud, angry voice.
   e. a and b

15. A detective and a therapist are working with a young child who was kidnapped to determine what occurred and in what order. They have provided stuffed animals, a toy car, some puppets, and various daily objects such as kitchen utensils, books, clothing, some toy buildings, etc. Following the child's lead, the detective "plays" with the child as she dramatically enacts her version of what happened. What theatrical element is being used?
   a. A puppet show
   b. Jungian psychology
   c. Creative dramatics
   d. Symbolism
   e. A musical

16. Which of the following is a principle actors follow?
   a. Allow skill and training to show in your acting.
   b. Speak your lines to someone rather than to yourself.
   c. The bigger the emotion, the more dramatically it must be expressed.
   d. Be fully aware of your performance and control.
   e. Always have the next line of dialogue in the front of your mind.

17. Compared to recorded history, is oral history more or less accurate?
   a. More accurate; it was first told by someone who was there.
   b. Equally accurate in its own way
   c. Less accurate; each generation forgets details and adds some that aren't original.
   d. Less accurate; the people passing down oral history are often not educated.
   e. More accurate; the people passing down oral history can stick with the truth rather than with a political agenda.

18. The history club has decided to do a reader's theater of an obscure 18ᵗʰ century British play they have come across. Which of the following best describes their production?
    a. Period costumes; full historically accurate staging; lighting done with candles for authenticity
    b. Period costumes; full historically accurate staging; lighting is dim to suggest authenticity
    c. Period costumes; minimal but historically accurate staging; low lighting for mood; actors improvise
    d. Minimal or no costumes; minimal or no staging; actors read from scripts
    e. Period costumes; no staging; actors read from scripts

19. The exercise called repetition used by Meisner in his acting training involves:
    a. Two actors repeating the same phrase back and forth repeatedly
    b. One actor repeating the same phrase over and over
    c. One actor speaking and another acting as a chorus
    d. Two actors speaking chorally
    e. All of the above

20. How does an actor best develop a character?
    a. Read the play to understand how the character relates to others.
    b. Learn lines quickly to internalize them.
    c. Find commonality with the character.
    d. Avoid obvious or stereotypical responses.
    e. All of the above

21. Speaking extemporaneously involves:
    a. Memorizing the speech so you don't need to read it
    b. Speaking energetically and quickly without knowing yourself what you'll say next
    c. Letting the audience see that you are not prepared so they will relate sympathetically
    d. Pausing to gather thoughts before speaking
    e. All of the above

22. Making a strong argument in a speech, conversation, or debate requires:
    a. Forceful delivery
    b. Acknowledging the opposing point of view with respect
    c. Demonstrating the weakness of the opposing view with mockery
    d. Seizing the floor when the opponent's point is strong
    e. Seizing the floor when the opponent's point is weak

23. Lincoln-Douglas debate format emphasizes:
    a. Logical thought, ethics, and philosophical point of view
    b. Logical thought, ethics, and passion
    c. Passion, control, and ethics
    d. Virtue, kindness, and compassion
    e. Strength, control, and determination

24. Among the types of debate formats used in high school and college debates are:
    a. Classical, extemporaneous, impromptu, moot court, and mock trial
    b. Classic, policy, simulated legislature, and spontaneous
    c. Extemporaneous, Montreal style, Australian universities, and online
    d. a, b, and c
    e. None of the above

25. The purposes of oratory are to:
    a. Influence, convince, persuade
    b. Inform, entertain, influence
    c. Inform, control, delight
    d. Delight, entertain, amuse
    e. All of the above

26. Metaphor, a rhetorical device, is used in oratory to:
    a. Compare two distinct things using "like" or "as"
    b. Surprise listeners
    c. Introduce a new idea via a familiar one
    d. Make the speech poetic and beautiful
    e. Cause listeners to think philosophically

27. Which of the following is true of a debate coach?
    I. A debate coach is highly trained in logic.
    II. A debate coach teaches a body of knowledge to team members.
    III. A debate coach nurtures and develops mental skills.
    IV. A debate coach questions and responds instead of leading and ordering.
    V. Debate coaches deserve respect; team members must never disagree with them.
    VI. A debate coach wears many hats; she raises money, reads arguments, and does administrative paperwork.
    a. I, II, III, IV, V, and VI
    b. None of the above
    c. I, II, III, and V
    d. I, II, V, and VI
    e. III, IV, and VI

28. Synecdoche is:
    a. A city in New York State
    b. Comparing two unlike things using like or as
    c. Two events that happen simultaneously in the act of public speaking, often a verbal event juxtaposed with a nonverbal one
    d. Substituting the part for the whole
    e. A term for the pregnant pause before the main point is delivered

29. The week-long National Speech and Debate Tournament offers Supplemental Events in which of the following categories?
    a. Extemporaneous Commentary, Expository Speaking, Prose Interpretation, Dramatic Irony
    b. Extemporaneous Speaking, Expository Commentary, Prose Interpretation, Dramatic Irony
    c. Impromptu Speaking, Expository Speaking, Prose Interpretation, Poetic Interpretation
    d. Extemporaneous Commentary, Expository Speaking, Prose Interpretation, Poetic Interpretation
    e. All of the above

30. Interpersonal communications can be unclear due to:
    a. Misinterpretation
    b. Assumptions
    c. Environmental context
    d. Relational context
    e. All of the above

31. In what way is a lucid dream intrapersonal communication?
    a. Every object in the dream is symbolic of the dreamer.
    b. The dreamer, in the midst of dreaming, is signaling herself that she is asleep and dreaming.
    c. In no way; dreams have nothing to do with communication.
    d. By speaking in her sleep, the dreamer is attempting to communicate.
    e. a, b, and d

32. One form of interpersonal communication common to businesses is gossip. The negative aspects of gossip are widely recognized. It causes hurt feelings, destroys self-confidence, and can be cruel. In what way might gossip be considered a useful form of interpersonal business communication from a manager's perspective?
    a. It offers a way of passing the buck.
    b. It clarifies status.
    c. It can be used to share unofficial information quickly.
    d. It strengthens social connections.
    e. In no way; gossip is always destructive.

33. How many meaningful facial expressions have been catalogued?
    a. 76
    b. 154
    c. 10,000
    d. 136,549
    e. Over a million, but many are variations within a category

34. Understood cultural "rules" regarding acceptable modes of expression that men and women share, those that are appropriate for men only, and those that are appropriate for women only are called:
    a. Gender display rules
    b. Gender distinction rules
    c. Gender distinction conventions
    d. Sexual characteristics
    e. Sexual display

35. Sub vocalization is:
    a. Tone of voice that shades meaning
    b. Groaning, moaning, whimpering, or other nonverbal vocal expressions
    c. Mentally "spoken" words when reading
    d. Talking without awareness, such as in one's sleep
    e. Poor enunciation

36. What do microexpressions communicate?
    a. Nothing; they are transitional muscular contractions as one facial expression changes to another.
    b. Fleeting, minor emotion
    c. Emotions that are being suppressed
    d. Passing thoughts
    e. Reactions to what is being heard

37. Which of the following behavior clusters are found in people with a high degree of interpersonal competence?
    a. Developed vocabulary, maintains relationships for many years, avoids conflict
    b. Prioritizes others' feelings, finds value in serving others, highly empathetic
    c. Self-disciplined, excellent language skills, interested in human nature
    d. Self-aware, maintains healthy relationships, uses positivity to resolve disagreements
    e. Strong communication skills, good listener, concerned with opinions of others

38. How might intrapersonal communication enhance interpersonal communication?
    a. Daydreaming is a type of personal rehearsal for a potential intercommunication.
    b. Reflecting upon a conversation can lead to deeper understanding of the communication's meaning.
    c. Keeping a journal creates self-awareness.
    d. Gesturing, a type of self-talk, adds to a message's meaning.
    e. All of the above

39. Within an office or organization, interpersonal communication can be seen as vertical or horizontal. The term vertical communication refers to communication that involves:
    a. A speaker and a listener
    b. Messages that descend from upper echelon to lower level employees, becoming less reliable with each drop
    c. A sender and a recipient
    d. Messages that move from the top down and from the bottom up
    e. A series of communications, each of which depends upon the previous communication for its meaning to become clear

40. Which of the following situations might affect someone's self-concept?
    a. Expecting someone to accept an invitation and being turned down
    b. Successfully teaching someone a skill you know well
    c. Failing an exam after studying hard
    d. Being the subject of gossip
    e. All of the above

41. An identity crisis arises when:
   a. The sense of a unified self through time is challenged.
   b. A primary relationship dissolves.
   c. An individual is the object of an attack.
   d. A group or team someone wants to join rejects him.
   e. All of the above

42 Identity achievement occurs when:
   a. An individual is accepted into a family, team, or group.
   b. An individual discovers she is fully self-enabled.
   c. An individual makes a commitment to a single identity.
   d. An individual rejects a person or situation that threatens her sense of self.
   e. None of the above

43. Two people on a first date are taking turns telling one another about themselves. They are communicating their histories, their aspirations, and details about their daily lives. This is an act of:
   a. Courtship
   b. Self-disclosure
   c. Self-assessment
   d. Self-revelation
   e. Self-sacrifice

44. Which of the following acts of self-disclosure is most revealing?
   a. Sharing details about long past events that were emotionally laden
   b. Sharing details about current events that are emotionally laden
   c. Offering a comprehensive timeline of one's personal history
   d. Holding back information you know will hurt the other
   e. b and c

45. How can a teacher best assess whether her lesson has been fully understood by students?
   a. Give them a 360 degree assessment.
   b. Ask them to complete a self-assessment.
   c. Ask them to write about the lesson in their journals.
   d. Ask them to explain the lesson back to her.
   e. All of the above are equally effective methods of assessment

46. Which three components does the Spitzberg & Cupach component model of communication competence include?
   a. Knowledge, skill, motivation
   b. Sender, receiver, message
   c. Desire, plan, achievement
   d. Concept, organization, delivery
   e. Creation, sharing, interpretation

47. A study group facilitator has one member who dominates the conversation and one member who is unwilling to participate at all. What is the best course of action?
   a. Open a group conversation in which members confront the domineering individual.
   b. Privately ask the domineering member to allow others to speak.
   c. Privately ask the reticent member to participate more.
   d. Nonverbally communicate to both members.
   e. b and c

48. Which of the following statements about discussions held to resolve an issue is/are true?
   I.   Each member of the group should get an equal amount of time to speak.
   II. All ideas are equally important, regardless of what they are or who said them.
   III. Individuals with greater knowledge should contribute more.
   IV. Individuals with greater knowledge should not be resented.
   V.   The floor should be held by each speaker in turn, and no interruptions should be allowed.
   a. I and II
   b. III and IV
   c. I, II, and V
   d. III, IV, and V
   e. I, II, IV, and V

49. Which of the following strategies for managing conflict within a group is a win/win?
   a. Compromise
   b. Accommodate
   c. Collaborate
   d. Compete
   e. Avoid

50. What are the drawbacks of compromise?
   a. Essential principles and goals can get lost.
   b. There is no clear winner.
   c. As a strategy, it is very time-consuming.
   d. It is often the result of bullying.
   e. All of the above

51. When is avoidance an appropriate strategy for a leader or member of a business team?
   a. Never; problems must be dealt with head-on.
   b. When the individual has little influence or will likely be ignored
   c. When more important things must be dealt with
   d. b and c
   e. When the situation has become uncomfortable

52. What is the first step in the reflective thinking or standard agenda approach to group decision making?
   a. Selecting group members
   b. Clarifying the issue or problem
   c. Brainstorming
   d. Writing the questions the facilitator will ask
   e. Deciding upon whether the group will be open, closed, or open by invitation only

53. A marketing group has assigned a team to a new ad campaign. The team is having their initial meeting. Someone suggests that everyone throw out as many ideas as possible without editing or suppressing any that may seem off the mark. Chaos erupts, yet by the end of the meeting the team has a clear idea of the direction they would like to go. This is called:
   a. Chaos theory
   b. Multiple minds
   c. Thunder thinking
   d. Brainstorming
   e. Groupthink

54. A group of very close church members are interviewing ministers. They share the same values and ideals, and are certain the community trusts them absolutely and believes they would never make a bad decision. The group's leader is very strong-willed and capable. This group:
   a. Has a healthy self-concept
   b. Lives their principles
   c. Is vulnerable to groupthink
   d. Is vulnerable to attacks from people of lesser values
   e. Is invincible and can handle any problems

55. Which of the following are negative outcomes associated with a group that has fallen under the influence of groupthink?
   a. Seeking only information that supports pre-existing positions
   b. Failure to consider a number of alternatives
   c. Failure to examine one another's ideas thoroughly
   d. Failure to have a contingency plan to fall back on
   e. All of the above

56. Research and experience have proven that abdicratic groups typically:
   a. Are difficult to penetrate and nearly impossible to challenge
   b. Are composed of group members who are happy with their relative positions
   c. Are able to accomplish more in less time than other types of groups
   d. Disintegrate quickly
   e. Are authoritarian

57. Four common leadership styles are:
   a. Autocratic, democratic, laissez-faire, abdicratic
   b. Autocratic, abdicratic, abracadabracatic, disincratic
   c. Autocratic, community-based, familial, abdicratic
   d. Autocratic, one-man-one-vote, cooperative, dissociative
   e. Autocratic, cooperative, collaborative, abdicratic

58. Initiator contributor, information seeker, opinion seeker, elaborator, coordinator, evaluator-critic, energizer, and procedural-technician are all examples of:
   a. Self-identifications
   b. Task oriented group roles
   c. Social group roles
   d. Anti-social group roles
   e. Individualistic group roles

59. Harrison Whitlock is writing a speech. He has researched the topic thoroughly and has a number of facts and statistics to include. He has completed an opening, outlined the purpose, and is in the process of collecting points to support his position. He will finish with a strong conclusion. This type of speech is a(n) _____ speech.
   a. Persuasive
   b. Introductory
   c. Demonstration
   d. Informational
   e. Toast

60. Which of the following is true about an informational speech?
   I. It should be no longer than 45 minutes.
   II. The speaker's position should be supported with sophisticated visual aids.
   III. Non-verbal communication should be incorporated.
   IV. The speech should be written in highly charged, emotionally strong language.
   V. It is acceptable to read the speech from a text, especially when a lot of visual aids are being used.
   a. I, II, III, IV, V
   b. II, III, V
   c. I, IV, V
   d. III
   e. IV

61. Esteban has been asked to speak to a group of music students about his work as a professional musician. He wants to talk about his instrument, the bass, and how he must make adjustments for the various sound systems and acoustics he must deal with. What type of speech should he present?
   a. Informational
   b. Persuasive
   c. Demonstration
   d. How-to
   e. Personal narrative

62. Before writing a speech, the writer needs to do an audience analysis, which considers which of these factors:
   a. Age, gender, culture
   b. Nationality, religious affiliation
   c. Skills and experiences with the topic
   d. Audience needs and interests
   e. All of the above

63. Yi's grandmother turns 90 this year. Yi has been asked to give a speech in her grandmother's honor. The grandmother's 9 living children, 32 grandchildren, and 57 great-grandchildren will be present, as well as family friends, neighbors, and members of the press. What should Yi include in her toast?
   a. Visual aids showing the family tree
   b. A timeline scroll that marks all the important events in her grandmother's life
   c. Funny and moving anecdotes about her grandmother and various members of the audience
   d. Historically accurate information about the times when her grandmother was young
   e. All of the above

64. Which of the following statements regarding eye contact is false?
   a. It suggests confidence and presence of mind.
   b. It lends a humanizing sensibility to a speech.
   c. Audience members are drawn into the presentation if the speaker makes repeated eye contact that lasts long enough to suggest emotional intimacy.
   d. It sparks audience interest because the occasion of the speech seems, on some level, to be a conversation in which they are engaged.
   e. It gives listeners the sense that the speaker is authoritative, knowledgeable, and in control.

65. Extemporaneously presenting a speech might be done because:
   a. It clarifies the major points in the appropriate order.
   b. The digitally produced visual aids add sophistication.
   c. It results in the audience adopting a can-do attitude and leads to action.
   d. It heightens the sense of immediacy and originality.
   e. a, c, and d

66. The company Mr. Gibbons works for hopes to make connections with another company in Japan. Because Mr. Gibbons is funny, uses body language dramatically, and isn't the least bit shy, he has been chosen to introduce his company's recent work in a brief after-dinner speech in Tokyo. While delivering his speech, he is horrified to discover that many of the audience members are nodding with their eyes closed. What is going on?
   a. He has offended them somehow; they are giving him the chance to save face.
   b. His dramatic nonverbal style has overwhelmed them.
   c. They are listening intently.
   d. They are bored.
   e. They've just eaten and are comfortable enough with him to drift off.

67. Public speaking is ultimately always about:
   a. Achieving the speaker's objectives
   b. Meeting the audience's needs
   c. Provoking deep thought
   d. a and b
   e. a, b, and c

68. Rehearsing a speech by videotaping it will help a speaker:
   a. Recognize effective nonverbal information
   b. Recognize confusing nonverbal information
   c. Recognize effective speech patterns
   d. Recognize where the speech loses focus
   e. All of the above

69. Public speakers want to give speeches that make their audience pay attention, but they also want to give speeches whose messages are meaningful enough to remain in audience member's minds. This can best be accomplished with:
   a. Simple language and stories
   b. Strict logical progression
   c. Sophisticated language and ideas
   d. Intense emotion and drama
   e. Eye contact

70. In the event of technology failure with a computer or projector, the speaker should:
    a. Make entertaining comments while trying to repair it.
    b. Ask for help from technologically savvy audience members.
    c. It depends upon the subject and the audience.
    d. Describe the visual aids since they can't be seen.
    e. Speak extemporaneously.

71. Nervousness can make inexperienced public speakers stammer, speak in a monotone, neglect gestures or overuse them, or talk too much or too little. Experienced public speakers:
    a. Have conquered nervousness through practice
    b. Mentally undress audience members to turn their own nervousness into amusement
    c. Use skills and techniques to manage nervousness
    d. Know they are in control
    e. All of the above

72. How should statistics, numbers, and percentages be used in a speech?
    a. The more the better; they prove points.
    b. The more the better; they demonstrate to the audience that the speaker knows his subject.
    c. The more the better; they will convince the audience.
    d. Judiciously and carefully; too many may confuse audience members.
    e. a, b, and c

73. Mr. Diallo feels that his speech is going very well. His audience seems engrossed; several have closed their eyes to concentrate, and a number of others are scribbling notes like crazy. A few are checking the conference materials. Mr. Diallo's audience is:
    a. Inspired by his presentation
    b. In agreement with his position
    c. Opposed to his position
    d. Disinterested in his position
    e. None of the above

74. Which of the following methods of assessment are useful for student presentations?
    a. Dialogue with audience
    b. Audience feedback with a rubric
    c. Videotape
    d. Self-assessment with rubrics
    e. All of the above

75. Cookie Baker is excited about her new job with a cookware company. She will appear at cooking shows, county fairs, exhibitions, and culinary schools to acquaint the audience with a new line of cookware. What type of speech should she employ?
    a. Informational
    b. Instructional
    c. Debate
    d. Demonstration
    e. How-to

76. Numerical data should be:
    a. Presented visually as well as orally
    b. Presented in the context of an image
    c. Repeated throughout the speech
    d. Translated into something the audience can relate to
    e. All of the above

77. What strategies might be useful for a leader who wants to introduce a change in a company's culture?
    I.   Announce the change; emphasize the transition will be smooth.
    II.   Encourage general questions, but discourage specific ones.
    III. Create a vision; ensure senior management members show enthusiasm.
    IV.   Have senior management members change their behaviors to align with new ideals; modify the structure of the organization to facilitate the changes.
    V.   Extinguish water-cooler gossip regarding the upcoming changes. Provide information regarding old behaviors no longer tolerated and new behaviors that will replace them.
    VI.   Remove employees who don't fit the new ideal; integrate new hires into the company's culture.
    a. I, II, III, IV
    b. I, III, IV, V
    c. III, IV, VI
    d. I, II, IV
    e. I, IV, V, VI

78. According to the two-step flow of communication model, ideas initially flow from _____ to _____.
    a. Speakers, listeners
    b. Mass media, society
    c. Opinion leaders, the public
    d. Mass media, opinion leaders
    e. None of the above

79. One mass communication theory holds that when an individual believes her position on a particular topic is not in alignment with that of most others, she will not speak up. This theory is called:
    a. Spiral of silence
    b. Don't ask, don't tell
    c. Silence is golden
    d. Safety in silence
    e. Groupthink

80. Which of the following statements about the spiral of silence is false?
    a. The spiral of silence has a temporally limited hold on public view.
    b. There must be a moral or ethical factor involved for the spiral to become active.
    c. Social consensus deactivates the spiral.
    d. Mass media has little effect on the spiral.
    e. All of the statements are true.

81. According to Marshall McLuhan, the medium is the message. This means:
   a. The medium in which the message appears affects how the message is read.
   b. An advertiser's message is easiest for the public to accept when it falls in the middle range of popular beliefs.
   c. Effective advertising should be transparent, as though it were channeled by a medium.
   d. Consumers do not like to imagine themselves at the far end of the spectrum; ads should be aimed at the average.
   e. All of the above

82. Some types of new media that scholars are turning their analytical eyes to include:
   a. Cable, wireless computers, Internet
   b. Internet, mobile phones, video games
   c. Internet, video games, faxes
   d. Internet, video games, semiotics
   e. Internet, gang signs, semiotics

83. The culturalist theory developed in the early 1990s holds that:
   a. Culture is determined by media.
   b. Media is determined by culture.
   c. The public uses mass media messages to interpret their own meanings.
   d. Mass media messages use the public to gain ever-widening influence.
   e. Influence and power feed and feed upon one another.

84. In television situation comedies, thin female actors are more often ____ by male characters, while heavy female actors are more often ____.
   a. Praised; insulted
   b. Protected; sacrificed
   c. Rejected; pursued
   d. Praised; ignored
   e. Treated politely; treated competitively

85. Which of the following is not an effect of new media?
   a. The way the public involves itself with media has changed.
   b. More diversity of cultural and political opinion is being expressed and supported.
   c. There is a heightened sense of personal responsibility for opinions.
   d. Consumers are more educated.
   e. Consumers are suffering from information overload.

86. ____ describes an individual who is focused on a medium's message. ____ describes an individual who is absorbing the message while doing something else. ____ describes an individual focused on another task while a medium is delivering a message.
   a. Absorbed; considering; distracted
   b. Absorbed; distracted; absent
   c. Primary involvement; secondary involvement; tertiary involvement
   d. First level involvement; second level involvement; disengaged involvement
   e. Single involvement; dual involvement; disengaged

87. The uses and gratifications model holds that motivations for attending to media include:
    a. The audience identifies with values or roles expressed, thereby reinforcing their behaviors and beliefs.
    b. The audience seeks a sense of relationship and security.
    c. The audience seeks information or knowledge.
    d. The audience wants to escape through entertainment.
    e. All of the above

88. The theory concerned with the effect advertising and voter campaigns have on behavior is called:
    a. Effects theory
    b. Causes theory
    c. Considerations theory
    d. Manipulations theory
    e. Control theory

89. Which of the following are political actors?
    a. Politicians
    b. Politicians and strategists
    c. Politicians, strategists, and interest groups
    d. Politicians, strategists, interest groups, and the media
    e. Politicians, strategists, interest groups, the media, and consumers

90. Videoconferencing, the Internet, mobile phones, and intranets and other information and communication technologies:
    a. Have changed the face of business
    b. Have created a global marketplace
    c. Have changed the face of politics
    d. Have negatively affected economies
    e. All of the above

91. Formative assessment is also called:
    a. Growth assessment
    b. Development assessment
    c. Cumulative assessment
    d. Educative assessment
    e. Peer assessment

92. One way in which objective assessment differs from subjective assessment is:
    a. Objective assessment is summative; subjective assessment is cumulative.
    b. Objective assessment is cumulative; subjective assessment is summative.
    c. Objective assessment has only one right answer; subjective assessment does not.
    d. Objective assessment can have numerous correct answers; subjective assessment cannot.
    e. Subjective assessments are often computerized; objective assessments are not.

93. In terms of teaching, moral motivation means:
    a. Recognizing and insisting upon fairness
    b. Being aware of how actions affect others
    c. Living one's moral convictions through action

    d.   Placing moral values above personal values
    e.   All of the above

94. Performance based assessment:
    a.   Evaluates a student's concert, speech, or other public performance
    b.   Is based upon real-life tasks
    c.   Is a formative assessment
    d.   Has been largely discredited
    e.   None of the above

95. A teacher is composing a test. Half of the questions involve discrete point items, which are:
    a.   Questions with multiple correct answers
    b.   Essay questions
    c.   Cumulative questions
    d.   Questions that require deductive reasoning
    e.   Questions that focus on one point only

96. Which of the following criteria might a teacher use to assess a student's public speaking project?
    a.   Chooses and fine tunes a topic for a specific audience
    b.   Communicates the thesis sufficiently
    c.   Ideas progress logically
    d.   Selects appropriate and quality support material
    e.   All of the above

97. A teacher has an English language learner in her speech class. His English is excellent, but his accent is pronounced. When he presents his class project, a speech about folk tales from his native country, the class is confused. It is difficult to understand what he is saying. This is probably because:
    a.   His accent is too strong.
    b.   He is making a lot of grammatical mistakes.
    c.   He is stressing words incorrectly.
    d.   He didn't practice enough.
    e.   All of the above

98. When selecting a text for a public speaking course at the high school level, the teacher should look for:
    a.   A comprehensive text
    b.   A text written at a level slightly above students' abilities
    c.   A text written at the level of students' abilities
    d.   A text that employs contemporary slang
    e.   All of the above

99. A teacher wants to give her public speaking students exciting topics so they will get involved with their material. Where can she find appropriate topics?
    a.   Online
    b.   From other teachers
    c.   From books
    d.   From her students
    e.   All of the above

100. Is it better to assign a topic that is extremely specific or one that is open to interpretation, and why?
   a. Specific, so students know what is expected of them
   b. Specific, to keep students on-topic
   c. Open to interpretation, so students can bring their own experiences into play
   d. Open to interpretation, because teenagers don't like being told what to do
   e. It completely depends upon the topic.

Multiple Choice Answers

1. E: Listening effectively requires the conscious use of a number of skills. First, the listener should focus on what's being said. The listener can show the speaker she's being heard by making eye contact or leaning forward. Forming an early opinion or judgment can cause a misinterpretation of the intended message, and becoming defensive shuts down an open mind. Paraphrasing and asking questions can help clarify the speaker's intended meaning. Paying attention to tone of voice, inflection, mood, or emotion is also an effective listening technique because they contribute to the message. Tapping on the table (c) is not an effective listening technique.

2. A: In both writing and speaking, effective communication involves a sender who initiates the communication and a receiver (audience) for whom it's intended. The message is the communication that is received, which may be different from what was intended. The channel is the medium by which the message travels. It might be an e-mail, a presentation, a commercial, or a verbal exchange. Feedback is how the receiver responds, and helps the sender know if the message arrived intact.

3. B: The environment in which a communication is initiated and received plays an important role in how that communication manifests, both because the environmental context contributes to meaning by offering reference, and because the environment can enhance or detract from the receiver's ability to process the message. Personal space (about 1 ½ - 4 feet) has a greater bearing on the formation or receipt of the message than does social space (about 4 – 12 feet). It's important to recognize that both social and personal space vary from culture to culture; what is acceptable in one may not be in another.

4. B: Relational messages, as opposed to content messages, are concerned with the relationship between a speaker and a recipient rather than with the overt subject of the communication. They may convey belonging, respect, or disapproval, among other things. They are frequently largely or entirely nonverbal; because of this, they may be supported with verbal feedback to confirm them. The content of the message, "Should I come over after work?" is a logistical request. If a speaker leans forward to touch a recipient who is weeping, the relational message is "Do you need my support?" The recipient might respond with a nod and a grateful look, or might clarify the speaker's offer by saying, "I won't be good company, but you can come."

5. D: Language comprehension doesn't necessarily involve sounds or speaking. For example, sign language and written language use different materials to form words. It does, however, require identifying words, knowing their meanings, recognizing how they are being used in the context of a sentence, understanding abstractions such as idioms or references, and drawing a conclusion regarding the message's meaning.

6. E: Listening is an essential communication skill. In any type of communication, participants spend a substantially greater amount of time listening than speaking. Listening is a learned skill as opposed to a natural, innate ability. Children learn to listen by modeling behaviors demonstrated by others and by practicing. They quickly learn that listening to tone, speed, and volume can offer important nonverbal clues about the overall meaning of a message.

7. E: Expressive language competency is the ability to express oneself orally. In order to use expressive language capably, the speaker must have control over nonverbal as well as verbal aspects of language. First, he or she must obviously know how to use oral language. Body language and gestures can add to or clarify the meaning of an oral message. For instance, turning away suggests dismissal, while leaning toward the recipient suggests inclusion. The tone in which a

- 155 -

statement is made can indicate irony, satire, or enthusiasm. It can also introduce emotional or psychological overtones. The context in which a statement is made also affects meaning.

8. D: Before delivering a central point in a speech, the speaker should stop talking for a moment. During that moment of silence, however, it's important not to disengage. Instead, the speaker should make eye contact, lean or step forward, take an audible deep breath, raise his or her eyebrows, or use other nonverbal methods to alert the audience that what follows is important.

9. B: Debate is a highly useful classroom technique in that it teaches the skills necessary for communication. Each participant must conduct research and consider what he or she knows about the subject; work collaboratively with other students to clarify beliefs and positions; present an argument that is logical, lucid, and on-point; listen to the response as well as to the other team's message; and respond when appropriate.

10. B: Aristotle's poetics, written around 335 B.C., is a philosophical text concerned with dramatic presentations and poetry. Poetic genres are categorized in terms of the vehicle of language (language, harmony, and rhythm); objects [agents (actors or symbolic objects) and actions]; and their representative modes, specifically tragedy, comedy, lyric poetry, epic poetry, and dithyramb, a hymn sung and danced by performers.

11. A: A hamartia is a flaw in a character's perception, belief, or personality which results in an action that leads to the undoing of that character or a situation. The hamartia might be an accidental error, an evil or wrong action, or a sin. While a hamartia might arise because of an evil done to another person, the action itself contains an element of innocence. It is never intended to cause the results it does.

12. E: Aesthetics is concerned with the appreciation of beauty (or ugliness) for its own sake. It examines how an object, whether a song, a dramatic monologue, a poem, a color, or another artistic element, affects the feelings and thoughts of a perceiver. Aesthetic appreciation is immediate and visceral, and is not concerned with whether an object is "good," socially acceptable, moral, ethical, politically correct, or practical. In other words, social judgments have no bearing on the value of an object with respect to its ability to move an observer.

13. A: One of the most important elements of a good story is words that create vivid images in the minds of listeners. Images are mental pictures, and are primarily created with sensory detail such as sound, aroma, texture, visual description, and sometimes taste. Vivid images can describe a detailed setting that springs to life in the listeners' minds, characters that are unique and easy to tell apart because of their individual descriptions, and action that is easy to imagine.

14. C: Creating a loud sound that isn't a verbal one will grab the students' attention because it is percussive and unexpected. Leaning forward on the desk makes the teacher appear larger and more powerful. Changing the pace of a verbal delivery alerts the listeners (or in this case, the non-listeners) that something important is being said. Deliberate pronunciation allows the teacher to place emphasis on certain syllables, which forces students to pay attention to the message. While screaming might be tempting, it causes listeners to turn away from the message rather than pay attention to it. When the teacher lowers her voice, it causes the students to lean forward in order to hear what is being said.

15. C: Creative dramatics involves an informal, usually spontaneous, acting out of a story or event. While it is theatrical in presentation, any staging is also spontaneous, and consists of objects at hand. Creative dramatics is often symbolic in nature, and the participants (as well as observers) recognize that the actors' movements, words, and choice of props all contain meaning that goes far beyond the surface. This means that not only are the actors involved in symbolic play, but the

- 156 -

listeners must also participate creatively by determining the symbolic importance of the performance.

16. B: Lines don't become part of a theatrical conversation unless the actor directs them towards a listener. Unskilled actors may memorize their lines and speak them according to the director's instructions, but if the actor doesn't have an internal conviction that his part of the dialogue is part of a conversation that is unfolding at that moment for the first time, the audience will sense it and the illusion will fail.

17. B: One way of looking at historical records, whether written or spoken, is that all records are produced based on the perspectives of individuals. All perspectives reflect perceptions, attitudes, beliefs, mores, and values. All perspectives are shaped by some kind of agenda, even if the historian is unaware he or she even has one. It can be said that history recorded by human beings will always be incomplete and flawed. Oral history, like written history, captures a period of time within some sort of perceptual framework. As the tale is passed from generation to generation, certain details that don't resonate will be dropped or replaced by others. In this way, a piece of oral history becomes composed of multiple layers over the years, each of which reflects not only the perspectives of the tellers, but also the teller's times.

18. D: Reader's theater, or RT, is used to support the reading of literature. While the form is rather fluid and can manifest in a number of ways, reader's theater is typically minimal in terms of production elements. The narrative, not the staging, is primary in importance. If there is any staging, it is simple or even symbolic. For instance, a large drawing of a chair may be used instead of a real one. Costumes are rarely used. Any that are used are symbolic or uniform. Actors don't memorize scripts. They are held by the actors, who refer to them as needed.

19. A: Sanford Meisner, who trained with method actor Lee Strasberg, developed a set of interconnected exercises that become increasingly more complicated as they progress. These exercises teach actors to draw upon their own emotional experiences and improvise around a situation. Repetition, one of Meisner's central exercises, involves two actors repeating the same phrase back and forth, with each repetition being somehow unique in that it is spoken as a reaction to the other actor's tone of voice, behavior, or other element used to add uniqueness to the phrase.

20. E: In order to develop a character, an actor must first understand the character. A thorough understanding of a play helps the reader understand how the character responds to other characters and situations. Internalizing dialogue helps the actor "own" the character's words. Finding commonality between the character and personal life experiences helps an actor relate to the character. Playing the character without making stereotypical or obvious choices is also important. For example, an irritable person doesn't snap at everyone constantly in real life, but only sometimes.

21. D: Speaking extemporaneously requires spontaneity. Being invited to say a few words at an award ceremony, being asked to elaborate on a point during a business meeting, or being asked to speak under other circumstances in which the individual does not have a speech prepared does not mean speaking without thinking. Among the techniques that make speaking extemporaneously appear easy is pausing for a moment before beginning to make eye contact or communicate a nonverbal message, such as an amused look. In this time, the speaker can gather a couple of thoughts on the subject and start by speaking slowly and with confidence. Keeping the speech brief and concentrating on relating to the audience are other techniques.

22. B: A strong argument is not made by forcing people to pay attention, interrupting another speaker, or belittling an idea, person, or group. These behaviors simply weaken the speaker's position because they each demonstrate in a different way that the speaker is not in control of his own ideas,

and must therefore try to control the situation by using emotion. The most successful arguments acknowledge the strongest points of the opposition, and then unemotionally dissect those points in order to find and demonstrate how they are flawed.

23. A: The Lincoln-Douglas debate format focuses on making a logical argument, communicating the speaker's ethical standards, and taking a philosophical position. This debate format is commonly used by debate leagues and in competitions. In this type of debate, 40-minute rounds are broken into 3-5 minutes of prep time and 13 minutes of speaking time for each debater.

24. A: Classical debate, an alternative to the more common policy debate, focuses on real-life discussions rather than abstract strategic arguments. Extemporaneous debate involves no pre-planning and very limited research. In an impromptu debate, which is less formal than other styles, each team member is given five minutes to speak. This is followed by a 10 minute discussion period and a brief rebuttal. Moot court and mock trial debates involve creating a courtroom environment and using a courtroom approach.

25. B: The reasons for public speaking are many: to teach, trade, punish, exhibit, advertise, apologize, denounce, plead, train, and reflect. These purposes, however, can be grouped into just three categories. A teacher lecturing students or a CEO addressing shareholders at an annual meeting are both using rhetoric to inform. A public speaker might also seek to influence an audience. A politician running for office, a missionary speaking to villagers, and an attorney arguing before a judge are all using oratory in this way. Finally, oratory can entertain. Examples of individuals that use oratory in this way include stand-up comedians and storytellers.

26. C: Every school child is taught that metaphor is the direct comparison of two different things. An example of a metaphor is: "The clouds are pillows of cotton." Looking more deeply into the heart of how metaphor operates, however, it is clear that it is an effective rhetorical device. Metaphor simultaneously allows for great linguistic economy while inviting listeners to embrace new ideas by linking them to ideas with which they are already comfortable and familiar.

27. E: A debate coach nurtures and develops students' mental skills. Debate coaches guide team members to understand and embrace their own ideas and express those ideas logically, aesthetically, creatively, and fully. Rather than instructing team members on how to handle a debate, the role of the coach is to listen and respond with questions so that the debater learns to fine-tune his argument. Coaches have many responsibilities in addition to encouraging individuals to think and express their unique ideas. They are often also responsible for practical tasks such as fundraising, scheduling, paperwork, and more.

28. D: Synecdoche is a rhetorical device in which a part of something is used to represent the entirety. Conversely, it may involve referring to an entire object to represent one specific manifestation. For example, referring to a business man as a "suit" is a figure of speech in which a part (his suit) is used to signify the man himself. Alternatively, when a thief tells his partner to run because "the law" is coming, the abstract idea of law is used to represent a specific individual who manifests it.

29. D: The National Speech and Debate Tournament offers Extemporaneous Commentary, Expository Speaking, Prose Interpretation, and Poetic Interpretation as Supplemental Events. Qualifying Events include Domestic Extemporaneous Speaking, Foreign Extemporaneous Speaking, Humorous Interpretation, Duo Interpretation, Dramatic Interpretation, Lincoln-Douglas Debate, Original Oratory, Policy Debate, Public Forum Debate, and Congressional Debate. Consolation Events are Impromptu Speaking and Storytelling.

30. E: Theoretically, no message arrives intact. Words ultimately don't mean the same thing to different people, so messages can easily be misinterpreted. A sender assumes recipients will interpret the

meaning of each word in the same way, which can result in interpersonal communications being unclear. Gender, culture, and age contribute greatly to how speakers formulate and interpret messages. The message's physical environment can contribute to confusion due to distractions. The relationship the sender and receiver share, as well as the relationships under discussion, all shade a message's meaning.

31. B: In the midst of a lucid dream, the dreamer "awakens" within the dream and recognizes it as such. The lucid dreamer "plays" with the dream as an artist plays with materials, exploring impossibilities and manipulating the dream in a way that is highly conscious. This is a very intimate form of intrapersonal communication. The dreamer is simultaneously utterly vulnerable and at the mercy of the dream, and also a God-like presence that can shape the dream however she desires.

32. C: Informal communications are both common and essential within an office environment. A savvy manager knows that gossip is how employees share information, rumor, and innuendo. A manager who wants to prepare his department for an upcoming change that has not yet been officially announced can simply drop a suggestive hint to the right person to make sure everyone in the department hears the news. To the gossips themselves, gossip enhances social bonding. Although it is informal, gossip is also a political communicative channel.

33. C: Just 43 muscles in the human face are responsible for roughly 10,000 distinct expressions. Some posit that expressions are culturally bound and therefore learned, while others believe they are universal, shared, and innately recognized. The most basic emotions—sadness, anger, fear, disgust, contempt, joy, and surprise—are shared with primates, who recognize their meaning not only when they appear on the faces of other primates, but also when they are observed on the faces of human beings.

34. A: Display rules is a term describing the shared, understood norms regarding acceptable modes of expression for specific groups in specific situations. Meanings assigned to emotions vary from culture to culture, from gender to gender, and across generations. Emotional expressions that are considered perfectly acceptable within a romantic relationship or between a child and parent may violate the unspoken display rules in an office, for example. As another example, women are permitted and even expected to express sorrow through crying in many cultures, while men are expected to deny such a "feminine" feeling. If it must be expressed, it must be expressed incognito, perhaps as anger or disappointment, both of which are acceptable gender display rules for men.

35. C: Subvocalization occurs during the act of reading. Although it is silent and internalized, the speaker "hears" the sounds of words, and in doing so creates a way to remember what was read. During subvocalization, some people, especially children, may move their lips as though they are speaking aloud. Some genres demand greater attention to subvocalization than others. For example, the cadences and aesthetic language choices of poetry beg the reader to "hear" the aural music in the midst of reading silently.

36. C: Microexpressions appear and vanish so quickly that up to 90% of observers don't register them at all. In fact, the owner of the face that wears them may not even be conscious of the feelings that create them. Microexpressions are the result of buried emotions. A liar is likely to briefly wear a series of microexpressions as he denies a truth. A lover breaking up with another may say one thing, but her face might reflect something else. Anger, sadness, fear, contempt, disgust, happiness, and surprise are triggered on a non- intellectual level and seize the body. A speaker who tries to suppress the associated expression is most likely condensing it into a microexpression. The speaker may be aware or unaware of its manifestation.

37. D: People with interpersonal competence are self-aware. They create and maintain healthy relationships by being honest with themselves and others. They disclose what they know and feel,

- 159 -

offer emotional support, and are willing to risk vulnerability in order to initiate and continue relationships that are important to them. Although empathy is associated with interpersonal competence, these individuals maintain a healthy dose of self-respect. Should the words or actions of another disappoint these individuals, they will bring their feelings out in the open. They will attempt to work with the other individual to resolve the issues that have brought negative feelings to light in a positive manner.

38. **E:** Intrapersonal communication is a dialogue with the self; the sender and receiver embody the same being. Intrapersonal communication is how we make sense of the unknown, frightening, or confusing. It is also how we practice how we will communicate with another. Daydreaming and journal keeping are both used to clarify one's feelings and thoughts, and to practice how to shape them into words. Private reflection upon a conversation that has ended keeps that conversation alive as the individual doing the reflecting discovers greater meaning. Gestures are the body's way of underscoring or adding information to a message, and are one way the body talks to itself. Patting your belly while telling someone you're hungry, for example, is a message to both the sender and recipient.

39. **D:** Vertical communication is passed from a higher level employer to one below him, or from a lower level employee to a supervisor or manager. Vertical communication is used to send formal messages to employees at various levels, to announce policy changes, to inspire, and to provide direction. Bottom up communication, also called upward communication, offers subordinates a formal means by which to deliver information to superiors, ask questions, or report on the status of an assignment. Both top down and bottom up modes of communication function inside a collection of understood rules that permit these communications to proceed efficiently.

40. **B:** Self-concept is related to self-awareness and self-esteem, but is not the same thing. Self-concept is the full collection of beliefs and perceptions an individual has about herself in all dimensions, including interpersonal, intellectual, creative, and logical skills. Self-esteem, in which the self assesses or judges the self, is a sub-category of self-concept, and self-awareness is simply a consciousness of self. Self-concept changes little through time because it is concerned with stable characteristics ("This is who I am") rather than passing conditions ("I am angry"). Self-concept is reinforced or enhanced when expectations are met. When they are not, it is not affected much, except in times of serious self-doubt. Therefore, while successfully teaching someone else a skill would reinforce someone's self-concept, being the subject of gossip, having an invitation rejected, or failing an exam would not likely drastically alter an individual's self-concept.

41. **A:** While the dissolution of an important relationship, being attacked, or being rejected can certainly affect one's self-esteem, an identity crisis is a radical unraveling in which an individual loses the connection with the self he knew in the past and the self he now knows himself to be. It is literally a sense of disintegration, a true loss of integrity. Such a split can result from a trauma such as war or other violence, a cultural shift, a period of soul-searching and reflection, and other transformative experiences.

42. **C:** Identity achievement is the result of an individual fully embracing a unified, single, integrated self-identity that integrates the totality of who she is. It follows a period of intense introspection or tremendous upheaval, and can occur at any point or at several points in an individual's life, from childhood through old age. After considering or experiencing a number of identities and finding one that is "the right fit," the individual will turn away from other identities that challenge the "true" one or subsume them if they are not contradictory to the primary identity.

43. **B:** Self-disclosure is communicating the things that are important to oneself with another. Some acts of self-disclosure are more telling than others. For example, telling a date that you fear spiders, love

hiking, and have a favorite aunt offers a glimpse into your emotional life, but nothing of major importance is being risked. Revealing that you've undergone several surgeries to remove scarring from a fire in which your identical twin died risks tremendous vulnerability. There is a cultural expectation that information disclosed at the beginning of a relationship is less intimate than that shared as the relationship deepens.

44. B: Emotionally intense events that occurred long ago gain a kind of mythology through time. We visit those events repeatedly at different stages of life, trying to understand what they meant, why they occurred, and what effects they had. We are, in truth, reforming the original event, shaping it into a story. All stories, even histories, contain elements of fiction. Objects or actions are symbolically transformed and charged with layers of meaning. Not all acts of self-disclosure are conscious. When consciously sharing a story about an event that occurred long ago, the teller is also unconsciously sharing another, more symbolic one.

45. D: The question is not concerned with assessing the students' competency in listening or learning, but with assessing the teacher's instruction. When a sender creates a message that is delivered to a receiver, there are many points along the way in which the message might become altered or ultimately be incompletely or incorrectly understood. Feedback, or the receiver's response, can take the form of questions, repeating back key information, or furthering the conversation. Feedback lets the sender know if the message needs clarification.

46. A: The Spitzberg & Cupach model of communication competence describes knowledge as the understanding of what a specific situation calls for in terms of behavior. Skill is knowing how to demonstrate that specific behavior appropriately, and motivation is the speaker's desire to make her communication clear in an appropriate way. When these three components are present, the speaker has achieved communication competency.

47. D: The facilitator should send a strong nonverbal message to each. When the domineering participant attempts to take over, the facilitator should stand, turn her back, and pointedly invite another member to speak. If the domineering member continues to talk, the facilitator should hold up her hand in a "stop" position directly at the individual and repeat her invitation to another member. By mirroring the quiet participant's movements, the facilitator will send a message that she is recognized and welcome in the group.

48. B: The purpose of this type of group discussion is to define an issue and then work toward its resolution. The purpose must remain central, and must not be eclipsed by emotional issues. While some of the discussion participants might feel slighted if they are interrupted, if someone disagrees with them and others concur, or if the group does not hold their ideas as highly as those of others, it would be inappropriate to display those feelings. Participants who have greater experience, knowledge, or skills related to the subject under discussion should be expected and invited to contribute more to the discussion. They should not be resented for their greater knowledge.

49. C: Collaboration relies upon the premise that working together is a framework in which everyone can achieve their secondary goals when the primary goal is reached. It works best when no one wants to be personally held solely responsible, when individuals are somewhat willing to be flexible, and when everyone wants to share in the credit. In a collaborative situation, an individual will willingly give up a position for the greater good, thereby participating in the ultimate success of the group.

50. A: In a compromise, all sides agree to give up something in order to play a role in gaining something more important. When both sides bend, no one feels they've been taken advantage of or manipulated. However, in the process of negotiating what will be given up, the danger is that a central ideal or essential part of the true goal will become eroded or erased entirely.

51. D: There are many situations in which avoidance is a useful, though usually temporary, strategy within a group. If a minor disagreement arises, it may be best to overlook it and focus on the goal at hand. In other words, avoidance is appropriate if more important things need to be dealt with. If a discussion has gotten out of hand, stepping away from the issues gives everyone a chance to calm down. An individual with little clout will reasonably prefer to avoid a confrontation rather than lose face. Avoiding making a decision is appropriate if more information is required, or when an acceptable answer has not yet become clear.

52. B: Standard agenda, or reflective thinking, is a six step process that systematically looks at a problem that requires a decision to be made. The first step is to clarify the issue or problem. Secondly, the problem must be analyzed. Next, given the goals of the decision, criteria must be chosen. Fourth, a comprehensive list of possible solutions must be gathered. Following this, each potential solution must be assessed using the criteria that were previously chosen. The most appropriate solution should then be selected. Finally, the selected solution should be applied.

53. D: Brainstorming is a useful technique for getting members of a group to think outside the box, generating unexpected ideas, and making unusual connections. In a brainstorming session, an idea is offered or a question is asked. Members are encouraged to begin rapidly generating ideas, saying them aloud. Interruption is allowed, and the sessions often erupt into a playful frenzy. Because ideas aren't being judged or categorized, brainstorming creates intense mental and creative energy.

54. C: Groupthink is a psychological phenomenon that is likely to manifest when a group's primary focus is on the solidarity of its members rather than on the task or purpose for which the group has been formed. "Groupthink" causes members to disown any individual thought that might disturb the group's amity. Members may be unaware or completely aware that they aren't in full agreement with a point of view or decision, but will push their own different ideas or ideals aside because they are unwilling to be seen by the others as different.

55. E: There are many negative outcomes and no positive ones to groupthink. Groupthink's ultimate goal is to preserve the status quo. Therefore, groups under the influence of groupthink cannot tolerate people who think for themselves, opposition, or even an idea just a shade different from their own "official" positions. These groups will seek only information that supports pre-existing positions, and typically have no contingency plan to fall back on. A group under groupthink influence will neither look for information that runs counter to their own beliefs, nor consider a range of alternatives. The group will not look too carefully at ideas the group approves of because the group believes itself to be infallible. Ultimately, groupthink causes its own demise because of its inflexibility. New members to a group might not be willing to accept the party line. Because they don't yet identify strongly with the group, they will be more willing to express other ideas.

56. D: Abdicratic groups typically disintegrate quickly. An abdicratic group is one in which there is no leadership, either because none of the individuals are willing to assume responsibility, or because the group holds an ideal that presupposes leadership is not necessary or desirable. A leaderless group will either pull itself apart because its members will go off in various directions, or it will experience no movement and, through the force of inertia, simply dissolve. The group may reorganize, but this time the leadership will be autocratic.

57. A: Autocratic leaders are strong-willed and authoritative. They do not allow decisions that do not work in their favor, further their cause, or benefit them in some way. Democratic style leadership gives authority to all group members, who make decisions together. Laissez-faire style leadership involves the group making its own decisions without interference from the leader, who acts only as a guide. Abdicratic groups recognize no authority in any of the members, and give equal freedom and responsibility to all.

58. B: All groups form around some kind of task. Roles such as initiator contributor (generates ideas), information seeker (gathers necessary information), opinion seeker (gathers group values), elaborator (clarifies), coordinator (finds connections between ideas), evaluator-critic (weighs group activities against an ideal), energizer (stimulates and inspires), and procedural-technician (handles logistics) are all essential. Other important roles include information giver (offers facts), opinion giver (offers positions about group concerns), orienter (changes the direction), and recorder (keeps the records).

59. D: An informational speech generally follows a formulaic format. The opening puts the topic of the speech in front of the audience and offers a thesis. A brief preview of what will be discussed and in what order is provided. A strong hook, often a humorous remark, is used to pull the listener in. The purpose of the speech is explained in a point by point fashion in the body of the speech. The conclusion reviews the information, circles back around to something that was said in the opening, and ends the speech with a flourish. In addition, informative (also called informational) speeches often use a number of facts, quotes, or statistics to support the speaker's position.

60. D: Informative speeches should be relatively short – typically under 20 minutes – so as not to overwhelm the audience. Some visual aids can be helpful, but should only be used to clarify the verbal message, not replace it. Eye contact, deliberate gestures, standing and moving with confidence, and other types of nonverbal communication should be used to enhance the speaker's message. The purpose of this type of speech is to inform, not to persuade or enflame. Therefore, the language should be simple, direct, and logical. A few notes are fine, but the speaker should be well prepared and not read from a script.

61. C: Demonstration speeches are designed to offer directions or instructions to an audience that explain how to do something. Before presenting a demonstration speech, it's important to know the degree to which the audience is familiar with the subject. If Esteban's audience is composed of graduate students in a well-respected music department, his presentation will need to be sophisticated enough to be of interest and use to them. High school students with little experience, however, will need a presentation they can understand.

62. E: Effective speeches are not written to appeal to anyone and everyone. A speech needs to be fine-tuned for its audience, who will receive it, interpret it, and apply it in ways that are meaningful within the framework of their own experiences. While no speech writer can accurately determine every detail of the lives of her audience, the more she knows, can find out, or can make an educated guess about, the better able she will be to fine-tune her message into something of lasting interest and value to her audience. Factors that should be considered include age, gender, culture, nationality, religious affiliation, the audience's skills and experiences with the topic, and the audience's needs and interests.

63. C: A toast is a type of ceremonial speech in which an event or person is honored and celebrated. These types of speeches should move the audience and cause them to have an emotional reaction to hearing about the subject. Toasts should not be used as an opportunity to educate. While the family tree or timeline might be fascinating to some of the older audience members, the younger ones lack the perspective to fully appreciate them. A mention of a historical fact or two is fine, but dwelling on history doesn't celebrate the individual. Stories about the person being honored in the toast and family and friends who are present in the audience interest everyone. They demonstrate character, are moving, and directly involve audience members.

64. C: Effective eye contact suggests confidence, piques audience interest, makes the speaker's message seem familiar, and suggests the speaker is an expert on her subject. Excessive eye contact, however, can cause considerable discomfort for audience members. Audience members enjoy being singled

out briefly and made to feel special. Holding a gaze for too long, however, removes the protective sense of anonymity, and can make someone in the audience feel embarrassed, uncertain, or even angry.

65. D: When done correctly, extemporaneous speaking has a sense of immediacy, vivacity, and originality that a canned or memorized presentation does not. Speaking extemporaneously requires a solid understanding of the material and the ability to respond to audience cues quickly. Extemporaneous speaking should also give the impression of informality. A joke, for instance, can establish a relaxed mood and create interest. It is important to note, however, that the impression of informality isn't the same as true informality. The speaker still needs to remain in control over the presentation.

66. C: Without knowing the habits and expectations of other cultures, it is easy to make a faux pas, accidentally offend someone, or misunderstand a nonverbal communication. In this case, the audience is simply concentrating. Listening with closed eyes is not only socially acceptable in Japan, but is also a sign of respect. Nodding agreement is also considered respectful. As a side note, Mr. Gibbons might want to tone down the humor in his presentation, especially humor that gently mocks himself or his country, as the Japanese find this offensive.

67. D: Ultimately, all types of public speaking come down to the speaker's objectives and how they relate to the audience's needs. Whether the speech is a toast designed to inform, persuade, or entertain, the speaker has a purpose or reason for presenting the speech, and the audience has a reason for listening to it. To be truly successful, a public speaker must meet his objectives and the audience's needs.

68. E: Rehearsing a speech is more than simply practicing it in order to learn the material. An effective speaker knows that everything she does contributes to or detracts from the overall meaning of the speech. A videotape offers both verbal and visual feedback, and can help the speaker become conscious of whether the gestures, eye contact, tone of voice, pitch, and speech patterns used are effective or ineffective. A videotape will show the degree to which visual aids are helpful or hurtful in terms of clarifying the message, and can also help the speaker recognize confusing nonverbal information and identify sections where the speech loses focus.

69. A: Audience members are most likely to retain the points of a speech or lecture if they are offered in the form of a story and the speaker uses language that is simple and direct enough to be transparent. The stories need to be simple, and must drive the speech directly toward an essential and clear point. Including anecdotes is most effective when the speaker uses storytelling techniques that will bring them alive, such as varying pace, pitch, and intensity, using body language to suggest a change in speakers, and using the stage to suggest a setting.

70. C: The approach a speaker should take in the event of equipment failure depends on the subject and the audience. For instance, a speaker who is presenting to a group of techno savvy young people might be saved by a volunteer from the audience. While the technology is being repaired, the speaker should ask for questions or carry on an informal, entertaining dialogue with the audience. On the other hand, a speaker presenting to a group of children will need to quickly switch into extemporaneous mode in order to keep the attention of the audience. A presentation being given to a group of scientists might rely heavily upon graphs, charts, and numbers. In this case, the speaker can illustrate points using a flipchart if the visuals cannot be repaired.

71. C: For most public speakers, nervousness is less of a problem when they are presenting to the type of audience with which they have considerable experience. The stakes are higher, however, when the audience or the material is new. Knowing about and using a handful of tricks, skills, and techniques that anticipate specific problems that can arise in the midst of speaking is an essential

part of successful speaking and dealing with nervousness. A few notes on a card will prompt a blank mind. Anticipating difficult or even hostile questions and preparing responses allows the speaker to continue with confidence. Sometimes, re-directing a feeling is all it takes. Channeling anxiety into excitement, for instance, will charge the speech with energy.

72. D: Appropriate numbers, statistics, percentages, and other data presented to strengthen a point will clarify concepts and help the audience understand what is being said. However, it should be kept in mind that it takes more time to comprehend the meaning of a number than it does to comprehend the meaning of a word. Numbers need to be processed, and presenting too many of them in a row will only befuddle the audience. Too much data is overwhelming, and will cause audience members to shut down. Therefore, this type of information should be used judiciously and carefully.

73. D: The audience is showing signs that they have disengaged. They are neither in agreement nor disagreement. Rather, they have tuned him out entirely. When an audience member is scribbling a lot of notes, those notes probably have nothing to do with the speech. Instead, the audience member is likely doing other work. Closed eyes might mean concentration, but could also indicate boredom. Studying a conference catalogue or other materials indicates that the audience member is disconnected from the speech. Other signs that an audience is distracted are staring, touching hair or face, sighing, foot tapping, whispering, dropping items, sprawling back in seats, and glancing around the room. When a speaker notes even a few members of the audience engaging in these actions, he needs to change pace, incorporate body language, and vary voice tone to recapture their attention.

74. E: When a student gives a presentation, several methods to help him understand what worked and what didn't should be used. Audience comments are useful if they're honest and clear. For instance, a popular student who has given a mediocre speech isn't helped by commentary that only praises her. Specific critiques, however, such as a student pointing out that the speaker's fiddling with her hair is distracting, are useful. Rubrics completed by students, the teacher, and the presenter can be extremely useful, both because a rubric looks at a number of specific areas, and because the presenter can see areas that everyone agrees need to be improved upon. A videotape will give strong, accurate feedback on the student's diction, speech patterns, voice tone, and nonverbal communication skills.

75. D: A demonstration speech, which combines the speaker's words with activities and visual aids, is a complex style of public speaking. To be successful, Cookie needs to know the speech inside and out to give the impression she is speaking spontaneously. Like an informational speech, a demonstration speech is organized into an introduction, a body, and a conclusion. Because she will be demonstrating as she speaks, it's important that Cookie uses simple vocabulary and direct statements rather than poetic or dramatic language and complex sentences.

76. E: When properly used, numerical data can enhance a speech and illuminate important points, but numbers on their own are hard to grasp. Presenting numbers verbally, and then showing them in a chart or graph helps the audience see the relationship between the numbers and the points presented in the speech. Translating numbers into a concrete image that audience members can relate to can be powerful. For example, the statement "By the time I finish this speech, seven more children will be diagnosed with cancer in the United States" brings the message home. Repeating this fact or the numbers associated with the fact at key points throughout the presentation will bring the information home in a way the audience will not forget.

77. C: A change in company culture is difficult, even if it's necessary. Lower level employees need to be reassured with a true vision infused with energy and hope for the future. Senior management members will need to change their behavior to align with the company's new ideals. Seeing senior

management enthusiastically embrace the changes, not just with their words but also through their actions, will further assure employees it is safe to trust the vision. Employees will have questions, and the leader must know how the organizational structure will be re-designed to facilitate upcoming changes. Employees who have displayed deviant behaviors prior to the change, such as chronic absenteeism or an unwillingness to work with others, must be purged. New hires that more closely align with the new model need to be brought in.

78. D: According to the two-step flow model developed by Lazarsfeld and Katz, mass media does not directly affect the public, but instead channels ideas through what they term opinion leaders. Opinion leaders are individuals who have the greatest ready access to a specific media, have an understanding of the ideas disseminated by mass media, and can spread those ideas by explaining or popularizing them to a more general audience.

79. A: The spiral of silence theory is concerned with both mass communication and political science. According to the theory, when people believe their position on a subject doesn't match the majority's, they remain silent rather than risk censure. It is called a "spiral" because the more confident those who hold the majority view feel, the more likely they are to voice their opinion. The more they voice their opinion, the less likely the opposition is to voice a different, opposing viewpoint. .

80. D: Mass media has a very strong influence over the spiral of silence because it shapes public opinion about an issue, and also reports or suggests that the majority opinion or viewpoint is the "correct" one. Mass media can also make it seem as though a local and minor issue is a much larger social concern, which invites the public at large to develop opinions (which are usually those the media has fed them). By reporting on the opinion of the majority, that opinion becomes the status quo.

81. A: According to McLuhan, a message cannot be divorced from the manner in which it arrives, and so the medium affects how a message is read. This suggests that in order to deliver the message the sender intends, an awareness of the characteristics of the medium is necessary. For example, a comic requires the creative involvement of the reader, who not only "hears" the voices of the characters, but also fills in the missing details from box to box.

82. B: Traditional media studies have focused on print media, including newspapers, books, magazines, journals, broadsides, brochures, flyers, coupons, and the like; visual media, including photographs, movies, videos, and television; and aural media, such as radio and recordings. New media has been studied as a subset of these, but that is changing. Interactive television, online videogames, mobile devices such as phones that bring the Internet wherever the user goes, digital media, videoconferencing, Twitter, Facebook, instant messaging, and more are beginning to be seen not as mere extensions of traditional media, but as entirely separate media types.

83. C: The culturalist theory is something of a marriage between two earlier theories. The limited effect theory of the 1950s claimed that media had a limited ability to influence people who were already knowledgeable about or experienced with a particular topic, and a greater ability to influence those who were less knowledgeable. The class dominant theory held that the media is controlled by an elite minority of corporate rulers who manipulate it to their advantage. The culturalist theory states that mass media, which is controlled by a tiny portion of the population, offers raw material— images, sounds, and vocabulary—intended to relay a message. Individuals take that material and craft or fine-tune their own messages based on their experiences and prior knowledge, meaning a single message can have multiple meanings when interpreted by different people.

84. A: A 2000 study of characters in situation comedies found that male characters were more likely to be given lines praising characters portrayed by thin female actors, and were more likely to be given lines insulting characters portrayed by heavy female actors.

85. C: The Internet, mobile devices, Twitter, Facebook, and other new media have altered the way information is received. In the past, television, radio, and newspaper scheduling controlled when and how content was received, as well as the nature of the content. As the public becomes increasingly more sophisticated in using the Internet, they have taken control over when they will receive content and what type of content they will receive. Members of the public have also gained a means by which they as individuals or groups can contribute to the pool of information. However, since the Internet allows for a great degree of anonymity, participants are able to express opinions or offer what they believe to be facts without assuming responsibility for the fairness or accuracy of their contributions.

86. C: Primary involvement is the term used to describe an audience fully focused on a medium's message. Reading a book, watching a television show, or listening to a debate demonstrates this type of involvement, which has the most immediate and strongest impact upon the audience. Secondary involvement means the audience is simultaneously absorbing the message and doing something else. A parent watching the news while preparing dinner is somewhat less open to the information being channeled. Tertiary involvement means the audience is paying little attention to the medium and is focusing primarily on something else. While part of the message may be received, it is less immediate and considerably less influential.

87. E: McQuail's uses and gratifications model finds that there are multiple, and oftentimes overlapping, reasons a consumer accepts a medium's message. A message that reinforces one's beliefs enhances his or her identity. Watching or reading about relationships gives an individual the illusion that he or she is involved in those relationships, and so the media is fully embraced. Consumers turn to media to gain specific information or escape the problems of their own lives through entertainment.

88. A: Proponents of the effects theory claim that the influence of media on values, beliefs, and behaviors is profound. This theory suggests that there is little autonomy in audiences. If the message is aggressive or convincing enough, they believe and behave as they are told to and do not seek further information elsewhere. One piece of information used to support the theory is the direct correlation between rising crime and violence in media reports, movies, and games and instances of these events in real life. Critics, however, point out that most viewers do not imitate behaviors they have been exposed to, and those who do generally have extenuating psychological conditions.

89. D: All forms of communication media contribute to and influence how a political message is issued and received. The media is a source of information, and only information that is offered can be received and reflected upon by consumers. This is a political act in itself. The form the message takes, the words chosen, and the visual presentation all contribute to the message's meaning. In politics, the media serves to entrench particular beliefs in those who already hold them and to sway those who have not yet made up their minds. It is obvious that politicians, political strategists, and interest groups have a role in shaping the political field. The media also plays an important role.

90. E: Information and communication technologies such as the Internet, mobile devices, intranets, networking, videoconferencing, and the like have radically changed the pace at which information can be disseminated, accessed, and shared. Videoconferencing and the Internet have resulted in changes in the way organizations and businesses are structured, giving them greater flexibility that has resulted in a rise in virtual offices, permitted the development of a global marketplace, and relocated jobs to nations where the labor force is plentiful and cheap. While making goods and services less expensive to consumers, it has also negatively affected economies. In some areas, job losses have been considerable. These technologies have also radically altered the way political

campaigns are run by surrounding voters with layers of information from every corner. In order to be successful, politicians must be sensitive to the ways younger voters use the Internet.

91. D: The purpose of formative, or educative, assessment is to support learning by offering feedback over the course of the learning experience. This is a diagnostic assessment used to determine the student's current level of knowledge and skills, specifically what the student is doing capably and what the student needs to focus on improving. A formative assessment can take many forms, including a rubric completed by the instructor, other students, or the student himself; informal verbal feedback; or a response journal.

92. C: Objective assessment allows for only one correct response. Subjective assessment, on the other hand, can have multiple correct responses or a correct response that can be worded in a number of ways. Among the types of objective assessment questions are multiple choice, true or false, and matching questions. Objective evaluations are frequently found online. Subjective assessments often consist of essay questions.

93. D: Placing the importance of moral values above personal ones is moral motivation. Justifying behaviors that don't fit within one's moral code, ignoring aspects of those behaviors in order to avoid confronting oneself, or denying a misaligned behavior when confronted by another all indicate a turning away from one's moral center. Prioritizing personal values (particularly contradictory ones) above moral values results in a schism in belief and behavior. When a teacher says one thing but does another, students become confused. When a teacher justifies behavior despite her moral values, students learn that they too can live unreconciled lives in which their responsibility for doing the right thing is changeable rather than absolute.

94. B: Performance based assessments are concerned with evaluating a student's overall performance of a particular skill, including the planning, execution, and analysis of that skill. This type of assessment is most often ongoing over a period of time. It can be informal in nature (such as conversations between teacher and student) or formal (such as assessments that follow a rubric). Performance based assessments are concerned with real-world tasks and experiences, such as delivering a public speaking performance, writing a speech, directing a play, or writing a review.

95. E: Discrete point items require knowledge of a single piece of information, such as the definition of a word. In contrast, an integrative question is one that tests the student's ability to consider more than one point simultaneously. A question that asks a student to complete two tasks, such as identifying the correct definition of a word and using it in a sentence, is integrative. An objective question has a single answer, while a subjective question is open to interpretation.

96. E: Among the skills a good public speaker must possess is the ability to select a topic and fine tune it for a particular, specific audience; clarify the information by sufficiently communicating the thesis; transition logically from point to point throughout the presentation; and support the speech's purpose or position with appropriate statistics, graphs, charts, or other professional quality visual aids. A teacher evaluating a student's public speaking skills should also look for appropriate word choice and sentence structure; naturalness of delivery; variation in pitch, intensity, and pace; appropriate nonverbal support; and comfort with spontaneous additions as appropriate.

97. C: Since the student's English is excellent, it can be assumed he has a good grasp of both grammatical structures and vocabulary. A pronounced accent is noticeable, but isn't sufficient cause for misunderstanding unless he is not differentiating between phonemes such as /b/ and /d/ or /l/ and /r/. Again, since his English is excellent, it can be assumed this is not the problem. Although it isn't clear if he failed to practice, such a failure wouldn't likely contribute to the audience's inability to understand what he is saying. It is common for non-native English speakers to place the accent

incorrectly on a single word or multiple words within an orally produced string. Doing so skews a listener's mental organization of sound units into words. This is most likely the problem.

98. B: The teacher needs to find a text that will challenge the students to learn. One that is written with language, structure, or ideas slightly beyond the students' current level will inspire them to grow. It's important, however, that the teacher select material that is within their grasp. If the ideas or language are far beyond what the students are currently capable of, they will not respond to it. A text that employs contemporary slang will have a limited shelf life. As the idioms go out of fashion, the book will rapidly become dated.

99. E: Potential topics for public speaking abound. As the teacher gets to know her students, she will become familiar with their interests, worries, hopes, and values. These areas offer a rich source of potential topics and material. Other teachers can make suggestions based upon what they know about students or about her students in particular. They can also make suggestions based upon their own areas of expertise. While her classroom text is sure to contain some interesting topic ideas, the teacher can broaden her search to books of every kind for inspiration. Finally, the Internet offers thousands of topic ideas for students at every grade level.

100. C: One mistake teachers make is assigning a public speaking topic that is far too narrow in focus to allow for personal interpretation. The ubiquitous "What I Did on My Summer Vacation" is such a topic. Because the premise lacks life, the writing and presentation will too. Selecting a topic that requires interpretation and can be interpreted in a number of ways allows each student to bring her own knowledge and experiences to the topic to make it resonate. For example, asking students to create a performance about something that has been lost permits one student to write about a lost love, another about a lost pet, another about the loss of a belief, and a fourth about being lost at sea.

Secret Key #1 – Time is Your Greatest Enemy

To succeed on the TExES, you must use your time wisely.

Pace Yourself

Wear a watch. At the beginning of the test, check the time (or start a chronometer on your watch to count the minutes), and check the time after every few questions to make sure you are "on schedule."

If you are forced to speed up, do it efficiently. Usually one or more answer choices can be eliminated without too much difficulty. Above all, don't panic. Don't speed up and just begin guessing at random choices. By pacing yourself, and continually monitoring your progress against your watch, you will always know exactly how far ahead or behind you are with your available time. If you find that you are one minute behind on the test, don't skip one question without spending any time on it, just to catch back up. Take 15 fewer seconds on the next four questions, and after four questions you'll have caught back up. Once you catch back up, you can continue working each problem at your normal pace.

Furthermore, don't dwell on the problems that you were rushed on. If a problem was taking up too much time and you made a hurried guess, it must be difficult. The difficult questions are the ones you are most likely to miss anyway, so it isn't a big loss. It is better to end with more time than you need than to run out of time.

Lastly, sometimes it is beneficial to slow down if you are constantly getting ahead of time. You are always more likely to catch a careless mistake by working more slowly than quickly, and among very high-scoring test takers (those who are likely to have lots of time left

over), careless errors affect the score more than mastery of material.

Secret Key #2 - Guessing is not Guesswork

You probably know that guessing is a good idea - unlike other standardized tests, there is no penalty for getting a wrong answer. Even if you have no idea about a question, you still have a 20-25% chance of getting it right.

Most test takers do not understand the impact that proper guessing can have on their score. Unless you score extremely high, guessing will significantly contribute to your final score.

Monkeys Take the Test

What most test takers don't realize is that to insure that 20-25% chance, you have to guess randomly. If you put 20 monkeys in a room to take this test, assuming they answered once per question and behaved themselves, on average they would get 20-25% of the questions correct. Put 20 test takers in the room, and the average will be much lower among guessed questions. Why?

1. The test writers intentionally writes deceptive answer choices that "look" right. A test taker has no idea about a question, so picks the "best looking" answer, which is often wrong. The monkey has no idea what looks good and what doesn't, so will consistently be lucky about 20-25% of the time.
2. Test takers will eliminate answer choices from the guessing pool based on a hunch or intuition. Simple but correct answers often get excluded, leaving a 0% chance of being correct. The monkey has no clue, and often gets lucky with the best choice.

This is why the process of elimination

endorsed by most test courses is flawed and detrimental to your performance- test takers don't guess, they make an ignorant stab in the dark that is usually worse than random.

$5 Challenge

Let me introduce one of the most valuable ideas of this course- the $5 challenge:

You only mark your "best guess" if you are willing to bet $5 on it.
You only eliminate choices from guessing if you are willing to bet $5 on it.

Why $5? Five dollars is an amount of money that is small yet not insignificant, and can really add up fast (20 questions could cost you $100). Likewise, each answer choice on one question of the test will have a small impact on your overall score, but it can really add up to a lot of points in the end.

The process of elimination IS valuable. The following shows your chance of guessing it right:

If you eliminate wrong answer choices until only this many remain:	Chance of getting it correct:
1	100%
2	50%
3	33%

However, if you accidentally eliminate the right answer or go on a hunch for an incorrect answer, your chances drop dramatically: to 0%. By guessing among all the answer choices, you are GUARANTEED to have a shot at the right answer.

That's why the $5 test is so valuable- if you give up the advantage and safety of a pure guess, it had better be worth the risk.

What we still haven't covered is how to be sure that whatever guess you make is truly random. Here's the easiest way:

Always pick the first answer choice among those remaining.

Such a technique means that you have decided, **before you see a single test question**, exactly how you are going to guess- and since the order of choices tells you nothing about which one is correct, this guessing technique is perfectly random.

This section is not meant to scare you away from making educated guesses or eliminating choices- you just need to define when a choice is worth eliminating. The $5 test, along with a pre-defined random guessing strategy, is the best way to make sure you reap all of the benefits of guessing.

Secret Key #3 - Practice Smarter, Not Harder

Many test takers delay the test preparation process because they dread the awful amounts of practice time they think necessary to succeed on the test. We have refined an effective method that will take you only a fraction of the time.

There are a number of "obstacles" in your way to succeed. Among these are answering questions, finishing in time, and mastering test-taking strategies. All must be executed on the day of the test at peak performance, or your score will suffer. The test is a mental marathon that has a large impact on your future.

Just like a marathon runner, it is important to work your way up to the full challenge. So first you just worry about questions, and then time, and finally strategy:

Success Strategy

1. Find a good source for practice tests.
2. If you are willing to make a larger time investment, consider using more than one study guide- often the different approaches of multiple authors will help you "get" difficult concepts.
3. Take a practice test with no time constraints, with all study helps "open book." Take your time with questions and focus on applying strategies.
4. Take a practice test with time constraints, with all guides "open book."
5. Take a final practice test with no open material and time limits

If you have time to take more practice tests, just repeat step 5. By gradually exposing yourself to the full rigors of the test environment, you will condition your mind to the stress of test day and maximize your success.

Secret Key #4 - Prepare, Don't Procrastinate

Let me state an obvious fact: if you take the test three times, you will get three different scores. This is due to the way you feel on test day, the level of preparedness you have, and, despite the test writers' claims to the contrary, some tests WILL be easier for you than others.

Since your future depends so much on your score, you should maximize your chances of success. In order to maximize the likelihood of success, you've got to prepare in advance. This means taking practice tests and spending time learning the information and test taking strategies you will need to succeed.

Never take the test as a "practice" test, expecting that you can just take it again if you need to. Feel free to take sample tests on your own, but when you go to take the official test, be prepared, be focused, and do your best the first time!

Secret Key #5 - Test Yourself

Everyone knows that time is money. There is no need to spend too much of your time or too little of your time preparing for the test. You should only spend as much of your precious time preparing as is necessary for you to get the score you need.

Once you have taken a practice test under real conditions of time constraints, then you will know if you are ready for the test or not.

If you have scored extremely high the first time that you take the practice test, then there is not much point in spending countless hours studying. You are already there.

Benchmark your abilities by retaking practice tests and seeing how much you have improved. Once you score high enough to guarantee success, then you are ready.

If you have scored well below where you need, then knuckle down and begin studying in earnest. Check your improvement regularly through the use of practice tests under real conditions. Above all, don't worry, panic, or give up. The key is perseverance!

Then, when you go to take the test, remain confident and remember how well you did on the practice tests. If you can score high enough on a practice test, then you can do the same on the real thing.

General Strategies

The most important thing you can do is to ignore your fears and jump into the test immediately- do not be overwhelmed by any strange-sounding terms. You have to jump into the test like jumping into a pool- all at once is the easiest way.

Make Predictions

As you read and understand the question, try to guess what the answer will be. Remember that several of the answer choices are wrong, and once you begin reading them, your mind will immediately become cluttered with answer choices designed to throw you off. Your mind is typically the most focused immediately after you have read the question and digested its contents. If you can, try to predict what the correct answer will be. You may be surprised at what you can predict.

Quickly scan the choices and see if your prediction is in the listed answer choices. If it is, then you can be quite confident that you have the right answer. It still won't hurt to check the other answer choices, but most of the time, you've got it!

Answer the Question

It may seem obvious to only pick answer choices that answer the question, but the test writers can create some excellent answer choices that are wrong. Don't pick an answer just because it sounds right, or you believe it to be true. It MUST answer the question. Once you've made your selection, always go back and check it against the question and make sure that you didn't misread the question, and the answer choice does answer the question posed.

Benchmark

After you read the first answer choice, decide if you think it sounds correct or not. If it doesn't, move on to the next answer choice. If

it does, mentally mark that answer choice. This doesn't mean that you've definitely selected it as your answer choice, it just means that it's the best you've seen thus far. Go ahead and read the next choice. If the next choice is worse than the one you've already selected, keep going to the next answer choice. If the next choice is better than the choice you've already selected, mentally mark the new answer choice as your best guess.

The first answer choice that you select becomes your standard. Every other answer choice must be benchmarked against that standard. That choice is correct until proven otherwise by another answer choice beating it out. Once you've decided that no other answer choice seems as good, do one final check to ensure that your answer choice answers the question posed.

Valid Information

Don't discount any of the information provided in the question. Every piece of information may be necessary to determine the correct answer. None of the information in the question is there to throw you off (while the answer choices will certainly have information to throw you off). If two seemingly unrelated topics are discussed, don't ignore either. You can be confident there is a relationship, or it wouldn't be included in the question, and you are probably going to have to determine what is that relationship to find the answer.

Avoid "Fact Traps"

Don't get distracted by a choice that is factually true. Your search is for the answer that answers the question. Stay focused and don't fall for an answer that is true but incorrect. Always go back to the question and make sure you're choosing an answer that actually answers the question and is not just a true statement. An answer can be factually correct, but it MUST answer the question asked. Additionally, two answers can both be seemingly correct, so be sure to read all of the answer choices, and make sure that you get

- 173 -

the one that BEST answers the question.

Milk the Question

Some of the questions may throw you completely off. They might deal with a subject you have not been exposed to, or one that you haven't reviewed in years. While your lack of knowledge about the subject will be a hindrance, the question itself can give you many clues that will help you find the correct answer. Read the question carefully and look for clues. Watch particularly for adjectives and nouns describing difficult terms or words that you don't recognize. Regardless of if you completely understand a word or not, replacing it with a synonym either provided or one you more familiar with may help you to understand what the questions are asking. Rather than wracking your mind about specific detailed information concerning a difficult term or word, try to use mental substitutes that are easier to understand.

The Trap of Familiarity

Don't just choose a word because you recognize it. On difficult questions, you may not recognize a number of words in the answer choices. The test writers don't put "make-believe" words on the test; so don't think that just because you only recognize all the words in one answer choice means that answer choice must be correct. If you only recognize words in one answer choice, then focus on that one. Is it correct? Try your best to determine if it is correct. If it is, that is great, but if it doesn't, eliminate it. Each word and answer choice you eliminate increases your chances of getting the question correct, even if you then have to guess among the unfamiliar choices.

Eliminate Answers

Eliminate choices as soon as you realize they are wrong. But be careful! Make sure you consider all of the possible answer choices. Just because one appears right, doesn't mean that the next one won't be even better! The test writers will usually put more than one

good answer choice for every question, so read all of them. Don't worry if you are stuck between two that seem right. By getting down to just two remaining possible choices, your odds are now 50/50. Rather than wasting too much time, play the odds. You are guessing, but guessing wisely, because you've been able to knock out some of the answer choices that you know are wrong. If you are eliminating choices and realize that the last answer choice you are left with is also obviously wrong, don't panic. Start over and consider each choice again. There may easily be something that you missed the first time and will realize on the second pass.

Tough Questions

If you are stumped on a problem or it appears too hard or too difficult, don't waste time. Move on! Remember though, if you can quickly check for obviously incorrect answer choices, your chances of guessing correctly are greatly improved. Before you completely give up, at least try to knock out a couple of possible answers. Eliminate what you can and then guess at the remaining answer choices before moving on.

Brainstorm

If you get stuck on a difficult question, spend a few seconds quickly brainstorming. Run through the complete list of possible answer choices. Look at each choice and ask yourself, "Could this answer the question satisfactorily?" Go through each answer choice and consider it independently of the other. By systematically going through all possibilities, you may find something that you would otherwise overlook. Remember that when you get stuck, it's important to try to keep moving.

Read Carefully

Understand the problem. Read the question and answer choices carefully. Don't miss the question because you misread the terms. You have plenty of time to read each question thoroughly and make sure you understand what is being asked. Yet a happy medium must be attained, so don't waste too much time. You must read carefully, but efficiently.

Face Value

When in doubt, use common sense. Always accept the situation in the problem at face value. Don't read too much into it. These problems will not require you to make huge leaps of logic. The test writers aren't trying to throw you off with a cheap trick. If you have to go beyond creativity and make a leap of logic in order to have an answer choice answer the question, then you should look at the other answer choices. Don't overcomplicate the problem by creating theoretical relationships or explanations that will warp time or space. These are normal problems rooted in reality. It's just that the applicable relationship or explanation may not be readily apparent and you have to figure things out. Use your common sense to interpret anything that isn't clear.

Prefixes

If you're having trouble with a word in the question or answer choices, try dissecting it. Take advantage of every clue that the word might include. Prefixes and suffixes can be a huge help. Usually they allow you to determine a basic meaning. Pre- means before, post- means after, pro - is positive, de- is negative. From these prefixes and suffixes, you can get an idea of the general meaning of the word and try to put it into context. Beware though of any traps. Just because con is the opposite of pro, doesn't necessarily mean congress is the opposite of progress!

Hedge Phrases

Watch out for critical "hedge" phrases, such as likely, may, can, will often, sometimes, often, almost, mostly, usually, generally, rarely, sometimes. Question writers insert these hedge phrases to cover every possibility. Often an answer choice will be wrong simply because it leaves no room for exception. Avoid answer choices that have definitive words like "exactly," and "always".

Switchback Words

Stay alert for "switchbacks". These are the words and phrases frequently used to alert you to shifts in thought. The most common switchback word is "but". Others include although, however, nevertheless, on the other hand, even though, while, in spite of, despite, regardless of.

New Information

Correct answer choices will rarely have completely new information included. Answer choices typically are straightforward reflections of the material asked about and will directly relate to the question. If a new piece of information is included in an answer choice that doesn't even seem to relate to the topic being asked about, then that answer choice is likely incorrect. All of the information needed to answer the question is usually provided for you, and so you should not have to make guesses that are unsupported or choose answer choices that require unknown information that cannot be reasoned on its own.

Time Management

On technical questions, don't get lost on the technical terms. Don't spend too much time on any one question. If you don't know what a term means, then since you don't have a dictionary, odds are you aren't going to get much further. You should immediately recognize terms as whether or not you know them. If you don't, work with the other clues that you have, the other answer choices and terms provided, but don't waste too much time trying to figure out a difficult term.

Contextual Clues

Look for contextual clues. An answer can be right but not correct. The contextual clues will help you find the answer that is most right and is correct. Understand the context in which a phrase or statement is made. This will help you make important distinctions.

Don't Panic

Panicking will not answer any questions for you. Therefore, it isn't helpful. When you first see the question, if your mind goes blank, take a deep breath. Force yourself to mechanically go through the steps of solving the problem and using the strategies you've learned.

Pace Yourself

Don't get clock fever. It's easy to be overwhelmed when you're looking at a page full of questions, your mind is full of random thoughts and feeling confused, and the clock is ticking down faster than you would like. Calm down and maintain the pace that you have set for yourself. As long as you are on track by monitoring your pace, you are guaranteed to have enough time for yourself. When you get to the last few minutes of the test, it may seem like you won't have enough time left, but if you only have as many questions as you should have left at that point, then you're right on track!

Answer Selection

The best way to pick an answer choice is to eliminate all of those that are wrong, until only one is left and confirm that is the correct answer. Sometimes though, an answer choice may immediately look right. Be careful! Take a second to make sure that the other choices are not equally obvious. Don't make a hasty mistake. There are only two times that you should stop before checking other answers. First is when you are positive that the answer choice you have selected is correct. Second is when time is almost out and you have to make a quick guess!

Check Your Work

Since you will probably not know every term listed and the answer to every question, it is important that you get credit for the ones that you do know. Don't miss any questions through careless mistakes. If at all possible, try to take a second to look back over your answer selection and make sure you've selected the correct answer choice and haven't made a costly careless mistake (such as marking an answer choice that you didn't mean to mark). This quick double check should more than pay for itself in caught mistakes for the time it costs.

Beware of Directly Quoted Answers

Sometimes an answer choice will repeat word for word a portion of the question or reference section. However, beware of such exact duplication – it may be a trap! More than likely, the correct choice will paraphrase or summarize a point, rather than being exactly the same wording.

Slang

Scientific sounding answers are better than slang ones. An answer choice that begins "To compare the outcomes…" is much more likely to be correct than one that begins "Because some people insisted…"

Extreme Statements

Avoid wild answers that throw out highly controversial ideas that are proclaimed as established fact. An answer choice that states the "process should be used in certain situations, if…" is much more likely to be correct than one that states the "process should be discontinued completely." The first is a calm rational statement and doesn't even make a definitive, uncompromising stance, using a hedge word "if" to provide wiggle room, whereas the second choice is a radical idea and far more extreme.

Answer Choice Families

When you have two or more answer choices that are direct opposites or parallels, one of them is usually the correct answer. For instance, if one answer choice states "x increases" and another answer choice states "x decreases" or "y increases," then those two or three answer choices are very similar in construction and fall into the same family of answer choices. A family of answer choices is when two or three answer choices are very similar in construction, and yet often have a directly opposite meaning. Usually the

- 176 -

correct answer choice will be in that family of answer choices. The "odd man out" or answer choice that doesn't seem to fit the parallel construction of the other answer choices is more likely to be incorrect.

Special Report: Additional Bonus Material

Due to our efforts to try to keep this book to a manageable length, we've created a link that will give you access to all of your additional bonus material.

Please visit http://www.mometrix.com/bonus948/texesspch7-12 to access the information.